Problems for
Computer Solutions
Using FORTRAN

WINTHROP COMPUTER SYSTEMS SERIES

Gerald M. Weinberg, *editor*

HENRY M. WALKER

Assistant Professor of Mathematics
Grinnell College

Problems for Computer Solutions Using FORTRAN

WINTHROP PUBLISHERS, INC.

Cambridge, Massachusetts

Library of Congress Cataloging in Publication Data

Walker, Henry M
    Problems for computer solutions using FORTRAN.

    Includes index.
    1. Mathematics—Problems, exercises, etc.—Data
processing. 2. FORTRAN (Computer program language)—
Problems, exercises, etc. I. Title.
QA43.W34   510′.08′54   79-26981
ISBN 0-87626-654-5

© 1980 by Winthrop Publishers, Inc.
   17 Dunster Street, Cambridge, Massachusetts 02138

10 9 8 7 6 5 4 3 2 1

BST
&
cop. 1

12.95

Contents

v

Foreword

Last year I had the misfortune to visit Henry Walker in Grinnell, Iowa—a misfortune because a tiny accident in tiny downtown Grinnell crippled our car for a week. In every *other* way, the trip was more than fortunate. Most fortunate of all was meeting Henry Walker and learning how Grinnell had achieved its outstanding record in the use of computers in teaching and learning.

Like many other small liberal arts colleges, Grinnell has gone on quietly for years building up its reputation for excellence in teaching. The Grinnell's of the nation don't get the publicity of the MIT's and Stanford's, but their students are probably the better for it. Unhappily, most of our textbooks seem to come out of the big universities, where teaching sometimes plays second fiddle to the game called "Research and Grants." Not being forced to play "publish or perish," the dedicated liberal arts teachers devote most of their spare time to their students, never thinking to write down what they've developed for sharing with the rest of us.

Knowing this, and knowing Grinnell's reputation for excellent teaching, I was elated to learn that we had a manuscript on programming originating at Grinnell. I read our sample chapters and was so pleased I arranged a visit to the campus. My wife, an outstanding teacher in her own right, saw the manuscript and asked if she could come along. Like me, she could see immediately that we had not just another introductory programming text, but an entire system of teaching backed up by a student-centered philosophy with which we could readily identify.

Much of the visit was concerned with publication problems we might encounter with such an unusual manuscript, but I was determined to work them out. I wanted to capture as much of the spirit of the Grinnell program as I could, and that spirit had reflected itself in the loving care that had been given to all phases of preparing the text. For instance, the original student text was reproduced using three colors to set off text, programs, and output. In this way, one of the major stumbling blocks was removed from the beginner's path, though at great trouble to the preparers.

But I need not belabor the virtues of the manuscript, for the reader need merely turn to any page to see the care that has been given to choice examples, layout, programming style, explanatory language, and especially to the problem sets around which the Grinnell course revolves. No, this is not your ordinary "Introduction to Programming." It's an exceptionally new, fresh book which every dedicated teacher will welcome. I've talked to several teachers who are planning to restructure their approach to introductory programming to follow the lead of *Problems for Computer Solutions*. . . . Some are using it for the text; some for the problems; but most for the text and problems together. I know it's given me an important new weapon in the war on ignorance and indifference about computers and programming. What more can a teacher ask?

Gerald M. Weinberg

Series Editor

Preface

This book provides the beginning programmer with an introduction to the fundamentals of computer programming, a review of several techniques illustrating applications of programming in a variety of different disciplines, and a collection of programming problems related to each of these disciplines. Its broad scope means that the book is appropriate for introducing FORTRAN programming to an extremely diverse audience.

This book grew out of the "Introduction to Programming" course at Grinnell College, which is taken by students ranging from freshmen to seniors, and from math and science majors to social science and humanities majors. In the course, all students learn the same programming concepts while concentrating their programming exercises on an area closely related to their own interests. Thus, a common set of lectures introduces programming to all students, while questions on problems or subject-oriented materials can be handled effectively during open laboratory sessions near computer terminals.

Part I introduces all readers to the same programming techniques and concepts. The book begins by assuming that the reader has had no contact with a computer. Chapter 1 outlines what a computer is and how it can be used. Technical details of computer hardware are omitted in favor of a general view of the machine. Chapter 2 then develops programming in FORTRAN from the beginning stages and proceeds through standard statement formats and programming concepts. Throughout Part I, examples are accessible to all readers.

The introduction to FORTRAN in Part I contains many sample programs, thereby enabling the reader to see specific examples that use the ideas being explained. Each program presented, together with the output it produces, has been run on a PDP-11/70 computer and thus gives the reader a working model of the techniques covered. Suggestions are offered on how programs can be written and how computer algorithms can be developed.

Part II contains chapters oriented to individual readers' interests and backgrounds. For example, the chapter on calculus discusses several computer techniques specifically related to calculus and gives a large number of problems using these techniques. These subject-oriented chapters are independent of each other, and each is coordinated with the programming presented in Part I. Thus, after reading the first sections on FORTRAN, the reader will be able to do the first problems in any of the subjects covered in Part II. Further, the subject matter in these chapters progresses from elementary to more advanced concepts, so that the programming problems can be coordinated with a first course in the subject being covered. For example, the calculus chapter uses rather few concepts at first, while later problems require a reasonable knowledge of the derivative or integral.

As this book has evolved at Grinnell College, several subject application chapters have been developed by various faculty members. Specifically, Charles Duke wrote the first versions of the physics problems; Eugene Herman wrote the linear algebra problems; Thomas Moberg contributed the precalculus statistics;

and John Vogel wrote both the chemistry and statistics with calculus sections. Further, the sections with general problems, algebra and trigonometry problems, and calculus problems have been revised several times by Eugene Herman and John Vogel, as well as by the author. I am very grateful to each of these individuals for their contributions to this book. I also wish to express my thanks to the Computer Services Department of Grinnell College, particularly to David Renaud, for their assistance in developing various aspects of this book, and to Mrs. Gladys Beaty for her expert typing of several drafts of the manuscript. Further, I want to thank Winthrop Publishers, particularly Robert Duchacek, for their considerable advice and assistance in editing and preparing the manuscript. Finally, I thank my wife Terry for her support and understanding especially during the time this book was being written and revised.

H. M. W.

Problems for
Computer Solutions
Using FORTRAN

PART 1

An Introduction to Programming Languages

CHAPTER 1

An Overview
of Computer Programming

Section 1.1: WHAT IS A COMPUTER?

A computer is popularly viewed as an intelligent being with an infinite capacity for solving even the most complex problems. While this is an interesting perspective, we will find that actually the computer must be told what to do in particularly straightforward and logical terms. The machine can carry out its instructions at a very high rate of speed, but it must be told precisely what steps to follow.

Before considering just how to tell the machine what operations we want it to perform, it is often helpful to have in mind a general picture of a computer. Thus, we begin with a brief overview of the components of a typical computer, concentrating on the conceptual framework of the machine and avoiding technical details.

A computer system consists of several components interconnected in various ways. A simple model is shown schematically in Figure 1.1–1.

The heart of the machine is the Central Processing Unit (CPU). This unit performs all computations and directs all other actions of the computer. It is the piece of hardware that controls the entire computer operation.

Attached to the CPU are various devices which allow information to be transmitted to and from the machine and which permit data to be stored. These devices can be divided into three categories:

(a) Input of information
  1. Terminal
  2. Card reader
(b) Output of data
  1. Terminal
  2. Card punch
  3. High-speed printer
(c) Storage of data
  1. *Disk*
  2. *Magnetic tape*

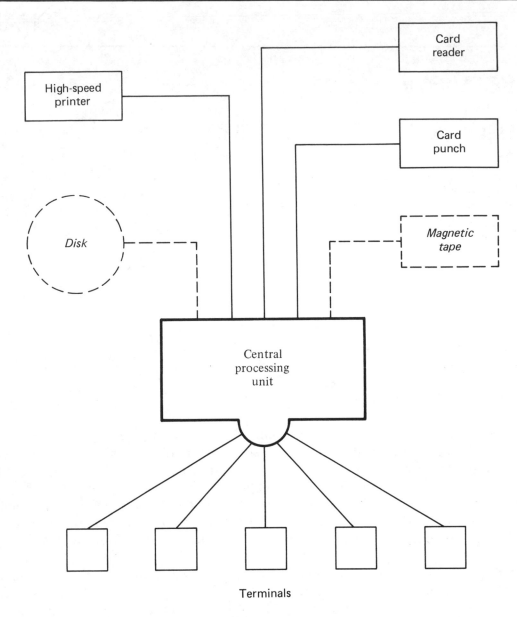

Figure 1.1–1.
Components of a Typical Computer

At any one time, we are likely to use only a few of these devices. It is worthwhile to realize, however, that these pieces of equipment are available. We will point out particular devices that are frequently used when we discuss batch and time-sharing processing in Sections 1.3 and 1.4.

We conclude this section by outlining the basic steps in running a simple computer application:

1. The user enters information into the CPU from cards or a terminal.
2. The CPU sometimes combines this information with additional data stored inside the machine or on disk or tape.
3. The CPU performs the operations specified by the user.
4. The results are printed on paper, cards, or a terminal, or stored on disk or tape.

Section 1.2: WHAT IS PROGRAMMING?

Now that we have a general idea of what components make up a computer, we turn to the problem of getting the machine to perform the job that we want.

In all applications, the machine must be given a step-by-step procedure for completing a desired task, and all instructions must be in a language that the computer can utilize. A sequence of instructions, written in a language usable by a computer, is called a *computer program.*

When writing a computer program, we must remember continually that all steps of our project must be stated in the correct order. In this respect, we can regard the computer as having several characteristics in common with a well-trained, but somewhat retarded monkey:

1. It is able to follow our instructions very quickly and accurately.
2. It does not analyze our instructions. It performs incorrect operations if we tell it to do so. It makes no judgments as to what we really mean, unless we write out our intentions explicitly.
3. It cannot fill in missing steps.
4. It will not change the order of our instructions. It will not correct us if we tell it to perform certain steps in an incorrect order.
5. It must be given instructions in a carefully defined format, or it will become confused. The omission of even a single comma may render it unable to continue processing our program.

The discussion in this section until now indicates that in our programming we must know precisely what steps we want the computer to follow. For example:

1. We must know precisely what information we want to use, and we must be certain that our data are entered into the machine.
2. We must decide what we want printed out and in what format on the page. We cannot merely say that we want the "appropriate" numbers printed. Rather, we must know specifically what output is desired.
3. On the basis of steps 1 and 2 above, we must determine all steps that are needed in order to obtain the output, and we must be able to decide in what order these steps should be executed.

Here we see that the programming process involves considerably more than writing in a special language that a computer can utilize. We must analyze the problem that we want to solve and decide what steps the computer must follow to find an answer.

Section 1.3: WHAT IS BATCH PROCESSING?

In Sections 1.1 and 1.2, we saw what a computer looks like, and we noted that instructions must be written in a language that the machine can use. We now investigate how to get our instructions into the computer and how to obtain the desired results.

Computer processing usually takes place in one of two modes, *batch processing* and *interactive time sharing.* Here we discuss the first of these modes, while the second is explained in the following section.

In simple batch processing, the main computer components used are the card reader, the central processing unit (CPU), and the printer (see Figure 1.3–1). Before approaching the machine, we prepare punched cards containing all the instructions and data that we will need. This self-contained card deck is then read into the card reader in one operation, the CPU performs the operations requested, and the output is printed.

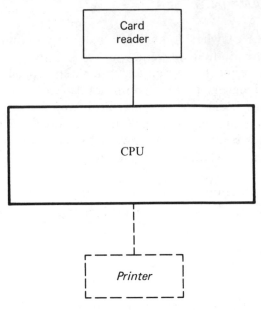

Figure 1.3–1.
Basic Computer Components
in Batch Processing

In this mode of computer operation, the card deck must contain all pertinent information before it is read into the machine. The format of the deck will vary from language to language and from machine to machine. However, the general characteristics of a card deck usually follow the example given below:

1 *//SAMPLE JOB (12345678), 'JOHN SMITH'*

1 A new JOB, with name SAMPLE, is being entered into the machine. The account number to be billed for the JOB is 12345678 and the programmer's name is JOHN SMITH.

2 *//EXEC ALGOLW*

2 The language used for the program that we wish to EXECute is ALGOLW.

3 *//SYSIN DD**

3 The program itself will begin with the next card. (The meanings of these specific words are technical and will not be discussed here.)

(ALGOLW program placed here.)

4 *%DATA*

4 The ALGOLW program itself has been given and the data for the program are about to be given.

(Data for program placed here.)

5 */**

5 ALGOLW program and data are complete.

6 *//*

6 JOB is finished. No further expense will be billed to account 12345678.

In batch processing, whenever a program is to be modified, the card deck is modified by adding or deleting cards, and the modified deck is resubmitted for reading into the card reader.

Section 1.4: **WHAT IS TIME SHARING?**

The time sharing operation of a computer differs from the batch processing discussed in the previous section in that time sharing allows the user to interact continually with the machine. The programmer sits at a terminal connected directly to the computer, and each user is allotted some storage space on the disk (see Figure 1.4–1). The programmer is allowed to use *part* of the CPU, and cards are no longer necessary since all materials can be stored in the machine.

When we want to use the computer to solve a problem, we begin by deciding what steps will be needed and we write (on paper) a program to do the job. When we come to a terminal, we find that our time is divided into three parts:

1. We must identify ourselves so that the machine will know what storage area our work is in and whom to bill for our work.
2. We proceed with our work, writing, modifying, or running programs, and/or changing data.
3. We must tell the machine when we are finished so that others will not have access to our work, and so that we will not be billed for the work of the next user.

These steps are illustrated in the following exchange with the computer. Here we use different type faces to distinguish the characters typed by us (*INPUT*) from the response of the computer (OUTPUT). As with batch processing, the exact format required may vary from one machine to another.

1 *HELLO*

    RSTS VØ7A-Ø2 GRINNELL COLL JOB 14 KB43 24-AUG-83 14:51
2 *#41,18*

1 This is our greeting to the machine to let it know that we want to begin working.

2 We type in our programming number in response to the request '#'. Note that 'Ø' and 'O' are distinct characters—the number zero and the letter oh, respectively.

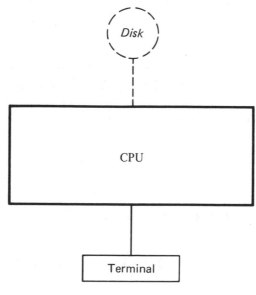

Figure 1.4–1.
Basic Computer Components
in Interactive Time Sharing

3 PASSWORD: - - - - - -

   *** WELCOME TO THE GRINNELL TIME-SHARING SYSTEM ***

3 This is where we type in the password that protects our work from tampering by other users. Others will not know our password, so they will be unable to use our materials. Note that the password is not printed on our screen.

4 READY

4 The computer is ready for us to begin typing.

5 *NEW WORK*

5 NEW is a command which indicates that we are going to type in a new program; WORK is the name given to this new program.

6 READY

6 The machine is ready for us to type.

7 *10 PRINT 'THIS IS A PROGRAM'*
8 *RUN*
9 WORK 14:57 24-AUG-83

7 We type in our program.
8 RUN makes our program execute.
9 The program name and the time are printed.

10 THIS IS A PROGRAM

10 This is the output from our program.

11 READY

11 The machine is ready for our next program.

12 *SAVE*

12 SAVE is a command to indicate that we want to save our program in our allotted space on disk for possible use at a later time.

11 READY

13 *BYE*

13 BYE is the way to say farewell to the computer.

14 CONFIRM: *YES*

14 The computer is programmed to make certain that we are serious about leaving.

In this time-sharing mode of operation, we spend more time interacting with the machine than in batch processing, where all instructions and data had to be punched on cards before the computer could be used. However, before we can use the computer in either mode of operation, we must have written out a program that will compute the desired results. This brings us to the final section before we start learning a programming language itself.

Section 1.5: WHAT IS AN ALGORITHM?

We have already noted that several things must be done before we can expect a computer to help us with a problem. These steps include:

1. formulating the problem carefully enough to know precisely what kind of data we have to start with and what results we want;
2. analyzing our problem to decide what major steps will be needed to compute the desired output;
3. writing out a program (on paper) that performs the steps we have decided upon;
4. typing out the program on cards or at a terminal.

A common tendency, particularly among novices, is for programmers to try to skip steps 1 through 3 and begin with step 4. The result is often an ill-conceived, difficult-to-understand, and inefficient program that *sometimes* produces correct results. Program instructions are often accidentally omitted. Corrections to these programs are often very difficult to make.

A much more reasonable approach is to concentrate on steps 1 and 2. Changes in a program are much easier to make before the program is written. For some programs, these steps can be done rather quickly. As problems become more advanced, however, we must be very careful to know exactly what we want and what we will be given.

Once step 1 is clearly defined so that we know what input can be expected and what output is desired, we must decide what procedures or algorithms will be needed. In more complex problems, this analysis in step 2 can be the most difficult part of the programming process.

A procedure called *top-down programming* is often helpful in constructing the algorithm that will perform the desired job. This procedure is indicated below:

1. Work in outline form, beginning with a few major steps that will do the job. These steps should be major headings and they may be quite general in nature.

2. Divide the major steps into smaller tasks. While these tasks are more specific than the major steps, there is no reason to cover all details at this point.

3. Continue subdividing each task, becoming more specific and detailed at each level, until all details are in place. At the end, all formulas should be included and all possibilities covered.

We can regard top-down programming as similar to approaching a city in a helicopter. We begin at the top, on a high general level where we get an overview of the city. We then proceed to more specific, detailed views or levels as we move toward the ground.

In the next chapter, we will find that the work of writing a program is very simple, given this outlined form. This approach of writing programs from an outline is illustrated by solving various programming problems in the next chapter, where we consider FORTRAN.

Example of Top-down Programming Problem

Outline a procedure to convert a temperature in Fahrenheit to one in centigrade and absolute.

1. An initial outline:
   I. Enter data
   II. Perform computations
   III. Print results
2. A more detailed outline:
   I. Enter data
       (A) Determine Fahrenheit temperature
   II. Perform computations
       (A) Compute centigrade temperature
       (B) Compute absolute temperature
   III. Print results
       (A) Print all three temperatures
3. A final outline, where we have looked up some formulas from a handbook:
   I. Enter data
       (A) Determine Fahrenheit temperature, F
   II. Perform computations
       (A) Compute centigrade temperature, C
           1. $C = \frac{5}{9}(F - 32)$
       (B) Compute absolute temperature, K
           1. $K = C + 273$
   III. Print results
       (A) Print all three temperatures
           1. Print F in column 1
           2. Print C in column 2
           3. Print K in column 3

CHAPTER 2

An Introduction to FORTRAN Programming

Section 2.1: INTRODUCTION

In Chapter 1, we saw that the computer must be given instructions for carrying out any application, and we noted that these instructions must be in a language that the machine can utilize. This chapter introduces one such language, called FORTRAN (FORmula TRANslation).

Historically, in 1956 FORTRAN became the first language designed to allow the non-computer specialist to use the computer. In particular, FORTRAN allowed especially easy use and efficient computation of mathematical formulas.

By 1958, a more advanced version, FORTRAN II, was introduced, and a later version, FORTRAN IV, appeared in 1962. With the general availability of these easy-to-use languages, FORTRAN II and FORTRAN IV were widely used, particularly for applications in science, mathematics, and statistics where many numerical computations were needed.

The various characteristics of FORTRAN II and FORTRAN IV were standardized in 1966, when specifications for American Standard Basic FORTRAN and American Standard FORTRAN, respectively, were published by the American Standards Association (now called the American National Standards Institute or ANSI). This made FORTRAN the first computer language to be given a national standard, and it implied that the same standard FORTRAN programs could be moved easily from one computer to another. This characteristic of standard FORTRAN contributed to the widespread use of FORTRAN today.

The present chapter describes an extension of standard FORTRAN which is used on the PDP-11 computer of Digital Equipment Corporation. This extended FORTRAN is used because it incorporates several additions that are available on many computers today and because standard FORTRAN has a rather limited capability for using disk files. The few differences between standard FORTRAN and the extended FORTRAN will be clearly indicated. With minor modifications, all techniques and programs in this chapter can be run in standard FORTRAN, except for the section on disk storage. (This section can be omitted without loss of continuity.)

We proceed by considering a large number of annotated programs. The annotations are designed to explain the structure of the language, while the programs will give the reader a variety of examples to consult when he begins writing his own programs.

Section 2.2: THE FIRST STEPS

Now that we have some idea of what a computer is and how to use batch processing, we can begin our study of the FORTRAN language. We start with an example.

Problem 2.2-1. Write a program to convert a Fahrenheit temperature to one in centigrade.

From a handbook, we find:

$$\text{Centigrade} = \frac{5}{9} \,(\text{Fahrenheit} - 32)$$

Now we write a program.

Major Steps for Problem 2.2-1

I. Determine degrees Fahrenheit.
II. Compute degrees centigrade.
III. Print result.
IV. Tell the machine we are done.

```
1       FAHR = 72.5
```
1 We indicate the number of degrees Fahrenheit that we have in mind.

```
2       CENTI = (5.0/9.0) * (FAHR - 32.0)
```
2 We compute the number of degrees centigrade.

```
3       WRITE (7, 38) CENTI
```
3 We write out the answer on device 7, which we take to be our printer. The spacing of the printout will be specified in a statement numbered 38.

```
4    38 FORMAT(F20.5)
```
4 We specify how the output is to be printed. Here, we will allow 20 spaces to print the number, including 5 places to the right of the decimal point. (We will discuss FORMAT more thoroughly in Section 2.4.)

```
5       STOP
```
5 We tell the machine to stop following our program.

```
6       END
```
6 END marks the last statement of every program.

When we run this program, we get

```
7            22.50000
```
7 The answer is given to 5 significant digits.

```
8 STOP
```
8 The machine stopped as requested.

From this example, we can make several observations:

(a)   FORTRAN programs can be written in a form closely related to our outline of the steps in a problem.

(b)   We must place FORTRAN statements in the correct order for solving our problem.

(c)   The text of our statements must be typed between columns 7 and 72 (inclusive). All text in column 73 or beyond is ignored in FORTRAN.

Columns 1–6 have special uses. For example, we may number a statement, such as FORMAT, by putting the number on columns 2–5.

(d)   The first two lines of the program illustrate a value (72.5, 22.50000) being assigned to a variable (FAHR, CENTI). FAHR or CENTI may be considered as a label or a name for a location within the CPU's memory, and these lines put the values 72.5 and 22.50000 into these locations.

(e)   A numeric variable in FORTRAN can be any combination of letters and numbers, beginning with a letter, and not exceeding 6 characters in length.

Valid FORTRAN variables are:

    MAY28
    T5X6KE

Invalid variables are:

    5T3 (starts with number)
    WHY? (invalid character)
    ALPHABET (over 6 characters)

(f)   Descriptive names can and should be used in writing programs, so we can understand what we are writing. The clearer our program, the more likely we have written it correctly.

(g)   The arithmetic operations of addition, subtraction, multiplication, and division are represented by +, −, *, /, respectively. Note that the symbol, '=', is used here to denote 'assignment' of values to variables; FORTRAN cannot 'solve' the second line of our program to get

$$FAHR = (9./5.) * CENTI + 32.$$

All variables that appear on the right side of an equal (assignment) sign must have been given values by previous FORTRAN statements.

(h)   When we want to print out an answer, we must say where the answer is to be printed. Here we used the number 7 in the WRITE statement, because we wanted our answer printed on device number 7.

The numbers for the various input and output devices may differ from one machine to another. In this text we will use the following numbering:

Number	Device
4	Disk file
5	Card reader
7	Printer

(i)   We must tell the computer when we want it to stop following our program.

In many extensions of standard FORTRAN, the STOP statement may be replaced by a statement

CALL EXIT

The CALL EXIT has a number of advantages in these extended versions of standard FORTRAN. Thus, in future programs, we will use this variation from the standard.

Integers and Real Numbers

Before we can consider additional examples, we must distinguish between integers and real numbers, since FORTRAN treats these two types of numbers in very different ways.

Customarily, we write numbers in any of three ways:

1. Integers.
2. Decimals.
3. Scientific notation.

Examples

1. -3, 17, 32767
2. -15.8, 2.71828
3. -5.7×10^8, 1.024×10^3

In FORTRAN, numbers can be written in each of these ways as well, although types 2 and 3 are both considered to be real numbers.

1. Integers (no decimal point)

2. Real numbers
   (a) Decimal notation (with decimal point)
   (b) Exponential notation
       Here E is used instead of the 10. Thus 1.024E3 is used to represent 1.024×10^3 or 1024.

Many computers restrict integers to be between -32768 and 32767, inclusive.
Frequently, real numbers are restricted to 8 significant digits and exponents must be between -38 and 38, inclusive.

As a further example, in the first program we wrote real numbers 5.0, 9.0, and 32.0. If we had written 5, 9, and 32 instead, then these numbers would have been considered integers.

In FORTRAN, unless explicitly stated, variables are assumed to be integers if they begin with the letter I, J, K, L, M, or N, and variables are assumed to be real otherwise.

For example KLEAN and NO are integers while CLEAN and ON are assumed to be real.

In our first program the variables FAHR and CENTI are both real numbers. However, we can override the above convention by stating at the beginning of the program that a certain variable is REAL or INTEGER.

This distinction between integer and real becomes particularly important when performing arithmetic because *arithmetic involving integers truncates all values to the right of the decimal point*.

The answer is not rounded off in integer arithmetic.

Thus 5/9 yields 0 since it is performed in integer mode, while 5.0/9.0 yields the real number 0.55555.

Thus, use of 5/9 in the first program would cause a result of 0 to be computed!
For example, 5/9.0 is not allowed in standard FORTRAN.

In standard FORTRAN, an arithmetic operation between a real number and an integer is not allowed. Rather a special function must be used to convert the integer to a real number before the arithmetic can be performed. (This function, called FLOAT, is discussed in Section 2.6.)

However, in most versions of FORTRAN now in use (such as that used on the PDP-11 series computer), arithmetic operations between real and integer values are allowed. The machine automatically converts the integer to a real number and the operation is then performed.

Thus, in most current editions of FORTRAN, 5/9. is allowed and it yields 0.55555.

In the next section, we will see how the distinction between real and integer mode can be used effectively.

Section 2.3: TWO EXAMPLES

We illustrate several ideas from the last section by considering two examples.

Problem 2.3–1. Convert yards, feet, and inches to meters. From a handbook, we find:

$$1 \text{ yard } = 0.914403 \text{ meters}$$
$$1 \text{ foot } = 0.304801 \text{ meters}$$
$$1 \text{ inch } = 0.0254001 \text{ meters}$$

We now write our program.

```
1       REAL METERS, INCH



2,3     YARDS = 2.

2,3     FEET = 5.

2,3     INCH = 2.7
4       METERS = .914403 * YARDS + .304801 * FEET
5     1        + .0254001 * INCH




6       WRITE (7, 15) YARDS, FEET, INCH, METERS

7    15 FORMAT(4F20.5)



8       CALL EXIT
        END
```

When the program is run, we get:

    2.0000   5.00000   2.70000   3.42139

From the fifth and sixth lines of our program, when we compute METERS, we see that FORTRAN performs arithmetic in the same order as in algebra. That is:

(a) Expressions within parentheses are done first.
(b) Multiplication or division is performed before addition or subtraction.

Major Steps for Problem 2.3-1

I. Determine number of yards, feet, and inches.
II. Compute meters.
III. Print results.
IV. Stop program.

1 We want METERS and INCH to be real numbers, not integers. However, since they begin with M and I, FORTRAN will assume they are integers unless we specify otherwise.

2 We specify the number of yards, feet, and inches.

3 We use a decimal point in each number, as the lengths are to be considered real, not integer.

4 We compute the number of meters.

5 If we run out of room on one line, we can continue our statement on the next line by typing "1" (or "2", "3", etc.) in column 6 and then writing the next part of our line.

6 We may print more than one number at a time.

7 We will allow 20 spaces, including 5 spaces to the right of the decimal point, for each of the 4 numbers.

8 We tell the machine to stop processing our program.

Note, however, that FORTRAN does not specify what order should be followed if several additions, subtractions, or multiplications are

14

(c) In terms containing division, evaluation proceeds from left to right.

Examples

	Expression	Result
(a)	7 * (5 – 2)	21
(b)	7 * 5 – 2	33
(c)	6/3 * 5	10

to occur. In many machines, this evaluation does proceed from left to right, although we should not rely on this. When in doubt, use parentheses.

(a) Subtraction in parentheses is done first.
(b) With no parentheses, multiplication is done before subtraction.
(c) In a term containing division, evaluation proceeds from left to right. Thus, 6/3 is computed first. The resulting 2 is then multiplied by 5.

In our next program, we rely heavily on the characteristics of integer arithmetic of FORTRAN.

Problem 2.3-2. Write a program to compute the quotient and remainder when one integer is divided by a second integer.

We will let our two integers be IFIRST and ISECND. Then we want QUOTient and REMAINder where

$$\text{IFIRST} = \text{QUOT} * \text{ISECND} + \text{REMAIN} \qquad (*)$$

If we divide this equation by ISECND in integer mode, we get:

$$\frac{\text{IFIRST}}{\text{ISECND}} = \text{QUOT} + \frac{\text{REMAIN}}{\text{ISECND}}$$

However, we know the REMAINder will be smaller than the number ISECND that we are dividing by. Thus, with integer arithmetic, REMAIN/ISECND is 0, and the above becomes:

$$\text{QUOT=IFIRST/ISECND}$$

Once we perform this computation to compute QUOT, we can go back to equation (*) and solve for REMAIN.

We can now write our program.

Outline for Problem 2.3-2

  I. Determine the numbers.
 II. Compute the quotient.
III. Compute remainder.
IV. Print results.

We add the I to FIRST and SECOND so FORTRAN will treat these numbers as integers.

```
1 C THIS PROGRAM COMPUTES THE QUOTIENT AND REMAINDER
1 C     WHEN ONE INTEGER IS DIVIDED BY ANOTHER


2      INTEGER QUOT, REMAIN

  C DETERMINE THE TWO INTEGERS
       IFIRST = 24
       ISECND = 10
```

1 A comment may be inserted into a program of FORTRAN by typing a "C" in column 1. The line is then treated as a comment and is ignored by the CPU.

2 We want QUOT and REMAIN to be integers.

```
C COMPUTE QUOTIENT AND REMAINDER
      QUOT = IFIRST / ISECND

3     REMAIN = IFIRST - QUOT * ISECND

C PRINT RESULTS
      WRITE (7, 123) IFIRST, ISECND, QUOT, REMAIN
4 123 FORMAT(4I15)
C COMPLETE JOB
      CALL EXIT
      END
```

3 Here we have solved the equation (*) for REMAIN.

4 Here we are allotting 15 spaces to print each of the 4 integers.

When the program is run, we get

      24   10   2   4

Note how closely this program follows our initial outline. This leads us to some final notes on program clarity.

Program Clarity

A primary goal in writing a program should be program clarity. A clearly written program is easy to modify and correct, and it is no more difficult to write than a program that is hard to follow. The following suggestions may be helpful.

(a) Use many comments in your program, stating what the program is doing. If the program is long, divide the program into parts and comment on each part. You may want to include your outline in the comments of the program.

(b) Use variable names that describe the variables. METERS or REMAIN immediately suggest what they represent, while D or N1 give little hint as to their meaning.

(c) Add parentheses in arithmetical expressions where they add clarity. It is always permissible to add parentheses, even if they are not technically needed.

(d) Insert spaces in your typing to add clarity. You may not put spaces within a number or variable (so .91 44 03 and MET ERS are not allowed), but they may be typed between any symbols.

Do not try to get everything on one line. The digit in column 6 allows you to spread your statement over several lines so the statement can be easily read.

(e) When you use a continuation card, indent the second and subsequent lines, so you can tell easily that they are all related to the first line of the statement.

The first program of the section illustrates this note.

(f) Do not be afraid to type a few extra characters for clarity. The time spent typing is usually recovered in correcting errors and in making later modifications to the program.

Section 2.4: **FORMATTED OUTPUT**

In the previous section, each of our programs printed four numbers as our output. However, these numbers were not labeled, so we had to remember what the numbers represented. As programs become longer and more numbers are printed, we find it is rather hard to keep track of which number is which. Thus, in this section, we consider how we can label the output and control the spacing of the printing.

We proceed by examining the WRITE statement and by discussing the FORMAT statement which specifies exactly how our output is to be printed. This is seen in the following example.

Problem 2.4–1. Write a program that converts quarts to liters. From a handbook, we find:

$$1 \text{ liter} = 1.056710 \text{ quarts (U.S.)}$$

Our program is

```
C THIS PROGRAM CONVERTS QUARTS TO LITERS
      REAL LITERS
      QUARTS = 4.
      LITERS = QUARTS / 1.056710
C PRINT OUTPUT
1     WRITE (7, 43) QUARTS, LITERS



2   43 FORMAT(5X, F10.4, 9H QUARTS =, F10.4, 7H LITERS)




      CALL EXIT
      END
```

Running the program yields

```
  4.0000 QUARTS =     3.7853 LITERS
```

The FORMAT statement above illustrates several ways output may be specified, including numbers, labels, and spaces.

A. Formatting Numbers

As with variables, we must consider integers and real numbers separately.

1. Real numbers
   We may specify either decimal or exponential notation.

Outline for Problem 2.4–1

 I. Determine number of quarts.
 II. Compute liters.
 III. Print output.
     Specify format of output.

1 We specify our printer, and we indicate that the format of the output will be given in a statement with number 43.

2 We have assigned the number 43 to the line by placing 43 in columns 2 through 5. The material in parentheses specifies how the line is to be printed, as described below.

Note: Real numbers are sometimes called *floating point* numbers.

For decimal notation, we write

$$Fw.d$$

where w gives the number of columns to be used for the printing and d gives the number of places to the right of the decimal point.

For exponential notation, we write

$$Ew.d$$

where w specifies the total width for the printing and d gives the number of significant digits.

Thus, 3.7853 in E10.4 format would produce

$$.3785\ E+01$$

Note that the total width w must include the 4 spaces for the exponent E+01.

2. Integers

Our specification of integers has the form

$$Iw$$

where w is the number of spaces to be allowed for printing the integer. If the integer takes fewer spaces, it is right-justified.

With either integers or real numbers, if we do not allow enough space for the number, an error results and probably a string of *'s would be printed.

F10.4 specifies 5 places to the left of the decimal point, then the decimal point (1 space), and finally 4 places to the right of the point for a total of 10 spaces, i.e.,

$$\underline{-----.----}$$

```
    ----- .----
         d=4
   w=10
```

E10.4 produces

```
.---- E---
        ↑
      + or
d=4    - sign

   w=10
```

I5 specifies 5 spaces for integers.

```
-----
 w=5
```

If we print the integer 13 in I5 format, we get

$$---\underline{13}$$

If we try to print 1234 in I3 format, we get

$$\mathbf{***}$$
$$\underline{---}$$

B. Text

We can specify text to be printed out by counting the number of characters we want printed (including spaces) and preceding the text by this number and by the letter H.

For example, if we want the text ' LITERS' printed, we count 6 letters plus 1 space for a total of 7 characters. Thus, our format statement includes

$$7H\ LITERS$$

H stands for Hollerith, who was a pioneer in the field of data processing.

Note: Many machines allow an extension of standard FORTRAN where the text may be placed in quotation marks instead of using the H format. For example, ' LITERS' could be used.

C. Spaces

We can insert spaces in a line of text by using X format. We simply precede the letter X by the number of spaces we want. Thus, 5X indicates we want 5 spaces skipped on our line of output.

We can also control the spacing between lines of output. In fact, in formatting the output, the first character is used to control the carriage of our output printer, according to the system shown in Table 2.4–1.

In our example, the 5X at the beginning of the FORMAT statement has the following effects:

(a) Space 1: From Table 2.4–1, we see that the blank indicated we wanted to skip 1 line vertically before printing our output.

(b) Spaces 2–5: We skip 4 spaces on the new line before trying to print the rest of our line.

Caution: The first character of every FORMAT statement for writing should be explicitly stated, so the vertical spacing is not left to chance.

As we have seen in our example, various types of format specifications may be combined in one FORMAT. Further, we may skip a line in writing by using a slash, /.

As an example, if we changed the FORMAT statement in our sample program to

```
43 FORMAT(1HØ, E10.4,19H QUARTS CONVERTS TO, F8.3, 7H LITERS)
```

the output would have the form

⟨double space⟩
.4000 E+01 QUARTS CONVERTS TO   3.785 LITERS

If we added a slash in the FORMAT to get

```
43 FORMAT(1H0, E10.4,19H QUARTS CONVERTS TO / F10.3, 7H LITERS)
```

then the output would be

⟨double space⟩
.4000 E+01 QUARTS CONVERTS TO
    3.785 LITERS

Finally, we note that FORMAT statements allow us to print titles as in the following revision of the previous program.

```
C THIS PROGRAM CONVERTS QUARTS TO LITERS
      REAL LITERS
      QUARTS = 4.
      LITERS = QUARTS / 1.056710
C PRINT OUTPUT
1     WRITE (7, 21)
```

Table 2.4–1

First Character	Vertical Spacing Before Printing
Blank	Single space
0	Double space
1	Jump to top of next page
+	Do not space (overprint on current line)

In the previous programs, we left a very wide field in printing a number (such as F20.5) so we would not accidentally print anything in this first column. In the future, we will follow the safer route of carefully controlling this first character.

1 Writing takes place where we place the WRITE statement. The FORMAT can be placed anywhere. Note the statement numbers in the WRITE statements need not be in order.

```
      WRITE (7, 18)
      WRITE (7, 43) QUARTS, LITERS
2     FORMAT (39H1THIS PROGRAM CONVERTS QUARTS TO LITERS)
      FORMAT (1H0, 4X, 6HQUARTS, 4X, 6HLITERS)
3     FORMAT (1X, 2F10.4)

      CALL EXIT
      END
```

2 The 1 after the 39H is for the carriage control.

3 Here, we want 2 numbers printed. Thus we could write $F10.4$, $F10.4$ or we can combine these as $2F10.4$.

Running the program yields

4

```
   THIS PROGRAM CONVERTS QUARTS TO LITERS
```

5

```
        QUARTS  LITERS
        4.0000  3.7853
```

4 We skip to a new page.

5 We double space here.

Section 2.5:   INPUT OF DATA

In Section 2.3, we wrote a program that converted yards, feet, and inches to meters:

```
      REAL METERS, INCH
1  10 YARDS = 2.
1  13 FEET = 5.
1  17 INCH = 2.7
      METERS = .914403 * YARDS + .304801 * FEET
    1        + .0254001 * INCH
      WRITE (7, 15) YARDS, FEET, INCH, METERS
   15 FORMAT(5F20.5)
      CALL EXIT
      END
```

1 We may number statements, using columns 2–5, even if we do not refer to these statement numbers in the rest of our program.

Here, we used statements 10, 13, and 17 to specify the number of yards (2), feet (5), and inches (2.7) we wanted to convert to meters. If we want to convert 3 yards, 2 feet, 7.9 inches to meters, we must re-write each of these lines to read

```
10 YARDS = 3.
13 FEET = 2.
17 INCH = 7.9
```

When we run the program again, we get

```
        3.00000          2.00000          7.90000              3.55347
```

If we want the conversion for several different sets of values, we must

1. rewrite statements 10, 13, and 17;
2. run the program with the revised lines.

This procedure can be simplified with the DATA or READ statements. If we replace these three lines by

```
DATA YARDS, FEET, INCH/3., 2., 7.9/
```

then the variables YARDS, FEET, and INCH will be assigned the corresponding values at the beginning of the program. Thus, the DATA statement specifies the initial values to be given to the variables mentioned. Then, if we want to run this program for several different sets of values, we only must change this one statement.

We note, however, that since DATA statements give initial values, they must be placed early in the program, immediately after any REAL or INTEGER statements. Further, the same variable may not appear in two DATA statements. Thus, the following is *not* allowed:

```
10 DATA YARDS, FEET, INCH/3., 2., 7.9/
13 DATA YARDS /2./
```

However, it is permissible for different variables to be in different DATA statements or for several lists of variables to be in such a statement. Thus, the following are allowed:

```
10 DATA YARDS /3./, FEET /2./
13 DATA INCH /7.9/
```

A second important way to assign values to variables is with the READ statement. Here, our program might have the form

```
        REAL METERS, INCH
1       READ (5, 12) YARDS, FEET, INCH
```

1 Here, we are directing the machine to read some numbers from device number 5, the card reader. As with the WRITE, we must specify what FORMAT statement will specify what columns to find the numbers in.

```
2    12 FORMAT(3F10.5)

       METERS = .914403 * YARDS + .304801 * FEET
     1      + .0254001 * INCH
       WRITE (7, 15) YARDS, FEET, INCH, METERS
    15 FORMAT(4F20.5)
       CALL EXIT
       END
```

2 We will expect the first number in columns 1–10, the second in columns 11–20, and the third in columns 21–30.

When this program is run, the READ statement sends the machine to the device specified (number 5 – card reader). The computer then reads a card, and assigns the numbers it finds in the specified columns to YARDS, FEET, and INCH. The values for YARDS, FEET, and INCH can then be changed for the next run of the program by retyping only the one data card.

Recall, from our example in Section 1.3 on batch processing, that after the program was written we wrote

```
%DATA
     (Data for program placed here.)
```

In the program at hand, we would write

```
%DATA
    3.        2.        7.9
```

Finally, it may happen that our card of data contains many numbers and we only want to use some of these values in our computation. For example, the card may look like

3.0   5.7832   314.159   2.000   7.9   271828.1828
↑   ↑   ↑   ↑   ↑   ↑
column 1   column 11   column 25   column 33 column 40 column 51

Here, we know that the first number will appear in the first 10 columns, the second in columns 33–39, and the third in columns 40–50.

In this case, we could write

```
1      READ (5,103) YARDS, FEET, INCH
      103 FORMAT (F10.5, 22X, F7.5, F11.3)
```

1 We will specify the spacing of our input in a FORMAT statement numbered 103.

Here, the first number will be in columns 1–10, then we must skip 22 columns before reading the next numbers.

In our example, each of the numbers read contained a decimal point, so the specification of the number of decimal places in the FORMAT statement was ignored. However, if no decimal point was found, then the last 5 columns (columns 6–10) would be treated as containing digits to the right of the decimal point, because of the 10.5 specification. Thus, using the above FORMAT statement, we could type the following line for our data.

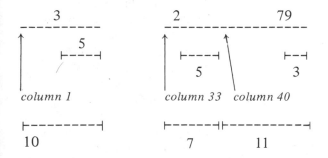

We now consider a final example.

Problem 2.5–1. Write a program that converts quarts and gallons to liters. Run the program for 5 gallons, 2.6 quarts and for 3 gallons, 3.2 quarts.

We decide that we will put both sets of data on the same data card, in the format

5   2.6   3   3.2
↑   ↑   ↑   ↑
column 1   column 11 column 21   column 31

We write the program

Outline for Problem 2.5–1

I.   READ values for quarts and gallons.

II. Compute liters.

III. Print result.

```
C THIS PROGRAM CONVERTS GALLONS AND QUARTS TO LITERS
      REAL LITERS
      READ (5, 1) GALLNS, QUARTS
1   1 FORMAT (2F10.9)




2     LITERS = (4 * GALLNS + QUARTS) / 1.056710
      WRITE (7, 2) GALLNS, QUARTS, LITERS
    2 FORMAT(1H , F10.5, 8H GALLONS, F10.5, 9H QUARTS =,
    1         F10.5, 7H LITERS)
      CALL EXIT
      END
```

1 The 5 is in column 1 for the first set of data. As 5 is not followed by a decimal point, we must tell the computer that the next 9 places are to the right of the decimal point.

2 Our conversion is based on the conversion factor listed in the previous section.

When this program is run, we get

```
5.00000 GALLONS   2.60000 QUARTS =  21.38714 LITERS
```

If we want to use the second set of data, we only change the FORMAT for our READing to

```
1 FORMAT (20X, 2F10.9)
```

Running this modified program gives

```
3.00000 GALLONS   3.20000 QUARTS =  14.38427 LITERS
```

Here we have used the same line of data for each program; we have only changed the specification of which numbers on the line should be used.

Section 2.6: ARITHMETIC FUNCTIONS

In Section 2.2, The First Steps, we saw that the mathematical operations, addition, subtraction, multiplication, and division, could be performed using the symbols +, −, *, and /, respectively. Here, we will see that other mathematical operations also can be done easily. We look at several classes of operations.

Exponents

On a card reader or on a terminal, it is not convenient to type exponents in their normal position as superscripts. For this reason, two asterisks ** are used. Thus

$$8^2 \quad \text{is written} \quad 8**2$$

As in algebra, exponentiation is done before all other operations. Thus, 2**3*5 is evaluated by computing 2**3=8 first and then multiplying by 5 to get 40. Similarly, 5*2**3=40. The exponents may be positive or negative and they may be either integers or real numbers. Note, however, that an error occurs in FORTRAN if a negative number is raised to a noninteger power.

A commonly occurring special case is the square root. Here $\sqrt{X}$ may be written X**.5, or a special function SQRT(X) may be used. These, together with other special functions, are shown in the following list, together with numerical examples. Unless otherwise specified, the list assumes the normal conventions that an integer variable begins with one of the letters, I, J, K, L, M, or N, and a real variable begins with any other letter.

Note: X must be a real number, not an integer, when using SQRT.

Function Code	Meaning	Examples
IABS(I)	Compute the absolute value, |I|, or |X|, of I or X.	5 = IABS(–5)=IABS(5)
ABS(X)		7.1 = ABS(–7.1)
FLOAT(I)	Converts the integer I to a real number.	3.0 = FLOAT(3)
AINT(X)	Give the truncated value of X as a real number	2.0 = AINT(2.3)
INT(X)	or as an integer. Thus, if X is written in a decimal expansion, the places after the decimal point are dropped.	–2 = INT(–2.3)
IFIX(X)	Converts the real number X to an integer.	2 = IFIX(2.0)
AMAX0(I1,I2, . . .)	Compute the maximum value of the integers	10.0 = AMAX0(7, 5, 10)
AMAX1(X1,X2, . . .)	I1, I2, . . . or real numbers X1,X2, . . . and	10.7 = AMAX1(7.3, 5.1, 10.7)
MAX0(I1, I2, . . .)	give the result as a real number or integer.	10 = MAX0(7, 5, 10)
MAX1(X1,X2, . . .)		10 = MAX1(7.3, 5.1, 10.7)
AMIN0(I1,I2, . . .)	Compute the minimum value of the integers	5.0 = AMIN0(7, 5, 10)
AMIN1(X1,X2, . . .)	I1,I2, . . . or the real numbers X1,X2, . . . and	5.1 = AMIN1(7.3, 5.1, 10.7)
MIN0(I1,I2, . . .)	give the result as a real number or integer.	5 = MIN0(7, 5, 10)
MIN1(X1,X2, . . .)		5 = MIN1(7.3, 5.1, 10.7)
SIGN(A1,A2)	ABS(A1) or IABS(1) is computed, and the	2.5 = SIGN (–2.5, 2.5)
ISIGN(I1,I2)	result is made positive if A2 or I2 is positive, the result is negative if A2 or I2 is negative, and the result is 0 if A2 or I2 is zero.	2.5 = SIGN (2.5, 2.5)
		–2.5 = SIGN (–2.5, –2.5)
		–2.5 = SIGN (2.5, –2.5)
		0 = SIGN (2.5, 0)
DIM(X1,X2)	Computes the positive difference of X1,X2 or	0.5 = DIM(5.6, 5.1)
IDIM(I1,I2)	I1,I2. That is, we compute X1–AMIN1(X1,X2)	0 = IDIM(5, 6)
AMOD(X1,X2)	Compute the remainder when X1 or I1 is	0.4 = AMOD(2.4, 1.0)
MOD(I1,I2)	divided by X2 or I2.	4 = MOD(24, 10)

Exponentials

SQRT(X)	Computes the square root of X, $\sqrt{X}$.	2. = SQRT(4.)
		9. = SQRT(81.)
EXP(X)	Computes $e**X$ or e^X, where e = 2.71828	2.71828 = EXP(1)

Logarithms

ALOG(X)	Computes the natural logarithm of X, $\log_e X$.	1. = ALOG(2.71828)
ALOG10(X)	Computes the common logarithm of X, $\log_{10} X$.	2. = ALOG10(100.)

Trigonometric Functions Note: All angles are assumed to be measured in radians!

We assume PI = 3.14159265

COS(X)	Computes the cosine of X, where X is measured in radians.	1. = COS(0.)
		0. = COS(PI/2.)

Function Code	Meaning	Examples
SIN(X)	Computes the sine of X, where X is measured in radians.	0. = SIN(0.) 1. = SIN(PI/2.)
ATAN(X)	Computes the arctangent (measured in radians) of X.	1 = TAN(PI/4.) 0.78 = ATAN(1.) (recall that 0.78 is PI/4.)
ATAN2(X1,X2)	Computes the arctangent (measured in radians) of X1/X2.	0.78 = ATAN (5., 5.)
TANH(X)	Computes the hyperbolic tangent of X.	1. = TANH(0)

Any of these functions may be used in any valid algebraic expression, as seen in the following:

Problem 2.6–1. Write a program that will READ the legs of a right triangle and compute the length of the hypotenuse and the size of the angles in degrees. (See Figure 2.6–1.)

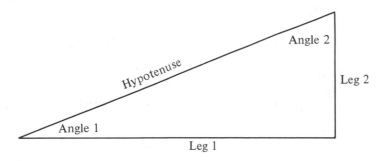

Figure 2.6–1
A Right Triangle

Recall that by the Pythagorean Theorem

$$\text{Hypotenuse} = \sqrt{(\text{Leg 1})^2 + (\text{Leg 2})^2}$$

and by trigonometry

$$\text{Angle 1} = \text{Arctangent (Leg 2/Leg 1)}$$
$$\text{Angle 2} = \text{Arctangent (Leg 1/Leg 2)}$$

and by geometry

$$\text{Degrees} = \frac{180}{\pi} \text{ radians}$$

We can now see what major steps are needed to solve the problem.

Outline for Problem 2.6–1

   I. Enter legs.
  II. Compute values.
      (A) Compute hypotenuse.
      (B) Compute angles in radians.
      (C) Convert radians to degrees.
 III. Print results.

The program becomes

```
C THIS PROGRAM COMPUTES THE HYPOTENUSE AND ANGLES
C OF A RIGHT TRIANGLE, GIVEN THE LEGS
      READ (5, 1) ALEG1, ALEG2
    1 FORMAT(2F10.5)
      HYPOT = SQRT(ALEG1**2 + ALEG2**2)
      RAD1 = ATAN(ALEG2 / ALEG1)
      RAD2 = ATAN(ALEG1 / ALEG2)
      DEG1 = 180. * RAD1 / 3.1415926535
      DEG2 = 180. * RAD2 / 3.1415926535
      WRITE (7, 2) HYPOT
    2 FORMAT(18H THE HYPOTENUSE IS, F8.4)
      WRITE (7, 3) DEG1, DEG2
    3 FORMAT(37H THE ANGLES, MEASURED IN DEGREES, ARE,
    1        F8.4, 5H AND , F8.4)
      CALL EXIT
      END
```

Running the program with the data card

```
   3.        4.
```

yields

```
THE HYPOTENUSE IS  5.0000
THE ANGLES, MEASURED IN DEGREES, ARE 53.1301 AND  36.8699
```

A table containing all standard FORTRAN functions is given at the end of Section 2.14.

Section 2.7: STATEMENT FUNCTIONS (SINGLE-LINE FUNCTIONS)

In the previous section, we saw that the computer could recognize certain arithmetical functions and that this simplified our program writing. Now we will see how to define our own functions.

We consider the following problem.

Problem 2.7–1. Compute the balance in a bank account after one year, given the principal and annual interest rate, if the interest is compounded annually, semiannually, quarterly, monthly, and daily.

From algebra, we find that if the interest is compounded N times a year, then at the end of the year

$$BALANCe = PRINcipal * (1+RATE/N)**N$$

Here, we must make the computation for the cases

$$N = 1, 2, 4, 12, 365$$

Consider the following program:

```
C THIS PROGRAM COMPUTES ONE'S BANK BALANCE AFTER 1 YEAR
C VERSION A
      REAL INTRST, MONTH
1     BALANC(PRIN, RATE, FREQ) = PRIN*(1. + RATE/FREQ)**FREQ


      READ (5, 1) PRIN, INTRST
   1 FORMAT (2F10.5)
2 C COMPUTATION OF VARIOUS BALANCES


3     ANNUAL = BALANC(PRIN, INTRST, 1.0)


4     SEMIAN = BALANC(PRIN, INTRST, 2.0)
      QUARTR = BALANC(PRIN, INTRST, 4.0)
      MONTH  = BLANC(PRIN, INTRST, 12.0)
      DAILY  = BALANC(PRIN, INTRST, 365.0)
  C PRINTING OF BALANCES
      WRITE (7, 2) PRIN, INTRST
5   2 FORMAT (5X, 'PRINCIPAL =',F8.2, 5X,
    1 'ANNUAL INTEREST RATE =',F7.4)


6     WRITE (7,3)


7   3 FORMAT (1H0, 4X, 'THE BALANCE AFTER ONE YEAR IS COMPUTED')

8     WRITE (7, 4)

    4 FORMAT (5X, 'BY COMPOUNDING AT VARIOUS INTERVALS')
      WRITE (7, 5) ANNUAL
9   5 FORMAT (5X, 28HANNUAL COMPOUNDING:        $, F10.2)

      WRITE (7, 6) SEMIAN
    6 FORMAT (5X, 28HSEMI-ANNUAL COMPOUNDING:   $, F10.2)
      WRITE (7, 7) QUARTR
    7 FORMAT (5X, 28HQUARTERLY COMPOUNDING:     $, F10.2)
      WRITE (7, 8) MONTH
    8 FORMAT (5X, 28HMONTHLY COMPOUNDING:       $, F10.2)
      WRITE (7, 9) DAILY
    9 FORMAT (5X, 28HDAILY COMPOUNDING:         $, F10.2)
      CALL EXIT
      END
```

1 We begin by defining our own function which will compute the balance.

2 The use of comments and indenting can help program readability. Note that the titles came from the major headings of the outline.

3 We want the value of the function, using FREQ=1.0 and using the values we read in for PRIN and INTRST.

4 Here we need FREQ=2.

5 As noted in Section 2.4, many extensions of FORTRAN allow text put in quotes as well as the H format.

6 Here we only want text written, and no variables are specified in the WRITE.

7 The 1H0 causes a line to be skipped.

8 Our title continues on a second line.

9 Here we must count spaces, so the output will be printed in columns. We use H format instead of quotes since we must count characters for the spacing and the H format emphasizes this counting.

If we run the program with the data card

```
1500.         .06
```

then we get the output

```
PRINCIPAL = 1500.00    ANNUAL INTEREST RATE = 0.0600

THE BALANCE AFTER ONE YEAR IS COMPUTED
BY COMPOUNDING AT VARIOUS INTERVALS
ANNUAL COMPOUNDING:          $    1590.00
SEMI-ANNUAL COMPOUNDING:     $    1591.35
QUARTERLY COMPOUNDING:       $    1592.05
MONTHLY COMPOUNDING:         $    1592.52
DAILY COMPOUNDING:           $    1592.76
```

This program illustrates how a statement function can simplify a program. At the beginning of the program (immediately after REAL or INTEGER specifications), we indicate the formulas for the functions that we will need. Then, later in the program, we can use the function, rather than writing out the entire formula each time.

This program illustrates how we can define our function. The statement function begins with the name of the function: *BALANC.*

> As *BALANC* begins with a B, the result of the function will be a real number. If we wanted the result to be an integer, we could add the declaration *INTEGER BALANC* either before or after the REAL declaration.

Once the name of the function is indicated, we must specify what variables the function has, by listing them in parentheses. Here, we are considering 3 variables, *PRIN, RATE,* and *FREQ.*

Finally, after an equal sign, we tell the computer the rule for computing the function. In this case, we give the formula for computing the balance.

Once the function has been defined, it can be used anywhere in the program, by writing the name *BALANC* and then giving the values to be used in computing the function. As seen in the middle part of the program, these values may be specified by giving a variable name, such as *PRIN* or *INTRST,* or by giving a number such as *1.0, 2.0, 4.0, 12.0,* or *365.0.* The computer then computes the value of the function following the normal conventions of algebra.

The program also illustrates that a variable name (*INTRST*) used in computing the function need not be the same as the name (*RATE*) used in defining the function. Since *INTRST* is the second variable listed in parentheses after the function name *BALANC* when the function is to be used, the machine will use its value for the second variable (*RATE*) listed in the definition of the function. Thus we see that we can use any variable names we wish in computing the value of a function, provided we list the variables in the order specified when the function is defined and providing corresponding numbers are both integer or both real.

> In the example, both *INTRST* and *RATE* are real numbers, since *INTRST* is explicitly declared to be real.

In the above example, we used the same value of *PRIN* and *INTRST* in the program and in the function. Only *FREQ* is being changed. In this situation, we can elect to specify only the value of *FREQ* as a variable for the function, and have the computer use the values of *PRIN* and *INTRST* as they are in the program. This leads to a revised program:

> When we used the function, we wrote all numbers with decimal points so they would be real numbers, corresponding to the real number *FREQ* in the function definition.

```
C THIS PROGRAM COMPUTES ONE'S BANK BALANCE AFTER 1 YEAR
C VERSION B
        REAL MONTH
1       BALANC(FREQ) = PRIN*(1. + RATE/FREQ) ** FREQ
```

> **1** As only FREQ is listed as a variable, the computer will use the

values for PRIN and RATE from the program in computing the function. Note the name INTRST in version A had to be changed to RATE to agree with the variable in the function.

```
       READ (5, 1) PRIN, RATE
     1 FORMAT (2F10.5)
  C COMPUTATION OF VARIOUS BALANCES
  2       ANNUAL = BALANC(1.)
  2       SEMIAN = BALANC(2.0)
  2       QUARTR = BALANC(4.0)
  2       MONTH = BALANC(12.0)
  2       DAILY = BALANC(365.0)
  C PRINTING OF BALANCES
          WRITE (7, 2) PRIN, RATE
        2 FORMAT (5X, PRINCIPAL = ,F8.2, 5X'ANNUAL INTEREST RATE =',F7.4)
```

2 The only variable allowed here is FREQ, as that is the only one specified in the definition of the function. The values for PRIN and RATE are as given in the READ statement.

(The remainder of the program is as in version A.)

In this case, we find that program clarity has been retained by simplifying the variables listed after the function. It may even be argued that clarity has been improved since here we can concentrate on the only variable changing, namely FREQ.

We must note, however, that it is possible to get carried away with abbreviation. Too much abbreviation of function variables can lead to programs that are harder to read and harder to correct.

A second use of statement functions is illustrated by the following.

Problem 2.7–2. Write a program that computes the value of the expression

$$i^2 + 2i - 1$$

for $i = 1, 2, 3, 4.$

In the following program, we write the expression as the function L(I).

Outline for Problem 2.7–2

I. Compute the value of the expression for the different values of i.

II. Print each value of the expression.

```
  C THIS PROGRAM COMPUTES THE VALUE
  C OF AN EXPRESSION L(I) FOR I = 1, 2, 3, 4.
  C VERSION A
  1       L(I) = I**2 + 2*I - 1

  C COMPUTE THE VALUE OF THE EXPRESSION AT 1, 2, 3, 4
          L1VAL = L(1)
          L2VAL = L(2)
          L3VAL = L(3)
          L4VAL = L(4)
  C PRINT THE VALUES OF THE EXPRESSION
          WRITE (7, 1)L1VAL
          WRITE (7, 2)L2VAL
          WRITE (7, 3)L3VAL
          WRITE (7, 4)L4VAL
```

1 The statement function defining L(I) must be placed at the beginning of the program.

```
2      1 FORMAT (5X, 'L(1) =', I5)
       2 FORMAT (5X, 'L(2) =', I5)
       3 FORMAT (5X, 'L(3) =', I5)
       4 FORMAT (5X, 'L(4) =', I5)
         CALL EXIT
         END
```

2 Program clarity is often enhanced by grouping all FORMAT statements together at the beginning or ending of a program. In this way, the FORMAT specifications are easy to find and modify when the need arises.

When the program is run, we get

```
L(1) =      2
L(2) =      7
L(3) =     14
L(4) =     23
```

Now, if we want to evaluate another integer expression at 1, 2, 3, 4, we only need to change the statement function. For example, if we want $L(I) = |I-2|$, we could use

$$L(I) = IABS(I-2)$$

Running the program gives

```
L(1) =      1
L(2) =      0
L(3) =      1
L(4) =      2
```

Note that another function can be used in defining the function L, as long as the other function has already been defined. Here the machine knows the IABS function, so IABS may be used. (This will be discussed again in Section 2.15, Function Subprograms.)

Thus, we see that the same program can be used for many functions, if we only retype the statement function each time. This saves considerable programming effort, as one program can be used for many functions.

Section 2:8: **LOOPS: PART I – THE DO STATEMENT**

When we computed the value of the expression $i^2 + 2i - 1$ in the previous section, we wrote a separate line for computing with $i = 1$, $i = 2$, $i = 3$, and $i = 4$. Then we had to write two additional lines (WRITE and FORMAT) to print each result. While the resulting program solved the problem given, it had two limitations:

1. While we used the same formula for each computation, we wrote a separate line for each value of i. A similar comment applies to printing even though a similar form was used each time.
2. The program would become long and tedious to write, type, and correct if we wanted a longer list of values for i.

For example, we would need an additional 48 lines if we wanted a table for $i = 1, 2, \ldots, 20$.

These difficulties are resolved in the following program:

```
C THIS PROGRAM COMPUTES THE VALUE
C OF AN EXPRESSION L(I) FOR I = 1, 2, 3, 4.
C VERSION B
1        L(I) = I**2 + 2*I - 1
C PRINT A TITLE FOR 2 COLUMNS
         WRITE (7, 1)
       1 FORMAT (9X, 'I', 6X, 'L(I)')
C COMPUTE I AND L(I)
2        DO 10 I = 1, 4



3            LVAL = L(I)




4    10      WRITE(7, 2) I, LVAL
     2       FORMAT(5X, I5, 5X, I5)
             CALL EXIT
             END
```

1 The program begins the same way as in version A.

2 We tell the machine to start here and to repeat the statements from here through the statement labeled as number 10 for $i = 1, 2, 3, 4$.

3 We compute the value of the expression. Indenting here is only to clarify how far the DO goes before repeating. The indenting is not required in FORTRAN.

4 We print the results.

When this program is run, we get

```
   I        L(I)
   1          2
   2          7
   3         14
   4         23
```

In reviewing this program, we see that the key steps involve only the 3 lines

```
DO 10 I = 1, 4
    LVAL = L(I)


10     WRITE (7, 2) I, LVAL
```

Here the DO statement tells the machine to repeat the lines through the statement labeled 10 for I = 1, 2, 3, 4.

If we wanted the expression tabulated for I = 1, 2, 3, . . . , 20, we would only have to change the DO statement to

```
DO 10 I = 1,20
```

If we wanted the tabulation to start with I = 5, we could write

```
DO 10 I = 5,20
```

With any of these versions of the tabulation program, we must observe that the placement of the statements

```
    WRITE (7, 1)
  1 FORMAT (9X, 'I', 6X, 'L(I)')
```

is important. When these lines were placed before the DO statement, they printed out titles as desired. However, if the program was revised to read

```
      DO 10 I = 1, 4
1         WRITE(7, 1)
          LVAL = L(I)
  10      WRITE(7, 2) I, LVAL
```

1   Here we are printing the title
    inside the DO loop.

then the computer would have printed the title for each value of I, as follows:

```
    I        L(I)
    1           2
    I        L(I)
    2           7
    I        L(I)
    3          14
    I        L(I)
    4          23
```

Before we can consider the next programs, we must expand upon our introduction to the CPU from Chapter 1. In particular, we must understand a little about how information is stored.

We can envision the CPU as containing a number of storage locations, much the same way as a post office contains a number of boxes for its customers. When we use a variable in a program, one of these locations is reserved for the variable. Thus, in the program above which tabulates the function *L*, we defined variables *I*, and *LVAL*, and the computer stores their values in the "post office boxes." Whenever *I* or *LVAL* are used in the calculations, the machine looks up the value in the corresponding location. When *I* or *LVAL* are assigned values, the machine stores the values in these locations (see Figure 2.8–1).

I		. . .	
LVAL		. . .	
		. . .	
⋮	⋮		⋮
		. . .	

Figure 2.8–1
The CPU Memory

With this background, we can describe what happens when the machine performs

$$MORE = LESS + 1$$

The machine goes to its memory and finds the value in the location for *LESS*. The computer then adds 1 and finally the result is stored in the location for *MORE*. Note that the machine does nothing with location *MORE* until after the computation is completed (see Figure 2.8–2).

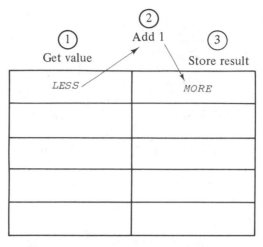

Figure 2.8–2
Performing MORE = LESS + 1

The same sequence can be used to explain the statement

$$X = X + 1.$$

This certainly is not valid mathematically, but it makes perfect sense to the computer in light of the above discussion (see Figure 2.8–3). The machine

1. finds the old value of X
2. adds 1.
3. stores the new value in location X (destroying the previous value)

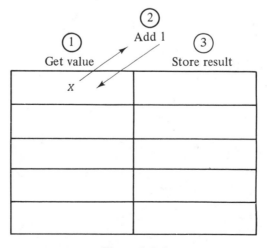

Figure 2.8–3
Performing X = X + 1.

For example, if we write

```
X = 2.
X = X + 1.
WRITE (7, 12) X
12   FORMAT (FIO.1)
```

then the program would print

3.0

We are now ready to consider two more problems.

Problem 2.8–2. Write a program to compute the average of N numbers.

We find from algebra that if the numbers are $X_1, \ldots, X_n$, then

$$\text{Average} = \frac{X_1 + X_2 + \ldots + X_n}{N}$$

In each of the following solutions, we use a variable ICOUNT to keep track of how many X-values we have already considered. Also, we use a variable SUM to keep track of the sum of X-values we have already considered.

In our program, we begin by READing the NUMBER of X-values we wish to average.

```
C THIS PROGRAM AVERAGES NUMBERS
C VERSION A
C INITIALIZE VARIABLES
      READ (5, 1) NUMBER
    1 FORMAT (I5)
      SUM = 0

C READ X-VALUES AND ADD THEM
      DO 2 ICOUNT = 1, NUMBER

         READ (5, 3) XVALUE
    3    FORMAT (F10.5)
         SUM = SUM + XVALUE

    2    CONTINUE


C COMPUTE AVERAGE
```

Outline for Problem 2.8–2

I. Enter the numbers and add.
   (A) Determine how many numbers are to be averaged.
   (B) Read each number.
   (C) Add the numbers.
II. Compute the average.
   (A) Divide the total by N.
III. Print the result.

1 Initially, we have not considered any X values, so SUM must start at 0.

2 Start here and proceed as far as statement number 2, for each of the values 1, 2, . . . , NUMBER.

3 Update the SUM based on the next XVALUE.

4 Repeat the read-in until all values are considered. The CONTINUE statement gives us a place to label the end of our loop as statement 2. Alternatively, we could have numbered the preceding statement

```
    2    SUM = SUM + XVALUE
```

5   AVG = SUM / NUMBER

    C PRINT THE RESULT
          WRITE (7, 4) AVG
        4 FORMAT (' THE AVERAGE IS ', F10.4)
          CALL EXIT
          END

5 Recall that most extensions of standard FORTRAN allow us to mix real and integer values. In this case, the computer will convert the integer to real before performing the operation. In standard FORTRAN, we must write

AVG = SUM/FLOAT(NUMBER)

When this program is run with the data

1   4
    5.0
    3.0
    1.0
    7.0

1 We will average 4 numbers.

the machine yields

THE AVERAGE IS   4.0000

In both of our examples of the DO statement, our loops have had the form

        DO label variable = first, last
                FORTRAN statements
label   last line of loop

Here, "first" and "last" are positive integer constants or variables and "variable" is always an integer variable.

In each case, the specified "FORTRAN statements" are executed for

        variable = first, first + 1, first + 2, . . . , last

If last is already greater than first, the specified statements in the loop are executed exactly once.

Thus, variable is increased by 1 each time the "FORTRAN statements" are executed.

Section 2.9: FURTHER EXAMPLES OF DO LOOPS

In the previous section, we have seen that DO statements allow us to perform the same piece of code several times. This concept is extremely important in much of computer programming, and so we consider several more examples that use DO loops.

Our first example illustrates a more extended form of the DO statement.

Problem 2.9–1. Compute the volume of a cylinder for the cases with the radius = 1, 2, 3 and height = 1, 3, 5 (see Figure 2.9–1).

From a handbook we find

Volume = π (radius)^2 (height)

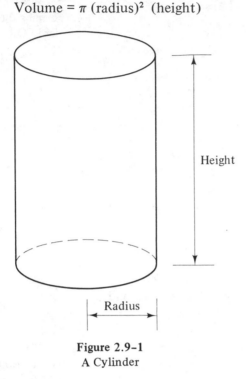

Figure 2.9–1
A Cylinder

Our solution uses 2 loops, one giving the radius its values and one giving the height.

```
    C THIS PROGRAM COMPUTES THE VOLUME OF A CYLINDER
1          INTEGER RADIUS, HEIGHT
    C PRINT THE HEADINGS
           WRITE (7, 1)
         1 FORMAT (5X, 'RADIUS', 5X, 'HEIGHT', 5X, 'VOLUME')
    C PRINT THE TABLE
2          DO 2 RADIUS = 1, 3

3              DO 3 HEIGHT = 1, 5, 2



                   VOL = 3.14159265 * (RADIUS**2) * HEIGHT
4        3         WRITE (7, 4) RADIUS, HEIGHT, VOL

         4         FORMAT (5X, I4, 7X, I4, 5X, F8.4)
5        2      CONTINUE

           CALL EXIT
           END
```

1 The variables in a DO statement must be integers.

2 This gives RADIUS the value 1, 2, 3 in succession.

3 For each value of RADIUS, HEIGHT will be set to 1, 3, and 5. The last 2 indicates that HEIGHT should be increased 2 at a time instead of just by 1 each time.

4 After the values are printed, we can go on to the next value for HEIGHT.

5 When all 3 values for HEIGHT are printed, we can go on to the next value for RADIUS.

When the program is run, we get

RADIUS	HEIGHT	VOLUME
1	1	3.1416
1	3	9.4248
1	5	15.7080
2	1	12.5664
2	3	37.6991
2	5	62.8319
3	1	28.2743
3	3	84.8230
3	5	141.3717

This example illustrates a more general format for the DO statement. The extended form

$$\text{DO label variable} = \text{number}_1 , \text{number}_2 , \text{number}_3$$

has exactly the same meaning as the previous form, except that the addition of number_3 allows the variable to be incremented by a size other than 1. As in the previous form, number_1, number_2, and number_3 must all be positive integer constants or variables and "variable" must be an integer variable.

This expanded DO statement gives us much more flexibility in constructing loops. However, we still must adapt this construction in many situations, as we see in the following problem.

Problem 2.9–2. Tabulate the expression $j^2 - 5j + 2$ for each of the following sets of values for j.

(a) $j = -5, -4, \ldots, 4, 5$
(b) $j = 10, 8, 6, 4, 2$

While this problem is very similar to the tabulation problem in the previous section, the restrictions on the DO statement prevent us from using statements such as

$$\text{DO 10 J} = -5, 5$$

or $$\text{DO 10 J} = 10, 2, -2$$

However, we can obtain the appropriate values if we perform a little arithmetic within our loop. For example, consider the following solution to part (a) of our problem.

```
C THIS PROGRAM COMPUTES THE VALUE
C OF AN EXPRESSION L(J) = J**2 - 5*J + 2
C FOR A RANGE OF J VALUES
1 C VERSION C
      L(J) = J**2 - 5*J + 2
C PRINT A TITLE FOR 2 COLUMNS
      WRITE (7, 1)
```

The variable is given the values
$$\text{number}_1$$
$$\text{number}_1 + \text{number}_3$$
.
.
.

until number_2 is exceeded. Thus, with $\text{number}_3 = 1$, this is exactly the same as the earlier form of the DO statement.

The first value for J must be positive.

The values for J must increase, rather than decrease.

1 Compare this program with the first of the previous section.

```
      1 FORMAT (9X, 'J', 6X, 'L(J)')
   C EVALUATE THE EXPRESSION AND PRINT THE RESULT
        DO 10 I = 1, 11
2               J = I - 6
                LVAL = L(J)
     10         WRITE (7, 2) J, LVAL
      2         FORMAT (5X, I5, 5X, I5)
        CALL EXIT
        END
```

2 We realize that if I takes on the values 1, 2, 3, . . . , 10, 11, then I - 6 or J takes on the values -5, -4, -3, . . . , 4, 5.

When this program is run we get

```
         J      -(J)
        -5        52
        -4        38
        -3        26
        -2        16
        -1         8
         0         2
         1        -2
         2        -4
         3        -4
         4        -2
         5         2
```

The key to this program was that we were able to relate the range we wanted (J = –5, . . . , 5) to a range which we could have in a DO statement (I = 1, . . . , 11). The same approach can be used to get the range specified in part (b), namely 10, 8, . . . , 2. In particular, we could change the first 2 lines of the loop of the previous program to read

```
DO 10 I = 2, 10, 2
   J = 12 - I
```

The next program illustrates an alternate approach to the problem. The DO statement here is only used to count the number of times that we have computed and printed an answer. Here we consider part (b) of our problem.

```
   C THIS PROGRAM COMPUTES THE VALUE
   C OF AN EXPRESSION L(J) = J**2 - 5*J + 2
   C FOR A RANGE OF J VALUES
   C VERSION D
        L(J) = J**2 - 5*J + 2
   C PRINT A TITLE FOR 2 COLUMNS
        WRITE (7, 1)
      1 FORMAT (9X, 'J', 6X, 'L(J)')
   C INITIALIZE J
1       J = 10
   C EVALUATE THE EXPRESSION AND PRINT THE RESULT
2       DO 100 I = 1, 5
3               LVAL = L(J)
3               WRITE (7, 2) J, LVAL
      2         FORMAT (5X, I5, 5X, I5)
4               J = J - 2
```

1 Our first case is when J = 10.

2 We want to consider the 5 cases, J=10, 8, 6, 4, and 2.

3 We compute and print the result for the given J value.

4 Before we make the next com-

putation, we must reduce J by 2 in order to get the next value that we want for J.

5 We are now ready to compute and print for the next J value.

```
5    100        CONTINUE

             CALL EXIT
             END
```

In the previous examples, we have tabulated integer expressions. The same ideas apply with real numbers.

Problem 2.9–3. Evaluate the expression

$$X^2 - 5*X \text{ for } X = .1, .3, .5, .7, .9$$

Here, we outline the main points of each approach used in the previous problem.

```
C VERSION A
        DO 100 I = 1, 9, 2
1            X = I/10.
             Y = X**2 - 5*X
   100       WRITE (7, 3) X,Y
```

1 When I is 1, 3, 5, 7, 9, then X takes on the appropriate values. Note that we must divide here by the real number 10.

The main points of the second approach are

```
C VERSION B
1       X = .1
2       DO 100 I = 1,5
             Y = X**2 - 5*X
             WRITE (7,3) X,Y
3    100       X = X +.2
```

1 We set X to the first value.

2 We want to compute and print 5 values.

3 Decimal numbers, such as .1 and .2, often cannot be stored exactly in the computer (because they are converted to the binary system from the decimal system in the machine). Integers, however, are stored exactly. Thus, this version adds inexact numbers to inexact numbers at this step, and these round-off errors can compound as the program progresses. This problem does not occur in version A, since the integer I will always be correct, so errors in division by 10 will not be compounded as the program proceeds. Thus, version A above is superior to this version B.

From these examples, we can observe several important points concerning the DO statement.

1. The DO statement allows us to repeat the same steps a specified number of times.

2.. While the DO statement performs this repetition on the basis of increasing values of an integer variable, we can repeat steps over other ranges and for real as well as integer variables by using a little arithmetic.

3. We can clearly identify what statements are repeated in a loop by indenting all statements in the loop following the DO statement itself.

Section 2.10: **LOOPS: PART II – THE IF AND
                   GO TO STATEMENTS**

In the previous section, we considered the program segment

```
      DO 10 I = 1, 11
          J = I - 6
1         LVAL = J**2 - 5*J + 2
   10     WRITE (7, 2) J, LVAL
    2     FORMAT (5X, I5, 5X, I5)
```

1 We write the formula out here instead of using the function from the previous section.

This program tabulated and printed a function's values for J = –5, –4, . . . , 4, 5. Before we started, we decided that the last value of J that we wanted was J = 5. However, in many applications, we may not know what final value we will want. This motivates the IF and GO TO statements.

We consider the following example.

Problem 2.10–1. Suppose we deposit a certain amount of money in a bank at a given interest rate with interest compounded quarterly. Write a program that will compute the balance in the account each quarter, stopping after the money has doubled.

We can use a formula similar to the one used in Problem 2.7–1 to compute the balance after each quarter. If PRINcipal is our initial deposit, INTRST is our interest rate and QUARTR is the number of quarters, then the balance is

$$BALANC=PRIN*(1+INTRST/4)**QUARTR$$

We now consider the following program that performs the desired computations.

Outline for Problem 2.10–1

I. Read the initial balance and the interest rate.

II. Print headings or titles.

III. For each quarter, compute and print the new balance.

IV. Continue step III until after the initial balance has doubled.

```
C THIS PROGRAM COMPUTES QUARTERLY BALANCES
C UNTIL AFTER THE INITIAL BALANCE DOUBLES
      INTEGER QUARTR
      REAL INTRST
C DETERMINE INITIAL VALUES
      READ (5, 1) PRIN, INTRST
    1 FORMAT(2F10.5)
```

```
1          QUARTR = 0
     C PRINT HEADINGS
           WRITE (7, 2) PRIN, INTRST
         2 FORMAT (20H INITIAL BALANCE = $, F10.2,
2        1         / 17H INTEREST RATE = ,F8.4)
           WRITE (7, 3)
3        3 FORMAT (1H0, //, 8H QUARTER, 5X, 7HBALANCE)
4          WRITE (7, 4) QUARTR, PRIN
         4 FORMAT (1H0, I5, 4X, 1H$, F10.2)
5    C COMPUTE FOR EACH QUARTER

       100 QUARTR = QUARTR + 1

6          BALANC = PRIN * (1 + INTRST/4) ** QUARTR
           WRITE (7, 5) QUARTR, BALANC
         5 FORMAT (1H , I5, 4X, 1H$, F10.2)
           TWICE = 2. * PRIN
7          IF (BALANC .LT. TWICE) GO TO 100
           CALL EXIT
           END
```

1 Before we start, we have computed interest for zero quarters.

2 Recall that / causes a line to be skipped.

3 1H0 skips double spaces. Then // skips 2 more lines.

4 We print the initial balance outside the loop, and we start our table by skipping a line from the titles.

5 Our loop starts here. We go on to the next quarter.

6 We compute and print the balance.

7 We want to repeat the process if the balance has not doubled. Thus, we check if BALANCe is Less Than twice the PRINcipal. If this is the case, our money has not doubled yet, so we must GO back TO line 100 where our loop started.

If we run the program with the data

```
1000.      .25
```

then our output is

```
INITIAL BALANCE = $    1000.00
INTEREST RATE =   0.2500

QUARTER       BALANCE

    0     $    1000.00
    1     $    1062.00
    2     $    1128.91
    3     $    1199.46
    4     $    1274.43
    5     $    1354.08
    6     $    1438.71
    7     $    1528.63
    8     $    1624.17
    9     $    1725.68
   10     $    1833.54
   11     $    1948.13
   12     $    2069.89
```

In this program, we compute and print successive balances. Then we compare BALANCe and 2* PRINcipal after each computation to determine if we can stop. When the money doubles (i.e., when BALANC $\geq$ 2*PRIN) then our test is no longer true, the computer no longer goes back to line 100, and we stop.

More generally, the IF statement has the following form:

IF (condition) (statement)

For example,

```
   IF (X.LT.0) WRITE (7,1)
1  FORMAT (' X IS NEGATIVE')
   IF (SKY. EQ. BLUE) RAIN = 0
   IF (GRASS.EQ.GREEN .OR. DIRT .EQ.BROWN) GO TO 83
```

(condition) is any expression that has a TRUE or FALSE answer. It may be made up of any logical combination of the following:

.LT.	Less than
.LE.	Less than or equal to
.EQ.	Equal to
.NE.	Not Equal
.GT.	Greater Than
.GE.	Greater than or equal to
.OR.	One or the other (or both)
.AND.	Both
.NOT.	Logical negation

With each of these examples, we see that the above *logical* IF statement can be used whenever an action is to occur only under some specified circumstances.

A particularly common situation arises when we want to go to different parts of a program, depending upon the value of a number or expression. In this situation, we can use a second form of the IF statement, as illustrated in the following problem.

The condition must be placed in parentheses. (statement) is any FORTRAN statement that the computer can perform, with the exception of a DO statement or another IF statement.

Problem 2.10–2. Write a program that reads a number and prints its square root if the number is nonnegative.

```
C THIS PROGRAM COMPUTES SQUARE ROOTS
        READ (5, 1) VALUE
      1 FORMAT(F10.5)
C DETERMINE IF VALUE IS NEGATIVE, ZERO, OR POSITIVE
1       IF (VALUE) 2, 3, 4
C VALUE IS NEGATIVE
      2 WRITE (7, 5)
      5 FORMAT (' THE NUMBER IS NEGATIVE YOU IDIOT!!')
2       GO TO 6
C VALUE IS ZERO
      3 WRITE (7, 7)
      7 FORMAT(' THE SQUARE ROOT OF ZERO IS ZERO')
2       GO TO 6
C VALUE IS POSITIVE
      4 ROOT = SQRT(VALUE)
        WRITE (7, 8) VALUE, ROOT
      8 FORMAT(' THE SQUARE ROOT OF ', F10.4, ' IS ', F10.4)
C ENDING
3,4   6 CONTINUE
4       CALL EXIT
        END
```

Outline for Problem 2.10-2

I. Enter number.

II. Compute and print the square root, if possible.

1 We consider the number VALUE.
  If VALUE < 0, then we go to statement 2.
  If VALUE $= 0$, then we go to statement 3.
  If VALUE > 0, then we go to statement 4.

2 When we finish this case, we skip over the other cases to get to the ending.

3 The CONTINUE statement allows us to mark this line, so we can number this place in the program as statement number 6.

4 We could also have written these two lines as

```
6       CALL EXIT
```

The version shown allows us to insert lines before ending, without having to retype the CALL EXIT line.

Running the program with data

`4.0`

yields

`THE SQUARE ROOT OF     4.0000 IS     2.0000`

Using the data

`0.0`

gives

`THE SQUARE ROOT OF ZERO IS ZERO`

Finally, using negative data produces

`THE NUMBER IS NEGATIVE YOU IDIOT!!`

The general form of this second type of IF statement is

IF (expression) number$_1$, number$_2$, number$_3$, . . .

The machine computes the value of the expression.

If the expression is negative, the machine goes to the statement labeled number$_1$.

If the expression is zero, the machine goes to the statement labeled number$_2$.

If the expression is positive, the machine goes to the statement labeled number$_3$.

As a final example of the logical and arithmetic IF statements, we note that in many instances we can use either of these constructions, although one may be somewhat clearer and simpler to use.

Thus, in the first program of this section, the lines

```
IF (BALANC .GT. (2.*PRIN)) GO TO 100
CALL EXIT
```

could have been replaced by

```
IF (BALANC - 2.*PRIN) 7, 7, 100
7 CALL EXIT
```

Further, in the second program, the lines

```
IF (VALUE) 2,3,4
2 WRITE (7, 5)
```

This form of the IF statement is called an *arithmetic* IF statement. (expression) is any arithmetic expression which can be computed and given a numeric value. Note that the expression must be placed in parentheses.

BALANC – 2.*PRIN will be positive precisely when BALANC is greater than 2.*PRIN.

could have been replaced by somewhat more complicated

```
      IF (VALUE .GT.0) GO TO 4
      IF (VALUE .EQ.0) GO TO 3
1     WRITE (7, 5)
```

1 If VALUE is neither greater than 0 nor equal to zero, then it must be less than 0, so we do not have to test this third case.

As with many other parts of programming, the choice of one form of IF over another depends on the simplicity and clarity of the program and upon which form seems to fit best with the programmer's logic and point of view at that stage of the program.

Section 2.11: ARRAYS

In all of the preceding examples, we could use a different name to identify a variable. However, in many applications, this may not be practical. We may want to be able to subscript our variables. This is illustrated in the following problem.

Problem 2.11–1. Write a program to read the numbers C_1, C_2, C_3, C_4, C_5, and compute the value of the polynomial

$$C_1 X + C_2 X^2 + C_3 X^2 + C_3 X^3 + C_4 X^4 + C_5 X^5$$

for the four values of X, 0, 1, 1.5, and 2.7.

Notes:

1. We write this program in a general form, so we will be able to modify it easily for higher degree polynomials.
2. We will also see how to add the constant term C_0 to the polynomial later.

Outline for Problem 2.11–1

I. Determine coefficients of polynomial.
II. Print titles.
III. Compute and print polynomial for each X value.
   (A) Determine value for X.
   (B) Add terms of polynomial.
   (C) Print value of polynomial for the given X.

```
C THIS PROGRAM TABULATES A FIFTH DEGREE POLYNOMIAL
C VERSION A
1       DIMENSION COEFF(5)


C INPUT COEFFICIENTS
2       READ (5, 2) COEFF

3     2 FORMAT(5F10.5)
```

1 We indicate that the largest subscript will not exceed 5. That is, we may consider COEFF(1), COEFF(2), . . . , COEFF(5), but we will never want COEFF(6).

2 We read in all 5 coefficients at one time.

3 The 5 desired coefficients are in fields 10 columns wide on the same card. If we wanted 1 coefficient on each of 5 cards, we could write

```
      2 FORMAT(F10.5)
```

```
C PRINT TITLE
      WRITE (7, 4)
    4 FORMAT('     X        POLYNOMIAL')
C WE COMPUTE AND PRINT 4 TIMES, ONE FOR EACH X-VALUE
4         DO 10 NUMBER = 1, 4
  C           DETERMINE X-VALUE
                 READ (5, 5) X
      5          FORMAT(F10.5)
  C          COMPUTE THE SUM OF THE TERMS
                 SUM = 0
5                DO 6 I = 1, 5



    6                  SUM = SUM + COEFF(I) * X**I
  C              PRINT ANSWER
                 WRITE(7, 7) X, SUM
      7          FORMAT(1X, 2F10.4)
  C              REPEAT FOR NEXT X-VALUE
     10              CONTINUE
          CALL EXIT
          END
```

4 The NUMBER of X values will be 4 when we are done. If we want another number of X values, we must change this statement to reflect this new number of values.

5 The polynomial is computed by finding

0

$C_1 X$

$C_1 X + C_2 X^2$

.

.

.

$C_1 X + C_2 X^2 + \ldots + C_5 X^5$

in successive times through the loop.

We will consider the polynomial

$$2X - 3X^2 + 4X^3 + 3X^4 - 5X^5$$

We use X values 0, 1, 1.5, 2.7.

When this program is run with the data

```
2.        -3.        4.         3.            -5.
0.
1.
1.5
2.7
```

we get

```
     X        POLYNOMIAL
  0.0000      0.0000
  1.0000      1.0000
  1.5000    -13.0313
  2.7000   -495.7511
```

Here we have used COEFF(1), . . . , COEFF(5) for the numbers C_1, . . . , C_5, and see that we can use subscripts by placing them in parentheses. With this notation, subscripted variables can be used in the same way as other variables. In programming, subscripted variables are called *arrays*.

We note, however, that when we use arrays, we must start with the DIMENSION statement. This statement is needed because, as we have already seen, the computer must use a separate location in the CPU for each variable. Thus, with subscripted variables, it must allocate a separate place for each of the numbers COEFF(1), . . . , COEFF(5). In allocating the space, the machine must know how much space might be needed, so we used

DIMENSION COEFF(5)

to allocate space for these 5 numbers. It is always permissible to specify more space than needed (provided the machine has enough space to meet your request). Thus, we could have used

```
DIMENSION COEFF(20)
```

in the above program. The machine would then have allocated space for COEFF(1) through COEFF(20). The locations for COEFF(6) through COEFF(20) would be available but not used.

However, an error will result if we tried to use more space than we specified. For example,

```
DIMENSION COEFF(4)
```

would be invalid in this program as we need COEFF(5) for our computations.

The next example shows how to eliminate several of the restrictions present in the previous program.

Problem 2.11–2. Write a program to read the degree N of a polynomial and the coefficients $C_0, \ldots, C_N$ and compute the value of the polynomial

$$C_0 + C_1 X + C_2 X^2 + \ldots + C_N X^N$$

for several values of X.

This problem requires 2 special techniques in FORTRAN programming.

1. We represent the coefficients $C_0, C_1, C_2, \ldots, C_N$ by the array elements COEFF(1), COEFF(2), . . . , COEFF(N+1).

2. We are not told how many X values will be required. Thus, we will agree to stop our tabulation of the polynomial when some certain X-value is read. In this case, we decide that we will never want to compute the polynomial for X = –9999. Thus, we will place the value –9999 at the end of our X-values to signify the end of the data.

We now can solve the problem.

Outline for Problem 2.11–2

I. Determine degree of polynomial.
II. Determine coefficients of polynomial.
III. Print titles.
IV. Compute and print polynomial for each X value.
   (A) Determine value for X.
   (B) Add terms of polynomial.
   (C) Print value of polynomial for the given X value.

As with the index I in the DO loop DO 6 I = 1,5, the allowed subscripts for arrays must be positive integers (zero is not allowed). Thus we must shift the subscript by 1 each time we compute $C_{i+1} X^i$, so we write

COEFF(I+1) *X**I

```
C THIS PROGRAM TABULATES AN N-TH DEGREE POLYNOMINAL, FOR N<= 100
C VERSION B
1      DIMENSION COEFF(101)
       INTEGER DEGREE, DEG1
C DETERMINE DEGREE OF POLYNOMIAL
       READ (5, 1) DEGREE
     1 FORMAT(I5)
C DETERMINE COEFFICIENTS OF POLYNOMIAL
```

1 If the degree of the polynomial were 100, we would need 101 coefficients, as seen in the note above.

```
2         DEG1 = DEGREE + 1
          DO 3 I = 1, DEG1
     3        READ(5, 2) COEFF(I)
3    2        FORMAT(F10.5)
  C PRINT TITLE
          WRITE (7, 4)
   4 FORMAT('          X          POLYNOMIAL')
  C COMPUTE AND PRINT POLYNOMIAL FOR EACH X-VALUE
  C     DETERMINE X-VALUE
     8        READ(5, 5) X
     5        FORMAT(F10.5)
```

```
4             IF (X .EQ. -9999.) GO TO 20
```

```
  C COMPUTE THE SUM OF THE TERMS
5             SUM = COEFF(1)
          DO 6 I = 1, DEG1
6    6           SUM = SUM + COEFF(I+1) * X**I
  C     PRINT ANSWER
              WRITE (7, 7) X, SUM
     7        FORMAT(1X, 2F10.4)
  C     REPEAT FOR NEXT X-VALUE
              GO TO 8
  C FINISH PROGRAM
    20 CONTINUE
          CALL EXIT
          END
```

2 DEG1 is the number of coefficients we will need.

3 We read the coefficients one at a time, with each one on a separate card. If we wanted to read eight numbers on each card, we could condense this DO loop by

```
READ(5,2)(COEFF(I),I=1,DEG
FORMAT(8F10.5)
```

The (COEFF(I), I=1,DEG1) has the same meaning as the DO loop, while the 8F10.4 tells the machine to read 8 values per card.

4 We decided to use the number –9999 to tell the machine that we wanted to stop.

5 We start the sum with the constant term.

6 Subscripts in standard FORTRAN can be integer numbers, integer variables, or certain integer expressions, such as

$$V + K$$
$$V - K$$
$$C * V$$
$$C * V + K$$
$$C * V - K$$

where C and K are integer constants and V is an integer variable. In PDP-11 FORTRAN and other extensions, any expression is permitted.

When we run this program with the data

```
1        5
2 0.
2 2.
2 -3.
2 4.
2 3.
2 -5
3 0.0
3 1.0
3 1.5
3 2.7
```

1 We will consider a 5th degree polynomial.

2 Here, we run the program on the same polynomial

$$0 + 2X - 3X^2 + 4X^3 + 3X^4 - 5X^5$$

3 We list the X-values we want.

4 *-9999.*

4 We end the X-values with -9999. Note in the program that the polynomial is never tabulated for this value of X. Instead, the machine just stops at this point.

we get

```
    X        POLYNOMIAL
 0.0000        0.0000
 1.0000        5.9999
 1.5000       24.9371
 2.7000      221.6872
```

An alternate approach to the last number convention (such as the -9999 in this program) is available on many extensions of standard FORTRAN. Here, we can read our cards until the end of the cards is encountered. At this point, we can specify (in the READ statement) what to do. In this extended version of standard FORTRAN, we could replace the lines

```
8          READ(5, 5) X

           IF (X .EQ. -9999.) THEN GO TO 20
```

by the single line

```
8          READ(5, 5, END = 20) X
```

When the end of the data cards is encountered, the machine goes to line 20.

A rather different example is given in the following problem.

Problem 2.11–3. A manufacturer requires 8 types of parts which are stored in 5 warehouses. These are represented in an inventory array, INVEN(P, W), where P is the type of part and W is the warehouse number. (See Table 2.11–1.)

Outline for Problem 2.11–3

   I. Determine inventory of each part for each warehouse.

  II. Compute the total number of parts in each warehouse.

 III. Compute the total number of parts of each type.

From the table, we find warehouse 3 does not contain any parts of type 7. Thus

INVEN (7,3) = 0

Table 2.11–1. Warehouse Inventory

Part Number	Warehouse				
	1	*2*	*3*	*4*	*5*
1	3	1	4	1	5
2	9	2	6	5	3
3	5	8	9	7	9
4	3	2	3	8	4
5	6	2	6	4	3
6	3	8	3	2	7
7	9	5	0	2	8
8	8	4	1	9	7

Write a program to input this table of inventories and

1. compute the total number of parts in each warehouse.

2. compute the total number of each type of part.

We now write a program which is divided into two parts, according to the problem.

```
  C INVENTORY PROGRAM
1         DIMENSION INVEN(8,5)
          INTEGER PART, WAREHS
    C INPUT INVENTORIES
2         READ (5, 1) INVEN




3       1 FORMAT(8I5)




  C COMPUTE THE TOTAL NUMBER OF PARTS PER WAREHOUSE
4         DO 2 WAREHS = 1, 5
              ISUM = 0
              DO 3 PART = 1, 8
5       3         ISUM = ISUM + INVEN(PART, WAREHS)
              WRITE (7, 4) WAREHS, ISUM

        4     FORMAT(' WAREHOUSE', I2, ' CONTAINS' I3, ' PARTS.')
        2     CONTINUE
  C COMPUTE THE TOTAL NUMBER OF PARTS OF EACH TYPE
6         DO 5 PART = 1, 8
              ISUM = 0
              DO 6 WAREHS = 1, 5
        6         ISUM = ISUM + INVEN(PART, WAREHS)
              WRITE(7, 7) ISUM, PART
        7     FORMAT(' THERE ARE ', I3, ' PARTS OF TYPE', I2)
        5     CONTINUE
          CALL EXIT
          END
```

1 We want parts 1 through 8 as the first subscript and warehouse 1 to 5 as the second subscript.

2 We read in all data. When no order is specified, the computer reads the numbers in one column at a time. Thus, this READ is the same as

> DO 100 I = 1, 5
> 100   READ INVEN(1,I), . . . ,
> INVEN(8,I)

3 We will put 8 numbers on each line of input, for convenience in typing. When 8 numbers are read, the machine will go to the next line to get the next 8 numbers. In all, 5 lines will be needed to get all 40 numbers requested.

4 We add down each column.

5 Note how the indenting makes it clear what is being done within each DO-loop.

6 This corresponds to adding across each row.

Running the program with the data from our table yields

```
WAREHOUSE 1 CONTAINS 46 PARTS.
WAREHOUSE 2 CONTAINS 32 PARTS.
WAREHOUSE 3 CONTAINS 32 PARTS.
WAREHOUSE 4 CONTAINS 38 PARTS.
WAREHOUSE 5 CONTAINS 46 PARTS.
THERE ARE 14 PARTS OF TYPE 1
THERE ARE 25 PARTS OF TYPE 2
THERE ARE 38 PARTS OF TYPE 3
THERE ARE 20 PARTS OF TYPE 4
THERE ARE 21 PARTS OF TYPE 5
```

```
THERE ARE 23 PARTS OF TYPE 6
THERE ARE 24 PARTS OF TYPE 7
THERE ARE 29 PARTS OF TYPE 8
```

With a small addition to the program, the cost of the items in each warehouse could be determined as well. In particular, we would need another array COST(8), giving the cost of each type of part. This array could be set up using

```
        DIMENSION COST(8)
        READ(5, 10)  COST
 10 FORMAT (8F10.5)
C DETERMINE THE TOTAL COST OF PARTS IN EACH WAREHOUSE
        DO 11 WAREHS = 1, 5
            TOTAL = 0.
            DO 12 PART = 1, 8
 12         TOTAL = TOTAL + INVEN(PART,WAREHS)* COST(PART)
            WRITE (7, 13) WAREHS, TOTAL
 13         FORMAT (' WAREHOUSE', I2, ' CONTAINS $', F5.2, 'WORTH OF PARTS')
 11         CONTINUE
```

Section 2.12: ALGORITHM DESIGN

In each of the programming problems we have considered so far, we started with a careful statement of the problem. Next we made an outline of the main steps required, and finally we wrote a program based on the outline. In this section, we look at this process more closely.

The importance of dividing a problem into parts cannot be over-emphasized in the programming effort. As problems become harder and programs get longer, a logical, carefully planned approach to programming becomes particularly essential. Long programs that are not carefully structured are virtually sure to give incorrect results. Thus, we should make a point of structuring our programming so we will be able to tackle harder problems as they arise.

Outlining is a particularly effective way of dividing a problem into parts. The outline has several important advantages.

A second approach, called *flow charting,* is another common way to achieve program structure.

1. An outline specifies major steps, and it allows us to break down large steps into smaller pieces.

2. An outline forces us to decide exactly what each step is to do.

3. An outline allows us to determine exactly what information will be needed in order to complete each step.

4. If we find our resulting program is in error, an outline serves as a useful guide to determine which part of the program is at fault.

5. If we want to modify our program after it is written, a good outline can help us decide just which parts need to be changed.

In outlining, we should try to make different sections of the outline independent. One section may be subdivided into several smaller parts. However, when the smaller pieces are done, this section should not rely on interaction with the next section. This is particularly useful and important when we decide to correct or modify a resulting program. If sections of the outline are closely interdependent, then a change in one section will be likely to cause a change in another one. Thus, a small change in one place may have considerable impact throughout the entire program. However, if sections are independent, then a correction in one section will not cause a new error in another section.

When we try to translate our outline into FORTRAN code, we may find several points helpful. First, we mention how to program loops.

1. It is often useful to concentrate on the key steps that are going to be repeated. We should not worry, initially, how we will start the process going. Rather, we should decide what process we need to repeat several times.

Example

We consider our program to compute

$$C_1 X + C_2 X^2 + \ldots + C_5 X^5$$

from Problem 2.11–1. Our outline was:

I.   Determine coefficients of polynomial.
II. Print titles.
III. Compute and print polynomial for each X value.
     (A) Determine value for X.
     (B) Add terms of polynomial.
     (C) Print value of polynomial for the given X.

In considering how to program part III(B), the key point is to compute a term $C_I X^{**} I$ and add this term. This gives rise to the lines

```
6    SUM = SUM + COEFF(I)*X*
```

In our example, we add line

```
DO 6 I = 1, 5
```

In our example, we need an initial value for SUM, so we add SUM=0.

2. Once we know what steps we want repeated, we add the statements that will repeat those steps. For example, we may use a DO construction to repeat the steps.
3. Next, we determine if any variables need to be set up initially, before the repetition can start. Also, we need to see if any special cases should be considered.

Other points on writing FORTRAN code from our outline may also be useful.

In our second example of the previous section, where we included a constant term, we must be sure the constant term, C_0 or COEFF(1), is included in the sum. Thus, here we use

$$SUM = COEFF(1)$$

1. If we cannot translate from our outline to FORTRAN easily, then we may need to break the outline into smaller steps. The FORTRAN program should evolve easily and quickly from the outline.

2. The GO TO statement allows us to jump from one section of our outline to another. We have already observed that the interdependence of sections of our programming can cause difficulties. GO TO's provide a particularly easy way to interconnect various sections of our outline, and we must be careful not to allow them to hurt the structure of our program.

Programs with many GO TO's may be considered as like being in a maze. At any time we are not sure how we got where we are and we have no idea where we are going. We have no overall sense of what is going on, and we are not sure what the result of any action is. (Some people consider such programs to be like cooked spaghetti.)

A GO TO can be useful if it goes to the beginning of the next section. However, we should not allow ourselves to branch into the middle of another section.

Branching into another section may be compared with parachuting into our maze above. Once we arrive, we have a particularly hard time deciding what is going on around us.

3. When typing our program, we can help the clarity of the result by following the same indenting scheme that we used in our outline. In particular,

   (a) We should start each section with a comment. (Perhaps we could use a sentence from the outline.)

   (b) All lines within a section or within a loop should be indented, so we can visualize the headings from the indented steps within the section.

   (c) The above formatting may take us a little longer to type. However, we are likely to make up this time in the ease of reading, correcting, and modifying our programs.

We summarize the various ideas in this section with the following principle.

Note: A typical reaction of beginners to sections like this is a feeling this structuring of programs is nothing more than a time-consuming luxury. These suggestions may seem like pedagogical techniques that are, in fact, superfluous. However, as our programs become longer, these ideas become progressively more important. As with a small maze, a short program with many GO TO's can be corrected using trial and error together with some luck. However, as the maze gets larger, these methods start to fail, and the programmer may starve to death before finding the way out.

> Programs should be divided into well-defined, independent, and clearly formatted pieces, and we should check that we are contributing to the goal at each stage of our work.

When this principle is carefully observed, programs can be relatively easy to write, and correcting and modifying our programs are easy to accomplish.

For those who are still skeptical of the value of structuring programs, perhaps the only response is to suggest that they defer their judgment until they gain more programming experience. Section 2.20 may provide a useful example.

In Section 2.2, we introduced two types of numbers in FORTRAN, integers and real numbers. These had the following characteristics.

1. Integers contained no decimal points and could be in the range −32768 to 32767 inclusive.

   Examples are −3, 17.

2. Real numbers contained decimal points and were stored in scientific notation. We noted real numbers customarily are restricted to 8 significant digits and exponents must be between −38 and 38 inclusive.

   Examples are −15.8, 2.71828, −5.7 × 10^8, 1.024 × 10^3. In this case, however, −15.8 and 2.71828 were stored as −1.58 × 10^1 and 2.71828 × 10^0, respectively.

We now consider three more types of data that are allowed in FORTRAN, namely,

(a) Double precision real numbers.

(b) Complex numbers.

(c) Logical values.

A fourth type of data, containing alphabetic characters, can also be used, although it must be handled rather differently. Thus, we defer a discussion of alphabetic information to the next section.

In this section, we begin by describing the meaning of each of these data types. Then we see how these types can be used, and finally we list all of the various functions available as part of the standard FORTRAN language, expanding our list from Section 2.6 on arithmetic functions.

Description of the Data Types

(a) *Double Precision Real Numbers*
We have seen that real numbers customarily are stored to about 8 significant digits. If we wish to have more accuracy, we may expand this to 17 significant digits using double precision. The range of exponents from −38 through 38 remains the same for both forms of real numbers.

(b) *Complex Numbers*
In many applications in science and mathematics, it is very useful to use the letter i to represent $\sqrt{-1}$, and to write numbers in the form $a + bi$, where a and b are real numbers. FORTRAN allows the pair (a, b) to be stored as one complex number.

(c) *Logical Values*
A logical expression is one that is either true or false. FORTRAN allows us to assign .TRUE. or .FALSE. to a logical variable.

Use of the Data Types

Whenever we want to use one of these types of data, we must

• tell the machine the type of data we will be storing in the variable;

We say we must *declare* the data type of the variable.

- be able to represent values of the data;
- be able to manipulate the data;
- be able to read and write the values of the variables.

(A) Declaration of Data Types

We have mentioned that variables starting with the letter I, J, K, L, M, or N are assumed to be integers in FORTRAN and all others are assumed to be real numbers. We also have seen that we can change this convention by explicitly stating INTEGER or REAL at the beginning of our program. We explicitly state that a variable will be of type DOUBLE PRECISION, COMPLEX, or LOGICAL by a similar statement at the start of our program.

Examples of Declarations

```
INTEGER VALUE
REAL NUMBER
DOUBLE PRECISION LONGER
COMPLEX AANDB
LOGICAL TORF
```

(B) Representation of Values for These Data Types

Numbers can also be of type DOUBLE PRECISION or COMPLEX by modifying how they are written. For example, real numbers can be written using an E before the exponent. Thus, the number 1024. or 1.024E3 is a real number. When we want a double precision real number, we replace the E by a D when we write the number.

Examples of Double Precision Real Numbers

1.2345678901234D5 represents

$1.2345678901234 \times 10^5$ or 123456.78901234

1.024D3 represents the double precision number 1.024×10^3 or 1024.

When we want a complex number, we write a pair of real numbers in parentheses and separated by a comma. (The real numbers are assumed to have the usual precision, not double precision.)

The logical values of true and false are written .TRUE. and .FALSE.

Examples of Complex Numbers

(1., 2.) represents $1 + 2i$

(1.024E3, .5) represents $1024 + .5i$

(C) Manipulation of Data for These Data Types

We can combine various values of these data types just as we did for arithmetic expressions. For example, we can write

1
```
    DOUBLE PRECISION LONGER
    LONGER = 1.2345678901234D3
    LONGER = 2D3*LONGER
```

2
```
    COMPLEX AANDB
    AANDB = (3., 4.)
    AANDB = AANDB - (1., 3.)
```

3
```
    LOGICAL TORF
    TORF = 3 .GT. 2
    TORF = .NOT. TORF
```

In standard FORTRAN we must still convert integers to real numbers before they can be combined with real data by arithmetic operation. This restriction is not present in most current extensions of FORTRAN now in use.

Value of the Expression

1 2.4691357802468D6

2 (1., 3.) representing $1 + 3i$

3 .TRUE. as 3 is greater than 2
   .FALSE. as before TORF
   was .TRUE.

Example

3.5 + (4/3) is not allowed in standard FORTRAN. However, in

The restriction of standard FORTRAN of not performing an arithmetic operation between an integer and a real number does not carry over to operations between other data types. Thus, even in standard FORTRAN, when an expression contains a real number and a double precision number or a complex number, the real number is converted to double precision or complex, respectively, when the two are combined. Note, however, that double precision and complex numbers may not be combined.

Further, integer, real, or double precision variables can be assigned values of type integer, real, and double precision. The type of the variable is simply changed before the assignment takes place.

However, integer, real, or double precision variables may not be given complex or logical values. Further, complex or logical variables may not be given values of any type but their own.

(D) Reading and Writing Values

We have already discussed in Section 2.4 the use of I format to read or write integers and the use of F or E format to read or write real numbers.

For double precision numbers, we use D format instead of E format. The format for D is otherwise the same as for E format.

For complex numbers, we write the format for two real numbers.

most extensions of FORTRAN 3.5 + (4/3) is allowed and it is evaluated by first dividing the integer 3 into the integer 4 to get the integer 1. This computation can be done completely in integer form, so no conversion is needed. This yields 3.5 + 1. Here both real and integer values are encountered, so the integer 1 is converted to the real number 1. before addition occurs. The result is 4.5.

Examples of Assignments

I = 5.3 gives the integer I the value 5. (The digits to the right of the decimal point are ignored.) R=5 gives the real number R the value 5.0.

Assignments NOT Allowed

$$
\left.\begin{array}{l}
I = .TRUE. \\
I = (3., 4.) \\
I = (3., 0.)
\end{array}\right\} \quad \begin{array}{l}
\text{assuming} \\
\text{I is an} \\
\text{integer}
\end{array}
$$

$$
\left.\begin{array}{l}
AANDB = 5. \\
AANDB = .TRUE
\end{array}\right\} \quad \begin{array}{l}
\text{assuming} \\
\text{AANDB is} \\
\text{complex}
\end{array}
$$

$$
\left.\begin{array}{l}
TORF = 1 \\
TORF = (0., 0.)
\end{array}\right\} \quad \begin{array}{l}
\text{assuming TORF} \\
\text{is logical}
\end{array}
$$

Examples

(a)   DOUBLE PRECISION LONGER
       LONGER = 1.024 D 3
       WRITE (7,1) LONGER
     1 FORMAT (1X, D10.4)

yields

1.02   D+03
├ - - -┤
  w=4
├- - - - - - - -┤
       d=10

(b)   COMPLEX AANDB
       AANDB = (3., 4.)
       WRITE(7, 2) AANDB
     2 FORMAT(1X,F10.2,F10.5)

yields

3.00   4.00000
├--┤   ├- - -┤
  2   5
├- - - - - - - -┤├- - - - - -┤
       10   10

For logical values, we use L format, which has the form L*w* where *w* is the number of spaces to be used in reading or writing. In writing, a T or F is printed in the first place and the remaining *w* – 1 spaces are left blank.

(c)   `LOGICAL TORF`
      `TORF = .TRUE.`
      `WRITE (7,3) TORF`
    `3 FORMAT(1X, L7)`

yields

```
T
├──────┤
    7
```

We now list all arithmetic functions that are available in standard FORTRAN.

Table of FORTRAN Arithmetic Functions

Function Code	Type of Input	Type of Output	Description
Conversions from One Data Type to Another			
FLOAT(I)	Integer	Real	Converts the integer I to a real number.
IFIX(X)	Real	Integer	Gives the truncated value of X as a real number or as an
INT(X)	Real	Integer	integer. Thus, if X is written in a decimal expansion,
IDINT(D)	Double	Integer	the places after the decimal point are dropped.
AINT(X)	Real	Real	
DBLE(X)	Real	Double	Converts real number to a double precision form.
SNGL(D)	Double	Real	Converts double precision number to a real number, by retaining only the first 7 significant digits.
CMPLX(X1,X2)	Real	Complex	Converts real numbers (X1, X2) to a complex number $X1+X2i$.
REAL(C)	Complex	Real	Gives the real part A of the complex number C=(A, B).
AIMAG(C)	Complex	Real	Gives the imaginary part B of the complex number C=(A, B).
Algebraic Functions			
IABS(I)	Integer	Integer	Computes the absolute value, |I|, |X|, |D| of I, X, D.
ABS(X)	Real	Real	
DABS(D)	Double	Double	
CABS(C)	Complex	Real	Computes the modulus, $\sqrt{A^2+B^2}$, of the complex number C=(A, B).
MAX0(I1,I2, . . .)	Integer	Integer	Computes the maximum value of the numbers specified.
MAX1(X1,X2, . . .)	Real	Integer	
AMAX0(I1,I2, . . .)	Integer	Real	
AMAX1(X1,X2, . . .)	Real	Real	
DMAX1(D1,D2, . . .)	Double	Double	
MIN0(I1,I2, . . .)	Integer	Integer	Computes the minimum value of the numbers specified.
MIN1(X1,X2, . . .)	Real	Integer	
AMIN0(I1,I2, . . .)	Integer	Real	
AMIN1(X1,X2, . . .)	Real	Real	
DMIN1(D1,D2, . . .)	Double	Double	
MOD(I1,I2)	Integer	Integer	Computes the remainder when the first number (I1, X1, or D1) is divided by the second number (I2, X2, or D2).
AMOD(X1,X2)	Real	Real	
DMOD(D1,D2)	Double	Double	

Function Code	Type of Input	Type of Output	Description
ISIGN(I1,I2) SIGN(A1,A2) DSIGN(D1,D2)	Integer Real Double	Integer Real Double	The second value, I2, A2, or D2, is given the sign of the first value, I1, A1, or D1.
IDIM(I1,I2) DIM(X1,X2)	Integer Real	Integer Real	Computes the positive difference, I1−min(I1,I2) or X1−min(X1,X2)
CONJG(C)	Complex	Complex	Computes the complex conjugate (A, −B) of the complex number C=(A, B)

Exponentials

Function Code	Type of Input	Type of Output	Description
SQRT(X) DSQRT(D) CSQRT(C)	Real Double Complex	Real Double Complex	Computes the square root of the number specified.
EXP(X) DEXP(D) CEXP(C)	Real Double Complex	Real Double Complex	Computes e^X, e^D, e^C, where $e = 2.71828\ldots.$

Logarithms

Function Code	Type of Input	Type of Output	Description
ALOG(X) DLOG(D) CLOG(C)	Real Double Complex	Real Double Complex	Computes the natural logarithm, $\log_e$, of the number specified.
ALOG10(X) DLOG10(D)	Real Double	Real Double	Computes the common logarithm, $\log_{10}$, of the number specified.

Trigonometric Functions

Note: All angles are assumed to be measured in radians!

Function Code	Type of Input	Type of Output	Description
COS(X) DCOS(D) CCOS(C)	Real Double Complex	Real Double Complex	Computes the cosine of the number specified.
SIN(X) DSIN(D) CSIN(C)	Real Double Complex	Real Double Complex	Computes the sine of the number specified.
ATAN(X) DATAN(D)	Real Double	Real Double	Computes the arctangent of the numbers specified.
ATAN2(X1,X2) DATAN2(D1,D2)	Real Double	Real Double	Computes the arctangent of X1/X2 or D1/D2.

Hyperbolic Function

Function Code	Type of Input	Type of Output	Description
TANH(X)	Real	Real	Computes the hyperbolic tangent of X.

Section 2.14: ALPHABETIC INFORMATION

In the previous sections, we have been able to label our output by writing a separate FORMAT statement for each number or by printing titles at the top of columns. In this section, we consider how to do more with alphabetic information.

We begin with a relatively simple example.

Problem 2.14–1. Compute the average of 5 test scores for each individual in a specific class. A typical set of data cards for a class will be in the form:

column 2	column 30	column 40	column 50	column 60	column 70
COOK, SUSAN	→51.	→92.	→43.	→60.	→72.
JONES, ROBERT	83.	77.	73.	72.	60.
SMITH, BARBARA	86.	98.	93.	99.	95.
WRIGHT, WILLIAM	73.	79.	85.	91.	97.

We would like the title of the class printed as well as the name of each student in the class.

Outline for Problem 2.14–1

  I. Read and print class title.

 II. Determine number of students in the class.

III. For each student:
    (A) Read data card.
    (B) Compute average.
    (C) Print results.

```
C THIS PROGRAM COMPUTES TEST SCORE AVERAGES
        DIMENSION TESTS(5)
        INTEGER PUPIL
C READ AND PRINT CLASS TITLE
1       READ (5, 1)
1     1 FORMAT(1X, 29H                                        )

2       WRITE (7, 1)



C DETERMINE NUMBER IN CLASS
        READ (5, 2) NUMBER
      2 FORMAT(I5)
C PRINT A TITLE FOR THE COLUMNS
3       WRITE (7, 6)

      6 FORMAT(5H NAME, 25X, 'TEST 1', 4X, 'TEST 2', 4X,
     1        'TEST 3', 4X, 'TEST 4', 4X, 'TEST 5', 4X, 'AVERAGE')
C ANALYZE EACH STUDENT
4       DO 3 PUPIL = 1, NUMBER
C       READ DATA CARD
            READ (5, 4) TESTS
5     4     FORMAT(1X, 28H                            , 6F10.5)

C       COMPUTE AVERAGE
            SUM = 0.
            DO 5 ITEM = 1,5
5               SUM = SUM + TESTS(ITEM)
            AVG = SUM / 5.
C       PRINT RESULTS
6           WRITE (7, 4) TESTS, AVG
      3     CONTINUE
        CALL EXIT
        END
```

1 We read the title of the class from 2–30 of the first card, putting this title in the H field of our FORMAT statement.

2 We print the same title that we read in by using the same FORMAT statement. Note, we needed the 1X in the FORMAT statement so we could print using same FORMAT without having to worry about our carriage control character.

3 We print a title for each column we will print out.

4 We will repeat this process for each student.

5 We read the student's name from columns 2–29 into the FORMAT statement and we read in the 5 TEST scores. (The last specification F10.5 is not used here, as TESTS has only dimension 5. See Note 6 for an explanation of this last F10.5.)

6 Here we print the name, scores, and average. Since we are printing 6 numbers here, we included the 6F10.5 in the FORMAT statement above.

When we run this program with the data

```
PROGRAMMING CLASS, FALL, 1985
    4
COOK, SUSAN                  51.     92.     43.     60.     72.
JONES, ROBERT               83.     77.     73.     72.     60.
SMITH, BARBARA              86.     98.     93.     99.     95.
WRIGHT, WILLIAM             73.     79.     85.     91.     97.
```

we get

```
PROGRAMMING CLASS, FALL, 1985
NAME                  TEST 1   TEST 2   TEST 3   TEST 4   TEST 5   AVERAGE
COOK, SUSAN           51.00000 92.00000 43.00000 60.00000 72.00000 63.60000
JONES, ROBERT         83.00000 77.00000 73.00000 72.00000 60.00000 73.00000
SMITH, BARBARA        86.00000 98.00000 93.00000 99.00000 95.00000 94.20000
WRIGHT, WILLIAM       73.00000 79.00000 85.00000 91.00000 97.00000 85.00000
```

This program illustrates that we can read alphabetic information into a FORMAT statement using H format and then we can print the same information out if we use the same FORMAT statement. However, this procedure has two limitations.

1. We must not read anything from column 1 into our H field, as the first column in printing is used to control the vertical spacing of our output.
2. We are not able to manipulate the alphabetic information in any way; we can only read it in and print it out in the same format.

We can see how to solve some of these problems in the following example.

Problem 2.14–2. Read columns 1–80 on each of 11 cards and print out the information read in columns 6–85 of the paper.

Outline for Problem 2.14-2

For each card:
(A) Read card.
(B) Print the data read.

```
C THIS PROGRAM INPUTS DATA AND PRINTS IT OUT AGAIN
      DIMENSION CARD (80)
1     DO 1 I = 1, 11
2         READ (5,2) CARD
2     2   FORMAT(80A1)

3         WRITE (7, 3) CARD
4     3   FORMAT(6X, 80A1)
      1   CONTINUE
      CALL EXIT
      END
```

1 We will work with 11 cards.
2 We will read 80 characters, 1 for each element in the array CARD.

3 We print the 80 characters.
4 The 6 spaces include 1 carriage control character

When we run this program with the data

Note that digits and punctuation can be included as well as letters.

THIS PROGRAM READS 80 CHARACTERS FROM EACH CARD, STORING EACH CHARACTER IN A
DIFFERENT ELEMENT OF THE ARRAY CARD. THUS, FOR THE FIRST LINE OF THIS TEXT,
WE HAD "T" STORED IN CARD(1), "H" STORED IN CARD(2), "I" STORED IN CARD(3), ETC.
THIS PROGRAM DEPENDS UPON A FORMAT, WHICH ALLOWS US TO READ AND WRITE
ALPHABETIC INFORMATION INTO AND OUT OF VARIABLES. HERE, THE A1 FORMAT TELLS
THE MACHINE TO STORE EXACTLY 1 CHARACTER IN EACH ELEMENT OF THE ARRAY CARD.
IF WE WANTED TO STORE THE INFORMATION 2 CHARACTERS AT A TIME, WE COULD HAVE
USED A2 FORMAT. A4 FORMAT WOULD HAVE ALLOWED US TO STORE THE INFORMATION
4 CHARACTERS PER ARRAY ELEMENT. WE NOTE, HOWEVER, THAT IF WE HAD USED A2 OR
A4 FORMAT, THEN THE DIMENSION OF CARD SHOULD BE CHANGED TO 40 OR 20,
RESPECTIVELY, SO WE WOULD STILL ONLY BE READING A TOTAL OF 80 CHARACTERS.

we get

```
THIS PROGRAM READS 80 CHARACTERS FROM EACH CARD, STORING EACH CHARACTER IN A
DIFFERENT ELEMENT OF THE ARRAY CARD. THUS, FOR THE FIRST LINE OF THIS TEXT,
WE HAD "T" STORED IN CARD(1), "H" STORED IN CARD(2), "I" STORED IN CARD(3), ETC.
     THIS PROGRAM DEPENDS UPON A FORMAT, WHICH ALLOWS US TO READ AND WRITE
ALPHABETIC INFORMATION INTO AND OUT OF VARIABLES. HERE, THE A1 FORMAT TELLS
THE MACHINE TO STORE EXACTLY 1 CHARACTER IN EACH ELEMENT OF THE ARRAY CARD.
IF WE WANTED TO STORE THE INFORMATION 2 CHARACTERS AT A TIME, WE COULD HAVE
USED A2 FORMAT. A4 FORMAT WOULD HAVE ALLOWED US TO STORE THE INFORMATION
4 CHARACTERS PER ARRAY ELEMENT. WE NOTE, HOWEVER, THAT IF WE HAD USED A2 OR
A4 FORMAT, THEN THE DIMENSION OF CARD SHOULD BE CHANGED TO 40 OR 20,
RESPECTIVELY, SO WE WOULD STILL ONLY BE READING A TOTAL OF 80 CHARACTERS.
```

The number of characters that can be stored in a variable depends upon the data type of the variable and it may also depend upon the particular machine we are using. On the PDP-11, Table 2.14–1 gives the

Table 2.14–1. **Maximum Characters per Variable Name Using FORTRAN on a PDP-11**

Data Type of Variable	Maximum Number of Characters
INTEGER	2
REAL	4
DOUBLE PRECISION	8
COMPLEX	8
LOGICAL	1

maximum number of characters that may be stored in each variable or in each element of an array. Any variable can be used to store fewer characters than this maximum. However, if we try to store too many characters, the last ones are omitted. For example,

```
1   DATA NUMBER/10HABCDEFGHIJ/
    WRITE (7, 1) NUMBER
  1 FORMAT(1X, A10)
    CALL EXIT
    END
```

1 We initialize the integer variable NUMBER, but since NUMBER is an integer, only the first 2 letters are stored. The rest are lost.

yields

```
        AB
2   |----------|
        10
```

2 In printing, the 2 characters are
right justified in the 10 spaces
specified in the FORMAT statement.

We now see how we can manipulate these characters once they are read into the machine.

Problem 2.14–3. Write a program that will read two names of 8 letters or less each and then print out the one that comes first in alphabetical order.

Outline for Problem 2.14–3

  I. Read 2 names.

 II. Determine which name comes first in alphabetical order.

III. Print out the appropriate name.

```
C THIS PROGRAM READS 2 NAMES AND PRINTS OUT THE ONE
C THAT COMES FIRST IN ALPHABETICAL ORDER.
C VERSION A
1       DOUBLE PRECISION NAME1, NAME2
C READ THE TWO NAMES
        READ (5, 1) NAME1
        READ (5, 1) NAME2
      1 FORMAT(A8)
C DETERMINE WHICH NAME COMES FIRST IN ALPHABETICAL ORDER
2       IF (NAME1 .LT. NAME2) GO TO 2
C NAME2 COMES FIRST
        WRITE(7, 3) NAME2



      3 FORMAT(1M, 'THE FIRST NAME IN ALPHABETICAL ORDER IS ', A8)
        GO TO 4
C NAME1 COMES FIRST
      2 WRITE (7, 3) NAME1
C ENDING
      4 CALL EXIT
        END
```

1 The 2 names, NAME1 and NAME2, are declared to be of type Double Precision, so that each will be able to accommodate up to the 8 letters required by the problem.

2 The relational operators such as .EQ., .LT., .GT., .GE., .NE., are applied to strings of characters to indicate alphabetical order. For example, *A* .LT. *B*, *CAT* .LT. *DOGGIE*, *HELLO* .LT. *HI* and *HI*.LT.*HIGH* as the first string occurs in alphabetical order in each case.

When this program is run with the data

```
SMITH
SAMPSON
```

the output is

```
THE FIRST NAME IN ALPHABETICAL ORDER IS SAMPSON
```

If we want to work with longer names, then we must store the characters in arrays and the comparison of the two names is a lot more involved. In particular, we must compare the first letters. If they are different, we know which name comes first. However, if the first letters are the same, we have to go on to the next letter. This is seen in the following program.

```
   C THIS PROGRAM READS 2 NAMES AND PRINTS OUT THE ONE
   C THAT COMES FIRST IN ALPHABETICAL ORDER
   C VERSION B
1          DOUBLE PRECISION NAME1, NAME 2
           DIMENSION NAME1(10), NAME2(10)
   C READ THE TWO NAMES
           READ (5, 1) NAME1
           READ (5, 1) NAME2
         1 FORMAT(10A8)
   C DETERMINE WHICH NAME COMES FIRST IN ALPHABETICAL ORDER

2          DO 2 ITEM = 1, 10


3              IF (NAME1(ITEM) .LT. NAME2(ITEM)) GO TO 3
4              IF (NAME1(ITEM) .LT. NAME1(ITEM)) GO TO 4
5        2   CONTINUE

6  C BOTH NAMES ARE IDENTICAL
           WRITE (7, 5)
         5 FORMAT (1X, 'BOTH NAMES ARE IDENTICAL')
           GO TO 6
   C NAME1 COMES FIRST
         3 WRITE (7, 7) NAME1
         7 FORMAT (1X, 'THE FIRST NAME IN ALPHABETICAL ORDER IS' ,
         1       /, 1X, 10A8)
           GO TO 6
   C NAME1 COMES FIRST
         4 WRITE (7, 7) NAME2
   C ENDING
         6 CALL EXIT
           END
```

1 We still want to store 8 letters in each element of arrays, NAME1 and NAME2, but here we will allow 80 characters altogether.

2 We will have to compare the first group of letters, then the second, then the third, etc., until we find a difference in the names.

3 Check if NAME1 comes first.

4 Check if NAME2 comes first.

5 If the names are the same so far, we must go on to the next group of letters.

6 If we compare all groups of letters and if we find no differences, then the two names are identical.

When this program is run with the data

UNIVERSITY OF ROCK CREEK
UNIVERSITY OF OKOBOJI

the machine prints

THE FIRST NAME IN ALPHABETICAL ORDER IS
UNIVERSITY OF OKOBOJI

As a final example of manipulating strings of characters, we consider the following problem.

Problem 2.14–4. Write a program that will input a word and translate the word into pig Latin.

Recall: To get a word in pig Latin,

1. take the first letter of the word and place it at the end of the word;

Outline for Problem 2.14–4

I. Enter word.

II. Translate to pig Latin.
    (A) Determine length of word.
    (B) Move second and sub-

2. add the letter "A' at the end of the word.

This leads to the following program:

```
C PIG-LATIN TRANSLATOR
1       DIMENSION WORD(80), PIG(81)




2       DATA ALET/1HA/, BLANK/1H /
  C ENTER WORD
        READ (5, 1) WORD
      1 FORMAT(80A1)
3 C DETERMINE LENGTH OF WORD
        DO 2 ITEM = 1, 80

4             LAST = 81 - ITEM

5             IF (WORD(LAST) .NE. BLANK) GO TO 8
      2       CONTINUE
  C MOVE SUBSEQUENT LETTERS OF WORD LEFT BY 1
      8 DO 3 LETTER = 2, LAST
      3       PIG(LETTER -1) = WORD(LETTER)
  C PUT FIRST LETTER AT END OF WORD
        PIG(LAST) = FIRST
  C ADD LETTER A
6       LAST = LAST + 1

7       PIG(LAST) = ALET
  C FILL THE REST OF PIG WITH BLANKS

8       LPLUS1 = LAST + 1
        DO 4 ITEM = LPLUS1, 81
      4       PIG(ITEM) = BLANK
  C PRINT THE TRANSLATED WORD
        WRITE (7, 5) WORD
      5 FORMAT(1X, 80A1)
        WRITE (7, 6)
      6 FORMAT(1X, 'TRANSLATED INTO PIG-LATIN GIVES')
        WRITE (7, 7) PIG
      7 FORMAT(1X, 81A1)
  C ENDING
        CALL EXIT
        END
```

When this program is run with the data

sequent letters of word left by 1.

(C) Put first letter at the end of the word.

(D) Add the letter "A".

(E) Put blanks following the translated word.

III. Print the translated word.

1 We allow our word to be up to 80 characters long, and we will store the characters one per array element so we can work with the letters individually. If the word is shorter than 80 characters, the last array elements may contain blanks. PIG will be our translated word.

2 In the program, we will need to work with the LETter A and with the character BLANK.

3 We will work backwards along the 80 characters read into WORD until we find one that is not blank.

4 As ITEM goes from 1 to 80, LAST will go down from 80 to 1.

5 We stop our searching when we find the first nonblank character.

6 There is one more letter in the pig Latin word.

7 Recall that we stored the character "A" in ALET at the start of the program.

8 We will start our blanks at the position one after our last character, "A".

FORTRAN

the machine gives

```
FORTRAN
TRANSLATED INTO PIG-LATIN GIVES
ORTRANFA
```

It is worthwhile to observe how well the final program corresponds to our outline of the steps to be performed.

Section 2.15: FUNCTION SUBPROGRAMS (MULTIPLE-LINE FUNCTIONS)

Throughout this chapter, we have emphasized techniques that increased program clarity and readability and that allowed programs to be modified easily. Thus, in Section 2.7, we used statement functions to specify our own functions, yielding programs that were easier to understand, correct, and modify. However, these functions had two major limitations:

1.   The functions had to be defined on one line.
2.   We could only get one answer from the function.

In this section, we see how to remove the first of these restrictions. In the next section we extend the discussion to consider both restrictions.

We begin by illustrating how we can write a function on several lines by returning to the computation of a balance in a bank from Section 2.7. The main equation for the computation was

```
BALANC(PRIN,RATE,FREQ) = PRIN*(1.+RATE/FREQ)**FREQ
```

This can be written on several lines as follows:

1	`FUNCTION BALANC(PRIN,RATE,FREQ)`	1 The name of the function, BALANC, is specified, followed by the variables to be used in the computation.
2	`BALANC=PRIN*(1.+RATE/FREQ)**FREQ`	2 The appropriate value is computed and this value is set equal to the function.
3	`RETURN`	3 We indicate that the machine should return to the program, now that we have completed our computation.
4	`END`	4 The end of the function is indicated.

This computation can be split into several steps, if desired.

1	`FUNCTION BALANC(PRIN,RATE,FREQ)` `  FACTOR=(1.+RATE/FREQ)**FREQ`	1 Part of the computation is per-

formed and stored as the variable FACTOR.

2   The balance is computed and designated as the value to be returned to the main program.

```
2        BALANC = PRIN*FACTOR
         RETURN
         END
```

Within the computation, we can change the value stored in BALANC, if we wish:

```
1        FUNCTION BALANC(PRIN,RATE,FREQ)
             BALANC=(1.+RATE/FREQ)**FREQ
2            BALANC=PRIN*BALANC

3            RETURN
             END
```

1   We store the intermediate value in the variable BALANC.
2   We revise the value BALANC to the final value we want.
3   The machine returns this final value of BALANC.

These examples illustrate the general format of a function subprogram.

(a)   The first line has the form

FUNCTION name (variables)

The name of the function and the variables must be given. The normal conventions concerning the data type of the function are followed.

Thus, function BALANC is assumed to be real. If we wanted a different type, we could specify INTEGER, REAL, DOUBLE PRECISION, COMPLEX, or LOGICAL when defining the function. Thus, if we wanted more significant digits in our function, we could specify DOUBLE PRECISION FUNCTION BALANCE(PRIN,RATE,FREQ)

(b)   Somewhere in the function, some value must be designated as the output of the function, although we may change this value within the function subprogram.

(c)   We must tell the machine when it is to stop computing within the function and RETURN to the main program.

(d)   The end of the function must be indicated with the word END.

When working with these multiple-line function subprograms, we must emphasize how the usage of variables in these subprograms compares with those found in single line, function statements.

First, in function subprograms and in function statements, the machine identifies the variables specified in parentheses in the first line of the subprogram with the variables specified when the function is used. Thus, when the above function

```
FUNCTION BALANC(PRIN,RATE,FREQ)
```

is used with the lines

```
REAL INTRST
READ(5,1) PRIN,INTRST
ANNUAL=BALANC(PRIN,INTRST,1.0)
```

(as was the case in Section 2.7, program version A) then the machine uses

(a) the value read for PRIN for the value of the variable PRIN in the function;

(b) the value read for INTRST for the value of the variable RATE in the function;

(c) the value 1.0 for the value of the variable FREQ.

In each case, we must be sure to use the same type of variable when we define the function as when we use the function. However, we can put any numbers into the function, and the machine will match each variable or array specified when the function is used with the corresponding variable specified when the function is defined.

In our example, all numbers or variables were REAL.

However, in contrast to what we saw with function statements, all other variables in function subprograms are considered to be unrelated to those in the rest of the program. Thus, if the function was

```
FUNCTION BALANC(FREQ)
BALANC=PRIN*(1.+RATE/FREQ)**FREQ
RETURN
END
```

then the machine would not know what values to use for PRIN and RATE, even if the main program contained the lines

```
READ(5,1) PRIN,RATE
ANNUAL=BALANC(1.0)
```

(as was the case in Section 2.7, program version B). Since PRIN and RATE are not mentioned explicitly as input into the function, the machine assumes that we are not identifying the PRIN and RATE in the function with those in the rest of the program.

This is exactly the opposite situation from the one we found for function statements in Section 2.7, where variables not specified in parentheses were taken from the context where the function was used.

This distinction between the variables specified as input into a function subprogram and those used within the subprogram itself is particularly noticeable when variables are found in both the function and in the rest of the program. This is seen clearly in the following function F, which is a function of X only, although Y is used both in the function itself and in the main program. (In the program, we number each line so we can refer to these lines later.)

```
C MAIN PROGRAM
     1     X = 2.
     2     Y = 3.
     3     Z = F(X)
     4     WRITE (7, 5) X, Y, Z
     5     FORMAT(' MAIN     ', 3F5.1)
     6     CALL EXIT
           END

C FUNCTION
       FUNCTION F(X)
     7        X = 5.
     8        Y = 7.
     9        F = X + Y
    10        WRITE (7, 11) X, Y, F
    11        FORMAT(' FUNCTION', 3F5.1)
    12        RETURN
              END
```

When we run this program we get

```
FUNCTION   5.0   7.0 12.0
MAIN       5.0   3.0 12.0
```

In order to understand this output, we go through the program step by step.

line 1: X is set equal to 2.

line 2: Y is set equal to 3.

line 3: We perform the function.

The variable X in the main program is identified with the variable X in the function. Thus, there is only one variable X for the entire program at this point.

line 7: X is set equal to 5.

line 8: A new variable called Y, which is known only to the function, is set equal to 7.

The variable Y in the main program is not affected, as that variable was not input into the function. Thus, at this point there are two distinct Y variables, which we could call $Y_{program}$ and $Y_{function}$. Here,

$$Y_{program} = 3$$

and $Y_{function} = 7$

line 9: F is set to the sum, which in the function is

$$X + Y_{function} = 5.+7. = 12.$$

line 10: We print the values found within the function. Thus, we print the values of X, $Y_{function}$, and F.

line 12: We return to the main program back at line 3.

$Y_{function}$ is discarded and only $Y_{program}$ or Y = 3, remains. X retains its new value of 5., as it was input into the function. (We say the value of X has been changed as a side effect of the function.)

line 3   (continued):
Z is set equal to F (= 12.0)

line 4: We print the values found within the main program. Thus, we print the values of X, $Y_{program}$, and Z.

line 6: Our program ends.

We will see more uses of function subprograms in the coming sections. At present, the major characteristics of these functions can be summarized as follows:

1. Functions, either single or multiple line, can be used to specify formulas that may be required in a program. This can be helpful for program clarity and for easy program modification.

2. Variables specified in parentheses when a function is defined are "dummy" variables. These variables are identified with those specified at the time the function is used. If the variables are modified within a function, the corresponding variables in the main program are altered.

3. Variables in *function statements* that are *not* specified in parentheses are "global" to the program where the statement is defined. These values are determined from context when the function is used.

4. Variables in *function subprograms* that are *not* specified in parentheses are "local" to the subprogram. The variables are considered distinct from the variables in the main program. Thus, if these variables are modified within a function, the values of the variables in the main program are unchanged.

Section 2.16: SUBROUTINES WITH FUNCTION SUBPROGRAMS

In the last section, we saw how we could write a function using several lines. This led us to *function subprograms,* which occupied several lines but which produced a single number as output. We begin this section by considering *subroutines,* which allow us to obtain several numbers as output. After this initial discussion of subroutines, we see how we can effectively combine function subprograms and subroutines in a single program.

We illustrate subroutines with the following problem.

Problem 2.16-1. Write a program to input N numbers and to calculate their sum, average, and product.

For clarity, we decide to write our program with each of the three

Outline for Problem 2.16-1

I. Input the data.
    (A) Enter the number N.
    (B) Enter the N values.

main steps of our outline clearly distinguished. This leads to the following program.

II. Perform the desired computation.
   (A) Compute the sum.
   (B) Compute the product.
   (C) Compute the average.
III. Print the answers.

```
C THIS PROGRAM COMPUTES THE SUM, AVERAGE, AND
C PRODUCT OF N VALUES
1       DIMENSION VALUES(100)
2       CALL INPUT (N, VALUES)

3       CALL COMPUT (N, VALUES, SUM, PROD, AVG)

4       CALL OUTPUT (N, SUM, PROD, AVG)

5       CALL EXIT
        END

6       SUBROUTINE INPUT(N, VALUES)

C THIS SUBROUTINE INPUTS THE DATA
7       DIMENSION VALUES(100)
C FIRST THE NUMBER  N  IS READ
        READ (5, 1) N
      1 FORMAT(I5)
C NEXT THE  N  VALUES ARE ENTERED, ONE AT A TIME
        DO 2 ITEM = 1, N
      2       READ (5, 3) VALUES(ITEM)
      3       FORMAT(F10.4)
8       RETURN
        END
9       SUBROUTINE COMPUT(NUMBER, ARRAY, TOTAL, PROD, AVG)

C THIS SUBROUTINE PERFORMS THE DESIRED COMPUTATIONS
10      DIMENSION ARRAY(100)

11      TOTAL = 0.
11      PROD = 1.

12      DO 1 ITEM = 1, NUMBER
            TOTAL = TOTAL + ARRAY(ITEM)
            PROD  = PROD  * ARRAY(ITEM)
12    1     CONTINUE
```

1. We will allow up to 100 numbers.
2. We enter the appropriate values, using the subroutine **INPUT** below.
3. We must compute the appropriate values, using the subroutine COMPUTe below.
4. We print out the appropriate numbers in the subroutine **OUTPUT**.
5. We go to the subroutine EXIT which tells the machine to finish our job.
6. We start the coding for our first subroutine after the coding of the main program.
7. As in the main program, VALUES is an array.

8. After we have read in the data, we return to the main program.
9. We begin the next subroutine. As with function subprograms, the machine identifies the variables specified here with those specified when the subroutine is called.
10. As in the main program, we need an **ARRAY**.
11. We initialize the variables TOTAL and PRODuct, so we can perform the additions and multiplication in a loop.
12. As with local variables in function subprograms, the machine assumes statement numbers in one subroutine or function or in the main program are not related to statement numbers in other subroutines, functions, or programs.

```
          AVG = TOTAL / NUMBER
13        RETURN
          END

14        SUBROUTINE OUTPUT(N, SUM, PROD, AVG)
   C THIS SUBROUTINE PRINTS THE DESIRED OUTPUT
          WRITE(7, 1) N
        1 FORMAT (' THERE ARE', I4, ' NUMBERS')
          WRITE (7, 2) SUM
        2 FORMAT ('      SUM =', F10.2)
          WRITE (7, 3) PROD
        3 FORMAT (' PRODUCT =', F10.2)
          WRITE (7, 4) AVG
        4 FORMAT (' AVERAGE =', F10.4)
          RETURN
          END
```

13 After performing the desired computation, we go back to the main program.

14 The OUTPUT routine begins.

If we run this program with the data

```
1    4
  7.
  5.
  3.
  9.
```

1 We will work with four numbers.

we get the output

```
THERE ARE    4 NUMBERS
      SUM =      24.00
  PRODUCT =     945.00
  AVERAGE =      6.0000
```

This program has several important characteristics:

1. The main program (the first few lines) is very short and easy to read, and it follows the outline clearly.
2. The program branches to each subroutine using the CALL statements.
3. When the subroutine is completed, the machine encounters the RETURN statement which sends the machine back to the line following the CALL.

When the program is run, the machine first executes the CALL INPUT statement, which sends the machine to the INPUT subroutine.

When all values are READ in the INPUT subroutine, the RETURN sends the machine back to the main program, to the line following the CALL INPUT (namely the line CALL COMPUT).

The CALL COMPUT sends the machine to the COMPUTe subroutine, where the computations are performed. The RETURN sends the machine back to the main program.

Finally, the CALL OUTPUT sends the computer to the OUTPUT subroutine and the RETURN sends the machine back.

The variables in a CALL statement are matched with those in the definition of the subroutine, just as with the function subprograms.

In this program, we must emphasize that the use of subroutines made the program (particularly the main program) extremely easy to read and understand. Further, we stress that the variables in SUBROUTINES have the same "local" or "dummy" qualities that we saw for function subprograms.

With this background, we can now turn our attention to the writing of large programs by dividing them into several parts. Each part performs just one task for us, and each part is self-contained. Further, when a part must contain more than a couple lines, we write it as a function or subroutine, so our main program remains concise and easy to understand.

As an example, we return to the pig Latin translator in Section 2.14. From our outline, we see several steps will require several lines of code, although we think of each step as a single operation. For example:

II-A.   Determine length of word.
II-B.   Move second and subsequent letters of word left by 1.
II-E.   Put blanks following the translated word.
III.   Print the translated word.

We now write a second version of our pig Latin translator, writing these steps as separate units. The first of these units yields exactly 1 number, so we will write it as a function. The second, third, and fourth units require a sequence of results (a shift, sequence of blanks, or several lines of output), so we write subroutines. In this program, we retain the titles from the previous version that correspond to our outline.

Outline for Pig Latin Translator

I.   Enter word.
II. Translate to pig Latin.
     (A) Determine length of word.
     (B) Move second and subsequent letters of word left by 1.
     (C) Put first letter at the end of the word.
     (D) Add the letter "A".
     (E) Put blanks following the translated word.
III. Print the translated word.

```
C PIG-LATIN TRANSLATOR
C VERSION B
      DIMENSION WORD(80), PIG(81)
1     DATA ALET/1HA/
```

1 We begin much the same way as before. We do not include BLANK/1H /here, however, as that variable is used only in determining the length of the word and in filling the end of the translated word with blanks. Thus, we defer the defining of BLANK until these subroutines.

```
C ENTER WORD
2     READ (5, 1) WORD
    1 FORMAT(80A1)

3 C DETERMINE LENGTH OF WORD
      LAST = LENGTH(WORD)
```

2 The code for this section is particularly short, so we write it out here.

3 As the determination of the length of the word requires several lines, we perform this operation in a separate function LENGTH below.

```
C MOVE SECOND AND SUBSEQUENT LETTERS OF WORD LEFT BY 1
4         CALL SHIFT(WORD, PIG, LAST)

C PUT FIRST LETTER AT END OF WORD
5         PIG(LAST) = WORD(1)
C ADD LETTER A
          LAST = LAST + 1
          PIG(LAST) = ALET
C FILL THE REST OF PIG WITH BLANKS, STARTING IN SPACE LAST+1
6         CALL BLANKS(PIG, LAST + 1)



  C PRINT THE TRANSLATED WORD


7         CALL OUTPUT(WORD, PIG)
  C ENDING
          CALL EXIT
          END


8         FUNCTION LENGTH(WORD)


9 C THIS FUNCTION DETERMINES THE POSITION OF THE LAST
  C      LETTER OF WORD
          DIMENSION WORD(80)
10        DATA BLANK/1H /

11        DO 2 ITEM = 1, 80
              LENGTH = 81 - ITEM
              IF (WORD(LENGTH) .NE. BLANK) GO TO 8
      2       CONTINUE
12    8   RETURN





13        END

14        SUBROUTINE SHIFT(WORD1, WORD2, LAST)







  C THIS SUBROUTINE MOVES THE LETTERS OF WORD1 INTO THE
  C      LETTERS OF WORD2, SHIFTING THESE LETTERS LEFT
  C      BY 1 IN EACH CASE
          DIMENSION WORD1(30), WORD2(81)
          DO 1 LETTER = 2, LAST
      1       WORD2(LETTER - 1) = WORD1(LETTER)
```

4   Shift is a subroutine, defined below, that performs the shifting process.

5   The last letter of the pig Latin word is added, following the code from the previous version.

6   Here, we use the subroutine BLANKS to add the blanks to the end of the pig Latin word. Note that we may enter the value LAST + 1 into the subroutine. In general, any arithmetic expression may be entered.

7   Subroutine OUTPUT will print both the original WORD and the pig Latin word.

8   The functions and subroutines are always listed after the main program.

9   As in the main program, WORD is an array.

10   In this function, we need to be able to identify a BLANK.

11   This part of our function follows the code of our previous version.

12   LENGTH has been revised during the execution of the function, until now it gives the position of the first nonblank character. This is the value we want returned in our function.

13   We are at the end of our function.

14   We begin our shifting subroutine. We will use 2 arrays, WORD1 and WORD2, which will be identified with WORD and PIG in the main program, and we will use the integer LAST.

<table>
<tr><td>15</td><td>

```
        RETURN
        END


        SUBROUTINE BLANKS(TEXT, LOWEST)
16 C THIS SUBROUTINE FILLS ARRAY TEXT WITH BLANKS,
   C BEGINNING WITH ITEM NUMBER LOWEST
```

</td></tr>
</table>

```
15    RETURN
      END


      SUBROUTINE BLANKS(TEXT, LOWEST)
16 C THIS SUBROUTINE FILLS ARRAY TEXT WITH BLANKS,
   C BEGINNING WITH ITEM NUMBER LOWEST


      DIMENSION TEXT(81)
17    DATA SPACE/1H /
      DO 1 ITEM = LOWEST, 81
   1      TEXT(ITEM) = SPACE
      RETURN
      END


18    SUBROUTINE OUTPUT(WORD1, WORD2)
   C THIS SUBROUTINE PRINTS THE RESULTS
      DIMENSION WORD1(80), WORD2(81)
      WRITE (7, 1) WORD1
   1 FORMAT(1X, 80A1)
      WRITE (7, 2)
   2 FORMAT(1X, 'TRANSLATED INTO PIG LATIN GIVES')
      WRITE (7, 3) WORD2
   3 FORMAT(1X, 81A1)
      RETURN
      END
```

15 The shifting has been completed, so we RETURN to the main program.

16 Notice how the use of comments at the first lines of each subroutine or function help us read and understand our program easily and quickly.

17 We are using the word SPACE for our blank space, so we will not confuse the subroutine BLANKS with a variable such as BLANK.

18 We will print the output in the same format as before.

While this version of our pig Latin translation uses the same input and produces the same output as our earlier version, the various sections are clearer to read and the resulting program is easier to debug and modify than the earlier program.

Section 2.17: COMMON STATEMENTS AND EXTERNAL STATEMENTS

In the previous two sections, we covered the main features of function subprograms and subroutines, and we saw several applications. Now we consider two additional features of FORTRAN that can be helpful in using these function subprograms and subroutines, namely,

1. COMMON statements.
2. EXTERNAL statements.

We will consider these topics separately.

COMMON Statements

When we discussed functions and subroutines in the previous two sections, we noted that the variables specified in parentheses at the beginning of the subprogram were "dummy" variables and other variables in the subprogram were "local" variables. When a function or subroutine was executed, the "dummy" variables were identified with other variables from the main program, while "local" variables were considered unrelated to variables elsewhere in the program. The "dummy" variables allowed us to use the same function or subroutine with different inputs. For example, the first program in Section 2.6 used the lines

```
RAD1 = ATAN(ALEG2/ALEG1)
RAD2 = ATAN(ALEG1/ALEG2)
```

to compute the arc tangent function for two different cases. However, in some situations, we want to use the same variables from the main program in the subprogram. In the program in the previous section where we computed the sum, average, and product of N values, for example, the program included:

```
DIMENSION VALUES(100)
CALL INPUT (N, VALUES)
CALL COMPUT (N, VALUES, SUM, PROD, AVG)       } main program
CALL OUTPUT (N, SUM, PROD, AVG)
CALL EXIT
END

SUBROUTINE INPUT(N, VALUES)                     } subroutine INPUT
DIMENSION VALUES(100)
        .
        .
        .
SUBROUTINE COMPUT(NUMBER, ARRAY, TOTAL, PROD, AVG)  } subroutine COMPUT
DIMENSION ARRAY(100)
        .
        .
        .
SUBROUTINE OUTPUT(N, SUM, PROD, AVG)            } subroutine OUTPUT
        .
        .
        .
```

Here the integer N in the main program is needed in each subroutine, the array VALUES is identified with arrays in the first 2 subroutines, and the numbers SUM, AVG, PROD in the main program are identified with numbers in the last 2 subroutines.

Since we never want to identify the "dummy" variables in these subprograms with any other variables in the main program, we may replace these "dummy" variables by variables in a COMMON statement. This would yield the following program:

```
      DIMENSION VALUES(100)
1     COMMON N, VALUES, SUM, PROD, AVG




2           CALL INPUT
2           CALL COMPUT
2           CALL OUTPUT
            CALL EXIT
            END
```

1 The COMMON statement begins the main program and each subprogram, coming after any dimension statements. As illustrated in subroutine COMPUT below, however, the dimension of array VALUES could be declared in the COMMON statement directly.

2 Since all variables needed are in COMMON, we do not put them in parentheses after the name of the subroutine.

3	SUBROUTINE INPUT DIMENSION VALUES(100)	3	As with the CALL statements above, we do not include the variables found in COMMON in parentheses after the name of the subroutine.
4	COMMON N, VALUES . . .	4	In this subroutine, we need the first two parts of COMMON, but we do not need the latter ones, so we omit these last ones.
5,6	SUBROUTINE COMPUT COMMON NUMBER, ARRAY(100), PROD, AVG . . .	5	Here, we use the names of the variables that we want in these subroutines. They need not be the same names as in the main program. However, the order of these variables must be in the same order as the corresponding variables in the main program.
		6	Note that we can combine the declaration of ARRAY in the COMMON, and the DIMENSION statement can be omitted.
7	SUBROUTINE OUTPUT COMMON N, FILL(100), SUM, PROD, AVG	7	Here we need the first value and the last three values in COMMON. However, to get to these last three values, we must skip over the array. Thus, we need an array to FILL the space of the array in COMMON. FILL takes up the desired space, but it will not be used in this subroutine.

In a second version of this program, we may decide to use COMMON for only some of these variables. We treat the other variables using the "dummy" variables discussed in the previous section. This alternate version is:

	COMMON N, VALUES(100) CALL INPUT CALL COMPUT (SUM, PROD, AVG) CALL OUTPUT (SUM, PROD, AVG) CALL EXIT END		
1	SUBROUTINE INPUT COMMON N, VALUES(100) . . .	1	Dummy variables, in parentheses after INPUT, are not needed, as all values needed are in COMMON.
2 2	SUBROUTINE COMPUT (TOTAL, PROD, AVG) COMMON NUMBER, ARRAY(100) . . .	2	Three dummy variables are needed here in addition to the values stored in COMMON on the following line.

```
3       SUBROUTINE OUTPUT (SUM, PROD, AVG)
        COMMON N
            .
            .
            .
```

3 As only the first value in COMMON is needed, we may omit the array from the COMMON statement.

We conclude the discussion with two additional comments concerning COMMON statements.

1. COMMON statements may be used in the same way in function subprograms as in subroutines, except that every function must contain at least one dummy variable (in parentheses following the function name).
2. The variable names specified in COMMON may not also be used as dummy variables (in parentheses following the function name).

EXTERNAL Statements

In the subprograms that we have considered up to now, we have seen how dummy variables in the subprograms can be identified with different variables in the main program at the time the subprograms are used. The EXTERNAL statement allows us to do a similar identification for functions and subroutines that we write. This is illustrated in the following problem.

Problem 2.17-1. Write a program that computes and prints the values of the functions:

$$f_1(X) = X^2 + 3X - 5$$
$$f_2(X) = X^3 - 2X + 5$$
$$f_3(X) = \sqrt{X}$$

for $X = 0, 1, \ldots, 5.$

Outline for Problem 2.17-1

I. Print titles.
II. Compute and print values for the first function.
III. Compute and print values for the second function.
IV. Compute and print values for the third function.

We write this program by writing one subroutine TABULate which does the computation and printing for a function F. This is seen in the following program.

```
C THIS PROGRAM COMPUTES AND TABULATES FUNCTIONS
1       EXTERNAL F1, F2, SQRT
C PRINT TITLES
        WRITE (7, 1)
    1 FORMAT (11X, 'X-VALUES')
        WRITE (7, 2)
    2 FORMAT (20X, '1', 9X, '2', 9X, '3', 9X, '4', 9X, '5')
C COMPUTE AND PRINT VALUES FOR FIRST FUNCTION
        WRITE (7, 3)
    3 FORMAT (1X, 'FIRST FUNCTION')
2       CALL TABULT(F1)
  C COMPUTE AND PRINT VALUES FOR SECOND FUNCTION
        WRITE (7, 4)
```

1 We indicate that these functions will be used as input to our subroutine TABULate.

2 The subroutine TABULate uses the function F1 in its computation.

```
     4 FORMAT (1X, 'SECOND FUNCTION')
3        CALL TABULT(F2)
  C COMPUTE AND PRINT VALUES FOR THIRD FUNCTION
         WRITE (7, 5)
     5 FORMAT (1X, 'THIRD FUNCTION')
4        CALL TABULT(SQRT)
  C ENDING
         CALL EXIT
         END

5        FUNCTION F1(X)
         F1 = X**2 + 3*X -5
         RETURN
         END

6        FUNCTION F2(X)
         F2 = X**3 - 2*X + 5
         RETURN
         END

  C TABULATION SUBPROGRAM
7        SUBROUTINE TABULT(F)
         DIMENSION VALUES(5)
  C COMPUTE FUNCTION'S VALUES
         DO 1 I = 1, 5
8            X = FLOAT(I)
9    1       VALUES(I) = F(X)
  C PRINT FUNCTION'S VALUES
         WRITE (7, 2) VALUES
     2 FORMAT (11X, 5F10.2)
10       RETURN
         END
```

3 TABULT uses function F2 in its computation.

4 The third set of computations in TABULT uses the third function SQRT.

5 The first function is defined.

6 The second function is defined.

7 The input to this subroutine is the function F.

8 We convert the integer I to the real number X.

9 Compute the value of the function for the given X value.

10 When the values are computed and printed for this function, we return to the main program.

When this function is run, we get

```
        X-VALUES
                  1          2          3          4          5
FIRST FUNCTION
               -1.00       5.00      13.00      23.00      35.00
SECOND FUNCTION
                4.00       9.00      26.00      61.00     120.00
THIRD FUNCTION
                1.00       1.41       1.73       2.00       2.24
```

Section 2.18: **DISK FILES**[†]

All programs up to this point have stored all of their data in the main memory of the CPU. This has certain advantages and disadvantages.

[†]*Note:* Disk file capabilities in standard FORTRAN are rather limited, although most extensions of the standard language expand these capabilities. This section begins by giving the basic techniques behind disk files in standard FORTRAN, and then it discusses additional details for the extended FORTRAN used on the PDP-11 computer series. Many of these details may also apply to other machines. However, the details of disk files discussed here are not used in the rest of this chapter, so this section may be skimmed or omitted without loss of continuity.

Advantages

1. The computer can process data in the main memory more quickly and efficiently than it can when data is stored outside the CPU.
2. Overhead costs for processing are reduced.

Disadvantages

1. All data must be READ from cards or from a terminal each time the program is run.
2. The amount of data is limited by the size of the main memory in the CPU.
3. All data inside the computer itself is destroyed after each program is run. No data is saved from one run to another, except what has been punched on cards.

When the amount of data in a program is comparatively small, these disadvantages are not significant, and entering each data each time a program is run is not a serious handicap. However, in many applications such as the inventory control program of Section 2.11, a great deal of data must be processed over many runs and these disadvantages become overwhelming.

In this section, we begin by presenting the basic ideas behind the use of disk files in standard FORTRAN for long-term, bulk storage. Then we turn to additional specific details concerning the use of these files. When we use these files, we may give up the efficiency of storing the data in fast memory, but we do solve the disadvantages listed above.

Basics of Disk Files in Standard FORTRAN

In standard FORTRAN, or in any of its extensions, we can think of the computer using a disk file instead of the card deck or the terminal. We consider the file as containing a sequence of lines, called *records* (just like a card deck or like paper in a terminal), and we use READ and WRITE statements to transfer data.

We always begin our use of disk files by assigning our disk file a logical number, just as the card reader has been given the number 5 and the printer has been given the number 7. Then we can use our READ and WRITE statements as before.

For example, if we have assigned the number 4 to our file, then we could print 5 lines on the file with the following program.

```
  C THIS PROGRAM PRINTS ON A FILE
1       WRITE (4, 1)

2     1 FORMAT ('THIS IS LINE NUMBER ONE')
        DO 2 NUMBER = 2, 5

3     2   WRITE (4, 3) NUMBER
      3   FORMAT ('THIS IS LINE', I2)
          CALL EXIT
          END
```

1 We print the first line according to the format specified on device 4, which is our disk file.
2 With disk files, the first character is usually not related to carriage control.
3 We print the subsequent lines.

When this program is run, nothing is printed at the terminal or on the printer, although the following is printed in our file.

```
THIS IS LINE NUMBER ONE
THIS IS LINE 2
THIS IS LINE 3
```

```
THIS IS LINE 4
THIS IS LINE 5
```

Similarly, information can be read from the file using the READ statement. For example, if our file contained

```
3.          5.
6.
```

THIS IS A TEST

and if our file is assigned the logical number 4, then we could use the following program.

```
C THIS PROGRAM READS A FILE
      DIMENSION TEXT(20)
C READING STARTS HERE
1     READ (4, 1) VALUE1, VALUE2
    1 FORMAT (2F10.2)
      READ (4, 2) VALUE3
    2 FORMAT (F10.2)
      READ (4, 3) TEXT
    3 FORMAT (20A1)
C PRINT VALUES AT PRINTER
      WRITE (7, 4) VALUE1, VALUE2, VALUE3, TEXT
    4 FORMAT (1X, 3F10.3, 5X, 10A1)
      CALL EXIT
      END
```

1 We READ from logical number 4 which is our file.

When the program is run we have

```
   3.00       5.00       6.00      THIS IS A TEST
```

Here, it is important to note that the READ and WRITE work exactly the same way for a file as for cards, terminals, and printers. That is, they always start at the first record (or line) and READ or WRITE subsequent records, one at a time. Each time a READ or WRITE occurs, we move on to the next record.

As an example of how this use of files can be employed, we return to part of the inventory program in Section 2.11.

Problem 2.18-1. A manufacturer requires 8 types of parts which are stored in 5 warehouses. These are represented in an array INVENtory (P,W) where P is the type of part and W is the warehouse number.

Write a program to input the table of inventories, store the table in the file SUPPLY.DAT, and compute the total number of parts in each warehouse.

We note how closely the outline and the following program follow that in Section 2.11. Only the few lines storing the data on the disk have been added.

We assume the disk file SUPPLY.DAT has been given the logical number 3.

Outline for Problem 2.18-1

 I. Determine inventory of each part for each warehouse.

 II. Store the data on the disk.

III. Compute the total number of parts in each warehouse.

```
C INVENTORY PROGRAM
      DIMENSION INVEN(8, 5)
      INTEGER PART, WAREHS
C INPUT INVENTORIES
      READ (5, 1) INVEN
    1 FORMAT(8I5)
C STORE INVENTORIES ON DISK FILE
      DO 10 PART = 1, 8
   10       WRITE (3, 11) (INVEN(PART, WAREHS),
     1            WAREHS = 1, 5)

   11       FORMAT (5I10)

C COMPUTE THE TOTAL NUMBER OF PARTS PER WAREHOUSE
      DO 2 WAREHS = 1, 5
            ISUM = 0
            DO 3 PART = 1, 3
    3             ISUM = ISUM + INVEN(PART, WAREHS)
            WRITE (7, 4) WAREHS, ISUM
    4       FORMAT(' WAREHOUSE', I2, ' CONTAINS',
     1            I3, ' PARTS.')
    2       CONTINUE
      CALL EXIT
      END
```

1 The program up to this point is identical with that in Section 2.11.

2 Only this section is added to the earlier program.

3 We write 5 numbers per record into the file.

4 The rest of the program is also identical with that in Section 2.11.

When this program is run with the data from before, we get

```
WAREHOUSE 1 CONTAINS 46 PARTS.
WAREHOUSE 2 CONTAINS 32 PARTS.
WAREHOUSE 3 CONTAINS 32 PARTS.
WAREHOUSE 4 CONTAINS 38 PARTS.
WAREHOUSE 5 CONTAINS 46 PARTS.
```

In addition, all of the values read into the array INVEN are saved in our disk file. Thus, if we want to compute the total number of each type of part, we can run a second program using this data. This follows many of the same steps as the second part of the inventory program of Section 2.11. (This time, for variety, we assume our disk file has been assigned logical number 6.)

Recall, the table used before was

Part	Warehouse				
	1	2	3	4	5
1	3	1	4	1	5
2	9	2	6	5	3
3	5	8	9	7	9
4	3	2	3	8	4
5	6	2	6	4	3
6	3	8	3	2	7
7	9	5	0	2	8
8	8	4	1	9	7

We read the table down the columns, so the first data card was

3 9 5 3 6 3 9 8

```
C INVENTORY PROGRAM, USING A DISK FILE
C PART 2
      DIMENSION INVEN(8, 5)
C READ INVENTORIES FROM DISK FILE
      DO 1 PART = 1, 8
```

```
1      1        READ (6, 2) (INVEN(PART, WAREHS),
       1             WAREHS = 1,5)
       2        FORMAT (5I10)
C COMPUTE THE TOTAL NUMBER OF PARTS OF EACH TYPE
       DO 5 PART = 1, 8
                ISUM = 0
                DO 6 WAREHS = 1, 5
       6            ISUM = ISUM + INVEN(PART, WAREHS)
                WRITE (7, 7) ISUM, PART
       7        FORMAT(' THERE ARE', I3, ' PARTS OF TYPE', I2)
       5        CONTINUE
       CALL EXIT
       END
```

1 We read the values from the disk file 5 numbers per record, using the same format as when they were stored there.

Running the program yields

```
THERE ARE 14 PARTS OF TYPE 1
THERE ARE 25 PARTS OF TYPE 2
THERE ARE 38 PARTS OF TYPE 3
THERE ARE 20 PARTS OF TYPE 4
THERE ARE 21 PARTS OF TYPE 5
THERE ARE 23 PARTS OF TYPE 6
THERE ARE 24 PARTS OF TYPE 7
THERE ARE 29 PARTS OF TYPE 8
```

Here we note that we did not need to read the data from the terminal or from cards again, since the information was already stored in the file during the previous program.

At this point, we have seen the major characteristics connected with disk files in standard FORTRAN:

1. We must assign a logical number to the disk file (although there is not a standard way to do this).

2. We can READ and WRITE on to the disk file using standard FORMAT statements, except that the first character of the line is rarely used for carriage control.

3. All READ and WRITE operations start with the first record (or line) of the file and proceed one record at a time to the end.
   (a) This characteristic makes it somewhat inefficient to update a single record using standard FORTRAN, since we must start at the beginning of the file even if we want to change a record near the end of the file.
   (b) Extensions of standard FORTRAN allow us more flexibility in updating files.

Disk Files in the Extended FORTRAN of the PDP-11 Computer

We now turn to the additional details of disk files in extensions of standard FORTRAN. We begin by discussing file names; then we see how to assign logical unit numbers to the files; next we see how to READ and WRITE whatever record is desired, regardless of where it is;

and finally we consider a new statement which can make this process more efficient.

File Names

We begin our discussion of disk files on a PDP-11 with a considera-tion of the names a file can have. The general format of a file name is

For example, 'TEXT.DAT', 'F78121.OUT', and 'PRBLEM.SET' are valid file names.

$$(name) . (extension)$$

Here the terms (name) and (extension) each are made up of digits and/or letters, with (name) having six or fewer characters and (extension) having three or fewer.

When specifying the disk files, any sequence of letters and digits can be used, although some conventions can be useful. The (extension) of the file should indicate the nature of the file. For example, .FOR indicates a FORTRAN program, .DAT indicates a file of data, .DOC indicates program documentation, and .PTR indicates a file to be printed on a high-speed printer.

We may have already encountered this format when we gave names to our programs. We normally use names such as LITERS.FOR or PROGRM.FOR when we create FORTRAN programs for use on the PDP-11.

The (name) of the file can indicate the project we are working on. Thus, we might use SUPPLY to name an inventory file, LATIN to name a passage from a Roman text, and CHECKS to record our transactions in our checking account.

Assignment of Logical Unit Number to File

Once we decide upon a name, such as SUPPLY.DAT, for our disk file, we must then assign it a logical unit name.

On the PDP-11, this is done using the ASSIGN subroutine.

The ASSIGN Subroutine

The ASSIGN subroutine, which is already stored by the system in the machine, can be used as in the following example.

The statement

```
CALL ASSIGN (3, 'SUPPLY.DAT', 10, NEW, 'NC')
```

On other machines, the role of the ASSIGN subroutine may be handled by statements given to the machine before the program is run. (This may be done in a specialized format called Job Control Language or JCL, which is beyond the scope of this text.)

does the following:

(a) Logical unit 3 is associated with the file name 'SUPPLY.DAT'.

(b) 'SUPPLY.DAT' is a file name containing 10 characters.

(c) 'SUPPLY.DAT' will be a NEW file.

(d) In writing on the file, the first column will *not* be for carriage control.

The more general form for using this subroutine is

```
CALL ASSIGN (unit number, filename, numbercharacters,
             status of file, carriage control)
```

Here we have already seen that the *unit number* is associated with the *filename.* The *numbercharacters* specification indicates how many characters there are in the *filename,* including periods. However, if *numbercharacters* is specified to be zero, then the *filename* is processed until the first blank or comma is found.

The *status of file* may be 'RDO', 'NEW', 'OLD', or 'SCR'. Here 'OLD' causes the computer to search for the specified existing file with the given name. If that file is not found, an error results, and the program terminates.

'RDO' is similar to 'OLD'. However, it does not allow us to change the file; we may READ from it but we may not WRITE. Any attempt to WRITE on the file (thereby changing what might have been on the file earlier) results in an error, and the program terminates.

'RDO' stands for ReaD Only.

'NEW' causes the computer to create a new, empty file with the given name.

> Any earlier file by that name is deleted.

'SCR' creates a new, temporary file for use during the program only. This file is deleted when the program ends.

'SCR' stands for SCRatch.

Finally, the *carriage control* may be either 'NC' or 'CC'. If 'CC' is specified, then the first column in each record of a WRITE is treated as a carriage control character. 'NC' indicates there is no carriage control in column 1.

With this subroutine, we can use a disk file in the same way as we have used cards or the line printer before. This is done in the following example, which completes the first program of this section, including the assignment of the logical unit number.

```
C THIS PROGRAM PRINTS ON A FILE
1       CALL ASSIGN (4, 'TEST.DAT', 8, 'NEW', 'NC')

2       WRITE (4, 1)
    1 FORMAT ('THIS IS LINE NUMBER ONE')
      DO 2 NUMBER = 2, 5
3   2       WRITE (4, 3) NUMBER

4   3       FORMAT ('THIS IS LINE', I2)
      CALL EXIT
      END
```

1 We will use logical number 4 for this NEW file.
2 The first record is filled with the 23 characters specified in the FORMAT statement.
3 We WRITE on records 2, 3, 4, and 5.
4 The FORMAT statement is used for files in the same way it was used for our cards, terminal, or printer.

General READ *and* WRITE *on Disk*

In previous examples, we would always READ or WRITE one record after another, just as we did with cards or the line printer. However, in some cases, we may wish to READ or WRITE on records in some other order. For example, if we store parts of an array on different records of a file, we may want to consider only part of the array at a time. In order to accomplish this on the PDP-11, we must:

1. use the DEFINE FILE statement to tell the computer some characteristics of our file;
2. include record number information in our READ or WRITE statements.

We consider each of the items in turn.

The DEFINE FILE statement is common to many extensions of standard FORTRAN.

The DEFINE FILE Statement

The DEFINE FILE statement tells the machine something of the nature of the records on the file. For example,

$$DEFINE\ FILE\ 3\ (8,\ 5,\ U,\ LINE)$$

indicates that the file with logical number 3 will have 8 records, each of which will have room for 5 integers. The U has technical significance and is the only letter allowed in the third position. LINE is a variable which will indicate the number of the record following each READ or WRITE.

The more general form of this statement is

$$DEFINE\ FILE\ \begin{array}{c}\text{logical}\\\text{number}\end{array}\left(\begin{array}{c}\text{number}\\\text{of records}\end{array},\ \begin{array}{c}\text{size of}\\\text{each record}\end{array},\ \begin{array}{c}U,\end{array}\begin{array}{c}\text{integer}\\\text{variable}\end{array}\right)$$

Here, the *number of records* corresponds to the number of cards in a card deck. *The size of each record* corresponds to the number of characters in our FORMAT statement. (If we do not allow enough room on a record for the FORMAT statements that we will use, then a single READ or WRITE will extend beyond the first record into the later ones.)

The *integer variable* may be used to determine what record we are working with at any part in the program. Whenever the machine READs or WRITEs on the file, the *integer variable* is set to the number of the next record.

Extensions of READ and WRITE

Previously, whenever we were READing or WRITEing one record after another, we always used the form

$$READ(u, f)$$
$$WRITE(u, f)$$

where u was the unit number and f was the number of our FORMAT statement. In FORTRAN IV PLUS on the PDP-11, if we wish to specify that we should work with record r of our file, then we use the following form:

$$\text{READ}(u'r)$$
$$\text{WRITE}(u'r)$$

Several observations are now in order.

1. These revised READ and WRITE statements do not permit us to specify what format we want to use within each record. Rather, the machine READs or WRITEs on the specified record, beginning at the start of each record until the values of the variables have been read or written. To some extent, our use of the DEFINE FILE statement allowed us to specify the characteristics of each record so that FORMAT is not as important as it might be otherwise. However, we must be careful not to depend upon a specific format when using this approach to disk files.

2. Because of the lack of FORMAT statements in this context, it is strongly advisable to always READ and WRITE on a file using the same number of variables and using the same type of variables (such as INTEGER or REAL).

3. We must allow enough room on each record for the data that we want to READ and WRITE. Here, we must know the amount of room required for each type of variable that we might use. This is shown in Table 2.18-1.

Table 2.18-1. Disk Storage Requirements on the PDP-11

Data Type	Storage to Allocate
Integer	1 unit
real	2 units
double precision	4 units
complex	4 units
logical	1 unit

We illustrate how these capabilities can be helpful in updating arrays stored on disk files by considering the following example.

Problem 2.18-2. Suppose the warehouse inventories, mentioned earlier in this section, were to be updated regularly. Specify a file structure to allow the file to be updated easily. Then (a) write a program to store the inventories in this new form, and (b) write a second program that will update any specified entry of this file.

As we did in Problem 2.18-1, we will store our inventory on 8 records, one for each PART, and each record contains the data for each of the 5 warehouses. With this background, we see that each record will have to contain 5 integers, so we must allow 5 units of storage for each record in our DEFINE FILE statement.

We now write our inputting program.

Outline for Problem 2.18-2(a)
For each part:
I. Read inventories of each warehouse.
II. Write those inventories on the disk file.

Outline for Problem 2.18-2(b)
I. Determine change to be made.
II. Read old values from appropriate record.
III. Make change in the appropriate record.

```
C INVENTORY PROGRAM, REVISED
        INTEGER PART
        DIMENSION INVEN(5)
C SET UP DISK FILE
1       CALL ASSIGN (3, 'SUPPLY.DAT',10, 'NEW', 'NC')

2       DEFINE FILE 3 (8, 5, U , LINE)

C FOR EACH PART
        DO 1 PART = 1, 8
C           INPUT INVENTORIES OF THAT PART
                READ(5, 2) INVEN
    2           FORMAT(5I5)
C           PRINT INVENTORIES ON THE FILE
3               WRITE(3'PART) INVEN

    1 CONTINUE
      CALL EXIT
      END
```

1   We want to create a NEW file here.

2   The file will have 8 records, one for each **PART**. Each record will hold 5 integers, one for each **WAREHOUSE**.

3   We write the data on the record for that **PART**.

We may now write our updating program. We will use the integer array IREC to store the data on a record of the file.

```
C INVENTORY UPDATING PROGRAM
        INTEGER PART, WAREHS
        DIMENSION IREC(5)
C DETERMINE WHAT CHANGE IS DESIRED
1       READ (5, 1) PART, WAREHS, NEW

    1 FORMAT (3I10)
C SPECIFY FILE

2       CALL ASSIGN (3, 'SUPPLY.DAT', 10, 'OLD', 'NC')
        DEFINE FILE 3 (8, 5, U, LINE)
C READ OLD VALUES FOR THE DESIRED PART
3       READ (3'PART) IREC
    2 FORMAT(5I10)
C MAKE CHANGE FOR THE DESIRED PART
4       IREC(WAREHS) = NEW

5       WRITE (3'PART) IREC

        CALL EXIT
        END
```

1   We determine what **PART** number and **WAREHouSe** number must have its inventory changed, and we read the NEW inventory value.

2   We specify an OLD file here, since we cannot update a file that does not exist.

3   We read in the record corresponding to the **PART** specified.

4   We change the inventory of the part for the desired warehouse.

5   Now that the inventory for the desired part is corrected in the CPU, we write the corrections back onto our disk file.

If we wanted to change our inventory for part 7, warehouse 3 to 4, we would run the program with the data

        7   3   4

No output is produced by the program at our terminal or on the printer since the machine is just changing the number in our file.

Caution! Since we have not asked the machine to print out the final file values, we do not have a convenient way of checking what is stored in the array; we cannot just look at some output. We must print the file from the disk file if we want to check it.

The FIND Statement

We close this section by mentioning the FIND statement which is useful in making our use of disk files more efficient.

When we are using disk files, some mechanical processes must be done by the computer in order to retrieve data. While this can be done rather quickly, it still takes some time for the computer to find the record we want to use. Thus, we may use the statement

$$FIND(u'r)$$

where u is a logical unit number and r is the record number. This statement starts the mechanical process going to find the specified record. If it appears well before a READ or WRITE, then the record may be found by the time we need it. The machine may perform other processing of statements between the FIND and the READ or WRITE while it locates our record. Thus, a sequence

$$FIND(u'r)$$
$$\vdots \quad \text{other statements}$$
$$READ(u'r)$$

may result in a reasonable savings of time in the machine. However, there is no advantage to

$$FIND(u'r)$$
$$READ(u'r)$$

since the machine is not given other work to do while it is finding the desired record.

Section 2.19: PROGRAMMING HINTS

Thus far in this chapter, we have discussed a large number of FORTRAN statements and programming techniques. We now present some general guidelines that can help make programming easier, faster, and more understandable. The comments fall into three main categories:

A. Program clarity
B. Output clarity
C. Error detection

Each program should be checked against these guidelines until clear programming has become a habit. The checklist shown on page 90 summarizes the main features of parts A and B.

A. Program Clarity

A clearly written, easy-to-read program is more likely to be correct, and mistakes, if any, are easier to find and correct.

1. The program should begin with comments identifying the problem being solved.
2. The program should be divided into logical steps.
   (a) Each step should begin with a comment.
   (b) Each line after the opening comment should be indented.
   (c) Whenever the step requires several lines, the step should be performed by a subroutine or function subprogram, so the main program is concise and easy to follow.
3. All function subprograms and subroutines must be grouped together at the end of the program.
   (a) Each subprogram should begin with a statement of what it is doing.
   (b) Whenever a function subprogram or subroutine consists of several smaller steps, each smaller step should be performed by a smaller subprogram. These smaller subprograms should (usually) be placed just after the calling subprograms and they should be indented, as in outline form, so the programmer can see what pieces are related to what larger pieces.
4. All variables, functions, and subroutines should be given descriptive names.
5. In each loop, the second and following lines should be indented.
6. The number of GO TO statements should be minimized.
   (a) Frequent use of GO TO yields code that is confusing, hard to read, and difficult to modify.
   (b) Abuse of the GO TO statement has led some expert programmers to advocate the elimination of the GO TO from programming languages. This has been done in some languages, such as SDL.
7. FORMAT statements should be placed where they can be found easily. In particular, they should either all be placed together at the beginning or end of each subprogram or they should be located immediately following the corresponding READ or WRITE statement.

B. Output Clarity

1. All printed output should be labeled clearly.
2. Spacing should allow the user to read the data easily.
3. When several values are printed in a table, the columns and rows should be identified. Titles or case numbers should be printed for easy reference.
4. When several sets of data are being processed, several spaces should be skipped after each set. Often, it is appropriate to start the output for each new data set on a new page.

C. Error Detection

1. When possible, the program should first be run with values where the answer is known.
   (a) The program's results should be checked against the known values.
   (b) The known cases should be sufficiently complete that all features of the program are used and checked.
2. After each step, WRITE statements may be added to check the progress of the program.
   (a) These statements should print a line identifier or the step name as well as the values of variables, so it will be clear where the printing is being done.
   (b) It is helpful to mark the extra write statements in some easily identifiable way, so they can be located quickly and removed easily when the program is found to be correct.

(c)   An example of such a statement is:

C   WRITE STATEMENT FOR DEBUGGING ********************
                                                              ↑
                                                   WRITE statement identifier

          WRITE(7,1000) VALUE1, VALUE2
   1000   FORMAT(' STEP ONE', 5X, 'VALUE1 =', F10.3, 'VALUE2 =', F10.3)
                                 ↑
                          step identifier   *values are printed and*
                                              identified in the output

3. Spelling is a particularly common source of error.
    (a)   The spelling of all variables should be checked very carefully.
    (b)   Special attention should be given to the letter O and the digit 0, since the computer treats these differently.
4. Care should be taken in choosing numbers for labeling statements.
    (a)   The numbers should be chosen in some logical order.
    (b)   If statement numbers are picked at random, the same number is likely to be used more than once, thereby yielding an error.
5. Particularly large numbers in results often indicate division by zero, while results of 0 often indicate multiplication by 0.
    (a)   All variables should be set initially to the desired values, so the computer will not make false assumptions.
    (b)   Particularly large errors are often due to lack of initializing a variable or to misspelling.
6. All loops should be designed to terminate eventually, regardless of possible data errors.
    (a)   The programmer should include a way for any loop to stop eventually. This may include counting the number of times a loop has occurred and stopping after a certain maximum number is reached.

Checklist for Program Clarity and Output Readability

Bad		Good			
1	2	3	4	5	

— — — — — *Overall program format*

— — — — — Program easy to read and understand

— — — — — Program divided into sections

— — — — — Sections begin with comments

— — — — — Comments help in interpreting program

— — — — — Indenting helps to clarify program logic and aids readability

— — — — — Descriptive variable names used

— — — — — Variables initialized

— — — — — Functions subprograms or subroutines used effectively where appropriate

— — — — — Mode-mixing is minimized

— — — — — *Overall input and output format*

— — — — — Output labeled clearly

— — — — — Output put in columns where appropriate

— — — — — Output neat, not cluttered

Section 2.20: **EFFICIENCY CONSIDERATIONS**

When considering the subject of efficiency, we must not lose sight of the principles of program clarity and readability. In almost all programming projects, the writing and debugging of a program takes a substantial amount of time. Sophisticated, intricate shortcuts are often very hard to correct and modify. Thus, if we write a program concentrating on efficiency and ignoring clarity, we may find that the few seconds saved in running the final program are overshadowed by hours of extra debugging.

We now turn to several areas where program efficiency can be increased:

A. Storage of intermediate values
B. Arithmetic
C. Functions versus formulas
D. Disk storage versus CPU storage
E. Computations in loops

Once again, we stress that we must continue to strive for readability and clarity, even when we are trying to increase efficiency.

A. Storage of Intermediate Values

While it is hardly surprising that it takes less time to do a computation once than to do it two or more times, this observation can lead to significant savings in computer time. For example, consider the following code from a program:

$$X = A + B/C$$
$$X = A - B/C$$
$$X = A**2 - 2* B/C$$

Here, we see that the quotient B/C is computed three separate times. After we observe this, we can decide to store this ratio after the first computation and use this result thereafter without repeating the division. The result might be:

$$RATIO = B/C$$
$$X = A + RATIO$$
$$Y = A - RATIO$$
$$Z = A**2 - 2*RATIO$$

Here, we have eliminated two divisions.

In general, it usually saves time and increases efficiency if a computation is saved when it is to be used several times within a program. Further, saving the computation may also increase clarity and eliminate chances for error.

B. Arithmetic

In all arithmetic, we must remember that it takes the computer time to convert from real mode to integer or from integer to real. Thus, it is worthwhile to minimize conversions from one mode to another. This is particularly significant in extensions of standard FORTRAN where mode mixing is allowed and where a programmer may mix modes unintentionally. For example, in the line

$$Z = X * 2$$

we are multiplying the real number X by the integer 2, so the 2 must be converted to a real number before the multiplication can occur. Adding decimal points to constants that we mean to be real solves the problem. Thus

$$Z = X * 2.$$

does not require the conversion of the 2. from integer to real, since 2. is already a real number.

We must also realize that the computer does not perform all arithmetic at the same speeds. Integer arithmetic is always done faster than arithmetic with real numbers. Further, various arithmetic operations require different amounts of time; in particular, addition and subtraction can be done quite efficiently, multiplication takes somewhat longer, division takes a little longer still, and exponentiation takes a considerable amount of time. The exact timings of these operations vary substantially from one machine to another. However, the relative time for the operations is likely to be similar among machines.

Table 2.20–1 presents some relative times for these operations (based on a particular PDP 11/70).

Table 2.20–1. Approximate Relative Times for Arithmetic Operations on the PDP 11/70*

Operation	Integer Arithmetic	Real Number Arithmetic
Addition	1	4
Subtraction	1	4
Multiplication	2	5
Division	3	6
Exponentiation	14	34

*In this table, 1 unit of time is taken as the time needed for the addition or subtraction of two integers.

These observations have several implications for program efficiency.

First, the use of integer variables can increase program efficiency substantially. Certainly, we must use real variables when our numbers will not be integers. (For example, 2.5 and 3.14159 must be stored as real numbers.) However, if we know the values of a variable will always be integers, we can save time if we use an integer variable.

Secondly, if a computation can be done in several ways, the approach used should be the one that uses the most efficient arithmetic operation. For example, 2.*A and A+A will both yield the same result. However, since addition is more efficient than multiplication, the A+A form will take less time. These savings are particularly noticeable when working with integers.

Next, if the same operations on real numbers can be done with multiplications or with divisions, the multiplications should be performed. For example, consider the following program segment:

$$A = W/5.$$
$$B = X/5.$$
$$C = Y/5.$$
$$D = Z/5.$$

Here we are performing four divisions. A more efficient approach would replace division by 5. by multiplication by 1./5. as follows:

$$RECIP = 1./5.$$
$$A = W*RECIP$$

$$B = X*RECIP$$
$$C = Y*RECIP$$
$$D = Z*RECIP$$

This revision contains an extra step, the first line. However, this line allows us to perform division only once, and we can use the faster multiplication in the remaining lines. (Of course, this approach is not possible with integer variables, because if all of these were integer variables, then IRECIP would be 0 unless the integer was ±1.)

Finally, parentheses can often be used to reduce the number of computations required. For example, the computation of $AX^3 + BX^2 + CX + D$ could be performed by any of the following expressions:

$$A * X**3 + B * X**2 + C * X + D$$
$$A * X * X * X + B * X * X + C * X + D$$
$$((A * X + B) * X + C) * X + D$$

In each case, 3 additions are required. However, the first case uses the very time-consuming exponential operation. The second case requires 6 multiplications while the last requires 3. Adding parentheses speeds up this computation substantially.

C. Functions Versus Formulas

When we considered the use of functions in Sections 2.6, 2.7, 2.15, 2.16, and 2.17, we found that they enhanced program clarity and that they allowed the same formula to be used in several places even though it was only defined once. These considerations are extremely important and they often outweigh any other factor. However, it should be stated that utilizing a function call requires a certain amount of overhead within the machine. If functions are called relatively few times, this overhead should not be a major concern of the programmer. However, if a short formula is to be used many times and if this formula is not expected to ever require modification, then the programmer should consider deleting the function and writing out the formula. This is particularly relevant within loops, and it will be discussed more in Part E, later in this section. The main point to be made here is that functions do require a little extra computer time each time they are used. Thus, their indiscriminate use can cause some inefficiency. However, once again we must stress that program clarity and ease of program modification should override any considerations in this area.

D. Disk Storage versus CPU Storage

In Section 2.18, where we described the advantages and disadvantages of storing data in the CPU, we noted that CPU data storage increases the speed of processing. The CPU operates completely by electrical circuits, so working with data in the CPU can be done very quickly without waiting for mechanical operations to be performed. In contrast, disk storage requires both mechanical and electrical operations, and thus it is substantially slower. This has several important consequences.

First, the number of times disk storage is referenced should be kept as low as possible. If the same value from the disk is going to be used several times, it may be faster to store the value in the CPU temporarily rather than refer back to the disk each time. This can be done by storing the value in the CPU.

Secondly, if we are working with an extension of standard FORTRAN that allows us to specify which record on a disk file is to be read, the information can be retrieved faster if the records are referenced in ascending order (for technical reasons). For example,

```
        DO 1 J = 1,100
1       READ (3'J) ARRAY(J)
```

uses the disk much more efficiently than

$$DO\ 1\ J = 1,100$$
$$K = 101–J$$
1   READ(3'K) ARRAY(K)

In general, to work with disk files efficiently requires a considerable technical background which is well beyond the scope of this chapter. However, the two guidelines above will allow some substantial savings in computer time.

E. Computation in Loops

Efficiency is a major consideration in loops, where the same steps are repeated many times. Thus, all of the comments made earlier in this section apply particularly in loops. We should be aware of storage of intermediate values, arithmetic efficiency, function usage, and disk storage in each loop. For example, the program

$$F(I,J) = I+J$$
$$K = F(I,J) \qquad \text{(Here, F is a function statement.)}$$
$$WRITE\ (7,10)\ K$$

may be quite reasonable, due to modification potential and clarity. The overhead due to one function call is small, and we may wish to ignore it.

However, if we had

$$F(I,J) = I+J$$

.

.

.

$$DO\ 1\ I = 1,\ 50$$
$$DO\ 2\ J = 1,\ 50$$
$$K = F(I,J)$$
2   WRITE (7,10) K
1   CONTINUE

then the overhead from using a function has been required many times (e.g., 2500 times). In this later case, we should be sure that clarity and modification ease merit the increased overhead.

Next in loops we should check that we are not performing the same computation needlessly. For example, consider

$$DO\ 1\ J = 1,20$$
$$X = 3$$
$$Y = X**J$$
1   WRITE (7,2) Y

Here we are setting X equal to 3 each of 20 times during the execution of the loop. A much more efficient program would be

```
            X = 3
            DO 1 J = 1,20
                Y = X**J
    1           WRITE (7,2) Y
```

Here, we have set X equal to 3 only one time, saving 19 operations. In this case, a simple reordering of the statements on a program increases efficiency with no loss of program clarity.

Finally, in loops, we must point out that some additional analysis of our problem can often yield substantial savings in our code. Returning to our program:

```
            X = 3
            DO 1 J = 1,20
                Y = X**J
    1           WRITE (7,2) Y
```

we note that we are performing exponentiation 20 times. However, we only want to print $X, X*X, X*X*X$, etc., and we can get one of these from the previous by just multiplying by X. Thus, our analysis of the program might lead to:

```
            X = 3
            TERM = X
            WRITE (7,2) TERM
            DO 1 J = 2,20
                TERM = TERM*X
    1           WRITE (7,2) TERM
```

Here we have replaced 20 computations with exponents by 19 multiplications, increasing the efficiency by a factor of more than 7.

Throughout programming, an awareness of these considerations of program efficiency can help us write programs that run quickly. After each program is written, a careful reading of it will often point out places where efficiency can be increased. However, in all programming, we should strive for program clarity and ease of program modification, and we should not allow these goals to be undermined.

Section 2.21: **EXAMPLE: PRINTING AN
ANNOTATED WEEKLY CALENDAR**

We conclude this chapter on FORTRAN programming with an example that incorporates many of the concepts of programming that we have encountered. After we state our problem to be solved, we indicate how we developed our outline of the solution, and we see how this outline led to the program itself. (The reader may wish to review how outlining fits into the programming process by rereading Section 2.12, Algorithm Design.)

Problem 2.21-1. Write a program that will print an annotated weekly appointment calendar including the following features:

(a)   The calendar includes the period 8:00 a.m. to 5:00 p.m. Monday through Friday.

(b)   Blocks of time on any day may be annotated, using one or more lines of comments. (Blocks of time may start on the hour, or at any quarter hour interval from the hour, and they may end at any similar time.)

(c)   The program should check that two appointments are not scheduled at the same time.

(d)   The calendar should have a title.

A sample of the output desired is shown in Figure 2.21–1.

We begin our solution with a simple outline.

I.   Enter title and appointments.   Outline: Draft 1
II. Print annotated appointment calendar.

Next, we analyze each of these major steps, turning them into smaller tasks.

I.   Enter title and appointments.
   (A) Enter title for the annotated calendar.
   (B) Enter desired appointments and annotations.   Outline: Draft 2
II. Print annotated appointment calendar.
   (A) Print title.
   (B) Print days of the week at the top of the calendar.
   (C) Print times and annotations.
   (D) Print line at bottom of calendar.

While some of these sections are now sufficient to program, other tasks are still too complex to handle directly. This is particularly true when we read in the annotations, checking that times do not overlap, and when we print each appointment.

When checking that times of appointments do not overlap, we must check the starting and ending times of each new appointment against each of the previous appointments.

When printing appointments, we must realize that once a line is printed, we cannot go back to it. Thus, for each quarter hour of time, we must print all annotated appointments, if any, for each day before going on to the next line.

We are now ready to expand the more complicated steps of our outline.

I.   Enter title and appointments.   Outline: Final Draft
   (A) Enter title for the annotated calendar.
   (B) Enter desired appointments and annotations.
      (1) Enter starting time and ending time of appointment and any annotation.
      (2) Check the starting time and ending time of the appointment against all previous appointments.
II. Print annotated appointment calendar.
   (A) Print title.
   (B) Print days of the week at the top of the calendar.
   (C) Print times and annotations.

```
OUTPUT FROM WEEKLY ANNOTATED APPOINTMENT CALENDAR

        MONDAY        TUESDAY       WEDNESDAY     THURSDAY      FRIDAY

 8:00!-------------!-------------!-------------!-------------!-------------!
     !             !             !             !MEET WITH    !             !
     !             !             !             !MARKETING    !             !
     !             !             !             !AND          !             !
 9:00!-------------!             !             !MR. MACKAY   !-------------!
     !STAFF        !             !             !             !BUDGET       !
     !MEETING      !             !             !             !MEETING      !
     !             !             !             !             !             !
10:00!-------------!-------------!             !-------------!             !
     !             !SEE DENTIST  !             !             !             !
     !             !             !             !             !             !
     !             !             !             !             !             !
11:00!             !             !             !             !-------------!
     !             !             !             !             !             !
     !             !             !             !             !             !
     !             !             !             !             !             !
12:00!-------------!-------------!-------------!-------------!-------------!
     ! LUNCH TIME  ! LUNCH TIME  ! LUNCH TIME  ! LUNCH TIME  ! LUNCH TIME  !
     !             !             !             !             !             !
     !             !             !             !             !             !
 1:00!-------------!-------------!-------------!-------------!-------------!
     !             !             !             !             !             !
 1:30!             !             !-------------!             !             !
     !             !             !PICK UP      !             !             !
     !             !             !MR. MACKAY   !             !             !
 2:15!             !             !AT AIRPORT   !-------------!             !
     !             !             !             !TAKE         !             !
     !             !             !             !MR. MACKAY   !             !
     !             !             !             !BACK TO      !             !
     !             !             !             !AIRPORT      !             !
     !             !             !             !             !             !
     !             !             !             !             !             !
 4:00!             !             !-------------!             !             !
     !             !             !             !             !             !
     !             !             !             !             !             !
     !             !             !             !             !             !
 5:00!-------------!-------------!-------------!-------------!-------------!
```

Figure 2.21-1
An Annotated Calendar

For each quarter hour:

(1) Determine if appointment and annotation is needed for this time.

(2) Each day when an annotation or appointment is appropriate, locate it and prepare to print appropriate information.

(3) Each day when no annotation or appointment is needed, prepare to print blanks.

(4) Print the appropriate line for the quarter hour.

(D) Print line at bottom of the calendar.

We are now ready to start translating the outline into FORTRAN coding. As we decide on how to proceed, we keep lists of various arrays and subprograms that we will want.

First, we note that much of the outline relates to various appointments and annotations for various times. Thus, we must first decide how an appointment and annotation will be stored, so we will be able to work with these appointments when necessary. (After all, we cannot write the coding for the appointments until we decide what form they will have.)

For each appointment we will need the day of the week, the starting and ending times and the text. We decide to store this in four arrays, with the Ith annotation specified by

$$\text{ANNDAY(I), ANNBEG(I), ANNEND(I), ANNTXT(I,1),}$$
$$\text{ANNTXT(I,2), . . . ,ANNTXT(I,15)}$$

The ANNotation DAY, ANNotation BEGinning time, and ANNotation ENDing time will all be integers, and the ANNotation TeXT will be a real array.

We will store these arrays together with the number of annotations, NUMANN, and the TITLE of the appointment calendar in COMMON.

For clarity in our program, we use a subroutine for each item in our outline that requires more than a few lines of code. Thus our first draft of the outline:

    I.   Enter title and appointments.
    II.   Print annotated appointment calendar.

will be translated into the main program

```
            CALL INPUT
            CALL OUTPUT
            CALL EXIT
            END
```

The INPUT and OUTPUT subroutines again are broken down into smaller subroutines.

We can input the calendar title and the appointment times and text, but we use a separate subroutine to CHECK if the newest appointment read in conflicts with any appointments already in.

As we begin to work with these appointments, we realize that we will need a concise way to store the starting time or ending time of an appointment. We decide to use a 24-hour clock for the hour. Since we only need to work with quarter hours, we will store the quarter of the hour by the integers 1, 2, 3, 4. The function CONVRT performs this conversion for us.

Also, when we input the days of the week, we want to use the standard English of MON., TUES., etc., or MONDAY, TUESDAY, etc. Thus, we will use a function NUMDAY to read the first three letters given and then produce the corresponding integer 1 to 5.

Thus, 8:00 translates to the integer 81, (hour = 8, quarter = 1), 11:45 translates to the integer 114 (hour = 11, quarter = 4), 5:15 p.m. translates to 17:15 on the 24-hour clock, which gives the integer 172 (hour = 17, quarter = 2).

When we consider the OUTPUT part of our program, we realize that we will have to decide upon the TEXT for each time of each day, and then we can PRINT the result. The array TEXT may be any of the following:

(1) Material from an annotation.
(2) Dashes ---- marking the starting or ending of an appointment.
(3) Blanks, so nothing is printed at that time for that day.

We use subroutines DASHES and BLANK to perform (2) and (3). However, we decide we must be a bit more careful in copying material from the annotations, as the text in an annotation may take up several lines. Thus, for each DAY, we will need an array ENTRY saying which annotation is to be printed, and we will need an array COLUMN to keep track of how much of the annotation is printed and where the next part to be printed begins. We use these arrays when we copy the material from the annotation to TEXT to be printed in COPyTeXT subroutine.

With the subroutines mentioned, we can write our finished program. Note how closely the program itself follows the outline we developed, and note particularly how the use of subroutines clarifies the step being done at each point.

```
 C THIS PROGRAM PRINTS AN ANNOTATED APPOINTMENT CALENDAR
1C DECLARATION OF VARIABLES
       INTEGER ANNDAY, ANNBEG, ANNEND
       COMMON TITLE(20), NUMANN, ANNDAY(50), ANNBEG(50),
     1    ANNEND(50), ANNTXT(50, 15)
 C INITIALIZATION
2      NUMANN = 0
3C ENTER TITLE AND APPOINTMENTS
       CALL INPUT
 C PRINT ANNOTATED APPOINTMENT CALENDAR
       CALL OUTPUT
 C ENDING
       CALL EXIT
       END

4      SUBROUTINE INPUT
 C THIS SUBROUTINE ENTERS THE NEEDED DATA
       INTEGER BEGHR, BEGMIN, ENDHR, ENDMIN
       INTEGER ANNDAY, ANNBEG, ANNEND
       DIMENSION TEXT(15)
       COMMON TITLE(20), NUMANN, ANNDAY(50), ANNBEG(50),
     1    ANNEND(50), ANNTXT(50, 15)
       DATA BLANKS/3H   /
 C ENTER TITLE FOR THE CALENDAR
       READ (5, 1) TITLE
     1 FORMAT(20A4)
 C ENTER DESIRED APPOINTMENTS AND ANNOTATIONS
 C     ENTER DATA
     4      READ (5, 2) WEEKDA, BEGHR, BEGMIN, ENDHR,
     1          ENDMIN, TEXT
```

1 The main program is particularly easy to read.

2 When we start, the NUMber of ANNotations is 0.

3 Each title in this main program is taken from our outline. The main program only considers the major headings of the outline.

4 This subroutine handles the first main heading of the outline, together with the main subdivisions of the main heading.

```
    2        FORMAT (A3, 7X, I2, 1X, I2, I2, 1X, I2,
   1              15A4)
    5    IF (WEEKDA .EQ. BLANKS) GO TO 3
    C    CHECK NEW APPOINTMENT AGAINST PREVIOUS ONES
             CALL CHECK (WEEKDA, BEGHR, BEGMIN, ENDHR,
   1              ENDMIN, TEXT)
    6    GO TO 4
    C ENDING
    3 RETURN
      END

    7        SUBROUTINE CHECK(WEEKDA, BEGHR, BEGMIN,
   1              ENDHR, ENDMIN, TEXT)
    C    THIS SUBROUTINE CHECKS THE STARTING AND ENDING
    C    TIMES OF THE NEW APPOINTMENT AGAINST ALL PREVIOUS
    C    APPOINTMENTS
             INTEGER CONVRT
             INTEGER DAY, BEGIN, END
             INTEGER BEGHR, BEGMIN, ENDHR, ENDMIN
             INTEGER ANNDAY, ANNBEG, ANNEND
             DIMENSION TEXT(15)
             COMMON TITLE(20), NUANN, ANNDAY(50),
   1              ANNBEG(50), ANNEND(50), ANNTXT(50, 15)
    C    CONVERT DATA TO STANDARD FORM
             DAY = NUMDAY(WEEKDA)
    8        BEGIN = CONVRT(BEGHR, BEGMIN)
             END   = CONVRT(ENDHR, ENDMIN)
    C    IF NO PREVIOUS APPOINTMENTS, WE MAY ADD THIS ONE
             IF (NUMANN) 10, 10, 1
    C    CHECK NEW APPOINTMENT
    1        DO 2 INDEX = 1, NUMANN
    9            IF (WEEKDA .NE. ANNDAY(INDEX)) GO TO 2
                 IF (BEGIN  .GE. ANNEND(INDEX)) GO TO 2
                 IF (END    .GT. ANNBEG(INDEX)) GO TO 5
    2        CONTINUE
    C    APPOINTMENT DOES NOT CONFLICT, ADD IT TO LIST
    10       NUMANN = NUMANN + 1
             ANNDAY(NUMANN) = DAY
             ANNBEG(NUMANN) = BEGIN
             ANNEND(NUMANN) = END
             DO 11 INDEX = 1, 15
    11           ANNTXT(NUMANN, INDEX) = TEXT(INDEX)
             GO TO 20
    C    APPOINTMENT CONFLICTS WITH EARLIER COMMITMENT
    5        WRITE (7, 3) WEEKDA, BEGHR, BEGMIN, ENDHR,
   1              ENDMIN
    3        FORMAT (' AN APPOINTMENT IS ALREADY SCHEDULED FOR ',
   1              A3, I3, ':', I2, ' TO ', I3, ':', I2)
    C ENDING
    20       RETURN
             END

             INTEGER FUNCTION CONVRT (HOUR, MINUTE)
    C    THIS FUNCTION CONVERTS A TIME IN HOURS AND
    C    MINUTES TO AN INTEGER, GIVING THE HOUR ON A
```

5 We conclude our annotations with a blank card.

6 Since the checking step involves several lines, we write the step as a separate subroutine.

7 Note how we indent this subroutine just as the checking in the outline is indented under the major heading "Enter title and appointments."

8 We combine the hour and minutes into a single integer.

9 We must check the day, starting time of each new appointment against all appointments that are made previously.

```
C      24 HOUR CLOCK AND THE QUARTER OF THE HOUR.
            INTEGER HOUR
C      CONVERT HOUR IF NECESSARY
            IF (HOUR .GT. 6) GO TO 1
            HOUR = HOUR + 12
C      CONVERT TIME TO THE INTEGER
       1    CONVRT = 10*HOUR + MINUTE/15 + 1
            RETURN
            END


       FUNCTION NUMDAY (WEEKDA)
C      THIS FUNCTION CONVERTS THE THREE LETTER ABBREVIATION WEEKDA
C      FOR THE DAY OF THE WEEK TO THE CORRESPONDING INTEGER
C      BETWEEN 1 AND 5
            DIMENSION ABBR(5)
            DATA ABBR(1), ABBR(2), ABBR(3), ABBR(4), ABBR(5)
       1       / 'MON', 'TUE', 'WED', 'THU', 'FRI' /
C      FIND DAY
            DO 2 INDEX = 1, 5
                IF (WEEKDA .EQ. ABBR(INDEX)) GO TO 4
       2    CONTINUE
C      INVALID ABBREVIATION
            WRITE (7, 3) WEEKDA
       3    FORMAT(1X, A3,
       1           ' IS AN INVALID WEEKDAY ABBREVIATION.')
            STOP
C      DAY HAS BEEN FOUND
       4    NUMDAY = INDEX
            RETURN
            END


       SUBROUTINE OUTPUT

C      THIS SUBROUTINE PRINTS THE ANNOTATED APPOINTMENT
C      CALENDAR
            INTEGER DAY, TIME, HOUR, QTRHR, ENTRY, COLUMN,
       1           FOUND
            DIMENSION TEXT(15), ENTRY(5), COLUMN(5)
            INTEGER ANNDAY, ANNBEG, ANNEND
            COMMON TITLE(20), NUMANN, ANNDAY(50), ANNBEG(50), ANNEND(50),
       1           ANNTXT(50, 15)
C      PRINT TITLE
            WRITE (7, 1) TITLE
       1    FORMAT (1H1, 20A4)
C      PRINT DAYS OF THE WEEK AT TOP OF THE CALENDAR
            WRITE (7, 2)
       2    FORMAT (1H0, 6X, 'MONDAY', 7X, 'TUESDAY', 6X, 'WEDNESDAY',
       1           4X, 'THURSDAY', 5X, 'FRIDAY')
            WRITE (7, 3)
       3    FORMAT (1H )
C      PRINT TIMES AND APPOINTMENTS
```

10 Hours between 1 and 5 are afternoon times, so we must add 12 to convert them to a 24-hour clock.

11 By looking at only the first three letters of the name of the DAy, we allow abbreviations as well as the full name.

12 If the WEEKDA is not recognizable, then we do not know how to proceed so we should stop. In this way, we can protect ourselves against incorrect data.

13 As with the INPUT part of the program, we use subroutine OUTPUT to do the second main part of our outline. We indent for each subheading in our outline.

```
14 C          CHECK 8:00 A.M. APPOINTMENTS
                  HOUR = 8
                  QTRHR = 1
                  DO 10 DAY = 1, 5
                     CALL NEWAPP (DAY, 81, ENTRY, COLUMN, FOUND)
      10             CONTINUE
   C          PRINT 8:00 A.M. LINE
                  WRITE (7, 11)
      11          FORMAT(' 8:00', '!', 5('-----------!'))
   C          ADVANCE TIME
15    20          QTRHR = QTRHR + 1
                  IF (QTRHR .LE. 4) GO TO 21
                  QTRHR = 1
                  HOUR = HOUR + 1
                  IF (HOUR .EQ. 17) GO TO 100
16    21          TIME = 10*HOUR + QTRHR


17                FOUND = 0



   C      FOR EACH DAY, CHECK APPOINTMENTS AND ANNOTATIONS
                  DO 30 DAY = 1, 5
   C          CHECK IF ANY APPOINTMENT IS CONTINUING
   C          OVER FROM THE PRECEDING HALF HOUR

18                   IF (ENTRY(DAY) .EQ. 0) GO TO 31

   C          APPOINTMENT DOES CONTINUE FROM
   C          PREVIOUS QUARTER HOUR
   C          CHECK IF APPOINTMENT ENDS
                     INDEX = ENTRY(DAY)
                     IF(TIME .EQ. ANNEND(INDEX)) GO TO 40
   C          APPOINTMENT DOES NOT END
   C          PRINT MORE OF THE ANNOTATION
19                   CALL COPYTX (DAY, INDEX, COLUMN(DAY),
       1                         TEXT)
                     GO TO 30

              APPOINTMENT ENDS
   C          PRINT DASHES AND DETERMINE IF NEW APPOINTMENT
   C          BEGINS
19    40             CALL DASHES (DAY, TEXT)
                     CALL NEWAPP (DAY, TIME, ENTRY, COLUMN,
       1                          FOUND)
                     FOUND = 1
                     GO TO 30
   C      ANNOTATION DOES NOT CONTINUE FROM THE PREVIOUS LINE
   C      CHECK IF NEW APPOINTMENT IS TO START AND SET UP TEXT
   C      TO BE PRINTED
      31             CALL NEWAPP (DAY, TIME, ENTRY, COLUMN, FOUND)
                     IF (ENTRY(DAY) .EQ. 0) GO TO 32
```

14 Since we will print a solid line at the 8:00 hour, in order to start our calendar, we must handle the printing of the hour separately.

15 When we go on to the next QuarTeR HouR, we must see if we must go to the next hour.

16 TIME is based on the 24-hour clock, as in FUNCTION CNVRT above.

17 FOUND tells us if an appointment begins or ends at this time. Before checking any appointments, we set FOUND = 0 to indicate we have not found a beginning or ending as yet. However, we change this to 1 if one is found later.

18 ENTRY(DAY) tells where the annotation for the present time and DAY is found. If the number is 0, no annotation is found.

19 Note how clarity is improved if we use the subroutine COPYTX, DASHES, or BLANK to copy some text, or to set up a line of dashes or blanks. Inserting the full code to do these jobs would greatly clutter the clean logical form we see here.

```
19                          CALL DASHES (DAY, TEXT)
                            GO TO 30
19      32                  CALL BLANK (DAY, TEXT)
   C                GO ON TO NEXT DAY
        30                  CONTINUE
   C            PRINT LINE
                            CALL PRINT (HOUR, QTRHR, TEXT, FOUND)
   C            GO ON TO NEXT QUARTER HOUR
                            GO TO 20
   C            FINISH BY PRINTING LINE FOR 5:00 P.M.
       100                  WRITE (7, 101)
       101                  FORMAT ('  5:00', '!', 5('------------!'))
   C            ENDING
                            RETURN
                            END


                    SUBROUTINE NEWAPP(DAY, TIME, ENTRY, COLUMN, FOUND)
   C                THIS SUBROUTINE DETERMINES WHAT APPOINTMENT, IF ANY, BEGINS
   C                AT THE TIME GIVEN
                            INTEGER DAY, TIME, ENTRY, COLUMN, FOUND
                            INTEGER ANNDAY, ANNBEG, ANNEND
                            DIMENSION ENTRY(5), COLUMN(5)
                            COMMON TITLE(20), NUMANN, ANNDAY(50), ANNBEG(50),
        1                       ANNEND(50), ANNTXT(50, 15)
                            IF (NUMANN .EQ. 0) GO TO 1
   C            CHECK EACH APPOINTMENT'S STARTING TIME
                            DO 2 INDEX = 1, NUMANN
                                IF (TIME .EQ. ANNBEG(INDEX) .AND.
        1                           DAY .EQ. ANNDAY(INDEX))
        2                               GO TO 3
        2               CONTINUE
                            GO TO 1
   C            APPOINTMENT FOR THIS TIME HAS BEEN FOUND
        3                   FOUND = 1
                            ENTRY (DAY) = INDEX
                            COLUMN(DAY) = 1
                            GO TO 4
   C            NO APPOINTMENT FOUND
        1                   ENTRY(DAY) = 0
                            COLUMN(DAY) = 0
   C            ENDING
        4                   CONTINUE
                            END


                    SUBROUTINE BLANK(DAY, TEXT)
20 C                THIS SUBROUTINE FILLS THE TEXT FOR THE
   C                GIVEN DAY WITH BLANKS
                            INTEGER DAY, DAY3
                            DIMENSION TEXT(15)
                            DATA SPACES/'    '/
                            DAY3 = DAY * 3
                            TEXT(DAY3 - 2) = SPACES
                            TEXT(DAY3 - 1) = SPACES
```

20 We put blanks in the 12 characters (3 array elements) for the day specified. Thus, we will not see any annotation for this time and day when the TEXT is printed.

```
              TEXT(DAY3)      = SPACES
              RETURN
              END


              SUBROUTINE DASHES (DAY, TEXT)
C     THIS SUBROUTINE FILLS THE TEXT FOR THE GIVEN
C     DAY WITH DASHES
              INTEGER DAY, DAY 3
              DIMENSION TEXT(15)
              DATA DASHES/'----'/
              DAY3 = DAY * 3
              TEXT(DAY3 - 2) = DASHES
              TEXT(DAY3 - 1) = DASHES
              TEXT(DAY3)      = DASHES
              RETURN
              END


              SUBROUTINE COPYTX(DAY, INDEX, COLUMN, TEXT)
C     THIS SUBROUTINE COPIES THE APPROPRIATE PART OF THE
C     ANNOTATION INTO THE LINE TO BE PRINTED
              INTEGER DAY, DAY3, COLUMN
              INTEGER ANNDAY, ANNBEG, ANNEND
              DIMENSION TEXT(15)
              COMMON TITLE(20), NUMANN, ANNDAY(50), ANNBEG(50),
     1               ANNEND(50), ANNTXT(50, 15)
              IF (COLUMN .GE. 16) GO TO 1
C     COPY ANNOTATION
              DAY3 = DAY * 3
              TEXT(DAY3 - 2) = ANNTXT(INDEX, COLUMN)
              TEXT(DAY3 - 1) = ANNTXT(INDEX, COLUMN
                  + 1)
              TEXT(DAY3)      = ANNTXT(INDEX, COLUMN + 2)
              COLUMN = COLUMN + 3
              GO TO 2
C     THERE IS NO TEXT LEFT TO COPY
     1        CALL BLANK (DAY, TEXT)
C     ENDING
     2        RETURN
              END


              SUBROUTINE PRINT (HOUR, QTRHR, TEXT, FOUND)
C     THIS SUBROUTINE PRINTS THE LINE FOR THE TIME
              INTEGER HOUR, QTRHR, FOUND
              DIMENSION TEXT(15), QUARTR(4)
              DATA QUARTR(1), QUARTR(2), QUARTR(3), QUARTR(4)
     1           / ':00'    , ':15'    , ':30'    , ':45'/
C     PRINT THE TIME IF AND ONLY IF FOUND = 1
              IF (FOUND .NE. 0) GO TO 4
C     TIME NEED NOT BE PRINTED
              WRITE (7, 2) TEXT
     2        FORMAT (6X, '!', 5(3A4, '!'))
              GO TO 3
C     TIME MUST BE PRINTED
     4        IHOUR = HOUR
              IF (IHOUR .LE. 12) GO TO 6
```

21 COLUMN points to the first part of the annotation that we want printed. After the next 3 segments (12 characters) are copied, we increase COLUMN so the next line will start with the next piece of text.

22 If no appointments begin or end at this time, then we do not print the time.

23 If an appointment does begin or end, then the time must be printed.

```
                      IHOUR = IHOUR - 12
      6               WRITE (7, 5) IHOUR, QUARTR(QTRHR), TEXT
      5               FORMAT (1H , I2, A3, '!', 5(3A4, '!'))
  C           ENDING
      3               RETURN
                      END
```

When we run this program to produce the weekly appointment calendar
shown, we need the following data:

```
OUTPUT FROM WEEKLY ANNOTATED APPOINTMENT CALENDAR
MONDAY        9:0010:00STAFF          MEETING
TUE.         10:0012:00SEE DENTIST
WED.          1:30 4:00PICK UP        MR. MACKAY AT AIRPORT
THURSDAY      8:0010:00MEET WITH      MARKETING  AND       MR. MACKAY
THURSDAY      2:15 5:00TAKE           MR. MACKAY BACK TO   AIRPORT
FRIDAY        9:0011:00BUDGET         MEETING
MON.         12:00 1:00 LUNCH TIME
TUES.        12:00 1:00 LUNCH TIME
WED.         12:30 1:45 LUNCH TIME
WED.         12:00 1:00 LUNCH TIME
THURSDAY     12:00 1:00 LUNCH TIME
FRI.         12:00 1:00 LUNCH TIME
```

←This line is left blank to indicate the end of our appointments.

Programming Problems

CHAPTER 3

General Problems

This chapter was written with Eugene Herman and John Vogel.

Section 3.1: **SORTING TECHNIQUES**

When a computer is used to store a large amount of information, it is often necessary to arrange the data in a specific order. We now consider several methods for placing numbers in ascending order. Only minor changes are needed to place numbers in descending order or to alphabetize alphabetic information.

In the following discussion, we assume we are given N numbers, A(1), A(2), . . . , A(N).

I. Swapping Numbers

One of the basic steps in any of the methods is the interchanging of two elements in the array. For example, if A(2) = 7 and A(3) = 4, it might be desired to interchange the two, so that A(2) = 4 and A(3) = 7.

We first observe that the statements

$$A(2) = A(3)$$
$$A(3) = A(2)$$

!!!Wrong!!!

do not work, for after A(2) = A(3), both elements are 4, and the 7 has been lost. Thus, we must introduce an extra variable, which we will call D, to hold the 7 during the interchange.

A correct sequence for interchanging elements A(I) and A(J) is

$$D \quad = A(J)$$
$$A(I) = A(J) \qquad !!!Correct!!!$$
$$A(J) = D$$

II. Bubble Sort, Improved Bubble Sort, Straight Selection Sort

In three sorting methods, the basic idea is the same. The elements A(1), . . . , A(N) are compared, and the largest is placed at the end, A(N). Then the elements A(1), . . . , A(N–1) are compared for the next largest, which is placed in A(N–1). This process continues, so that in general the elements A(1), . . . , A(I) are compared and the largest in this list is placed in A(I). The variations in the methods occur in how the largest element is found and when elements are interchanged.

(a) Bubble Sort

The simplest approach is the Bubble Sort. First, A(1) and A(2) are compared. If A(1) > A(2), then they are interchanged, so that at the end of this step A(2) ≥ A(1).

Next, A(2) and A(3) are compared. Again, if A(2) > A(3) a swap occurs. When this step is complete, we will have A(3) ≥ A(1) and A(3) ≥ A(2).

In general, A(J) and A(J+1) are compared. An interchange occurs, if necessary, so that after this step A(J+1) ≥ A(J). When this process occurs for J = 1, 2, . . . , I–1, the largest element in A(1), . . . , A(I) will be A(I). This proces is performed by the following DO loop.

```
        JTOP = I – 1
        DO 501 J = 1, JTOP
             IF (A(J) .LE. A(J+1)) GO TO 501
             D = A(J)
             A(J) = A(J+1)
             A(J+1) = D
501          CONTINUE
```

The sorting process is completed by repeating the above sequence for I = N, N–1, . . . , 2. A sample program follows, with an example.

```
        DO 500 K = 2, N
             JTOP = N + 1 – K
             DO 501 J = 1, JTOP
                  IF (A(J) .LE. A(J+1)) GO TO 501
                  D = A(J)
                  A(J) = A(J+1)
                  A(J+1) = D
501               CONTINUE
500          CONTINUE
```

Note in this last program that as K = 2, 3, 4, . . . , N, then N + 2 – K gives the sequence N, N – 1, . . . , 2 that we want for I. Therefore we use the computation JTOP = N + 1 – K.

Example: Bubble Sort. (Elements compared are underlined; * indicates a swap.)

Original array	8	13	11	6	5	12
Step 1	8	13	11	6	5	12
Step 2	8	11*	13*	6	5	12
Step 3	8	11	6*	13*	5	12
Step 4	8	11	6	5*	13*	12
Step 5	8	11	6	5	12*	13*
Step 6	8	11	6	5	12	13
Step 7	8	6*	11*	5	12	13
Step 8	8	6	5*	11*	12	13
Step 9	8	6	5	11	12	13
Step 10	6*	8*	5	11	12	13
Step 11	6	5*	8*	11	12	13
Step 12	6	5	8	11	12	13
Step 13	5*	6*	8	11	12	13
Step 14	5	6	8	11	12	13
Step 15	5	6	8	11	12	13

I = 6, I = 5, I = 4, I = 3, I = 2

(b) An Improved Bubble Sort

Two significant improvements can be made to speed up the Bubble Sort.

1. We observe that when considering the elements A(1), . . . , A(I), if the last swap is made for A(J), A(J+1), then the remaining elements A(J), . . . , A(I) must be in order. Thus, the next time through the DO loop for J, we need not check the last elements if no interchanges were made.

   This is accomplished by eliminating the DO loop for I. Instead, JTOP is initially set to N−1 and a variable LAST is used to record each time a swap occurs. Then, after each loop for J, LAST will equal the index where the last interchange occurred, and A(LAST), . . . , A(N) must be in order. In the next DO loop for J, we set JTOP = LAST. This continues until LAST = 1. In the example, this would eliminate steps 12, 14, and 15.

2. We observe that if no swaps are made during a DO loop for J, then the entire array must be completely ordered. Therefore we add a counter to record the number of swaps performed in the DO loop for J. When the counter is 0, we can stop.

With these improvements, the number of comparisons is usually reduced by 10% to 20%. However, the number of swaps is not changed (WHY?).

(c) Straight Selection Sort

In both the Bubble Sort and the Improved Bubble Sort, many interchanges are performed in the process of finding the largest element in A(1), . . . , A(I). An alternate approach is to use a pointer P (initialized to 1) to indicate the index of the largest element. Thus, instead of comparing A(J) and A(J+1), the elements A(P) and A(J) are compared. If A(J) > A(P) then we set P = J, but no interchange is performed. An interchange is performed only at the end of each DO loop for J, when necessary. The two nested loops remain much the same, with minor changes in the initial and ending values of each loop.

Analysis of the Bubble, Improved Bubble, and Straight Selection Sorts

In each of these three methods, a very large number of comparisons and swaps is needed, on the average, to complete the ordering process. For example, in the Bubble Sort and the Straight Selection Sort, N*(N − 1)/2 comparisons are needed. If N is reasonably large (e.g., 250), the number of comparisons becomes outrageously big. The Improved Bubble Sort is fairly good if the array is already close to being ordered. However, if the numbers in the array are random, the Improved Bubble Sort still requires a huge number of comparisons and swaps.

We therefore seek an alternative technique. The following method is significantly better, but is conceptually more involved and it requires a somewhat longer program.

III. Heap Sort[†]

The idea behind a Heap Sort is quite different from all of the preceding methods. Consider the following diagram:

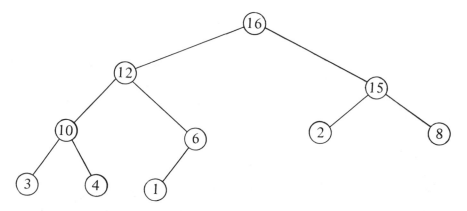

This figure is called a *binary tree*; each element (or node—the circled numbers) in the tree has two offspring nodes, as shown. Thus (16) has offspring (12) and (15) while both (4) and (3) have (10) as parent. Note at the bottom of the heap, we have run out of nodes, so that (6) has only one offspring and (2), (8), (4), (3), and (1) have none.

In addition, the above tree is also partially ordered, in that the number of each parent is ⩾ the numbers of each of its offspring. Once the tree is partially ordered, the elements can be completely ordered fairly easily, as follows.

The first (and largest) element on the tree is interchanged with the last element, and the last element is then ignored. The diagram becomes:

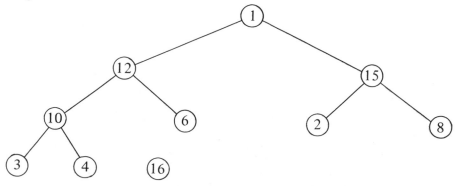

[†]Due to J. W. J. Williams; for more details see *CACM*, 7 (1964), 347–348.

We now put the resulting tree back into a partially ordered state. Since only the (1) has been moved in the present tree, that is the only node we must look at. Upon considering its two offspring, we observe that if the (15) and (1) are swapped, then the left half of the tree will be partially ordered (since $15 \geqslant 12$). Making this swap, we have

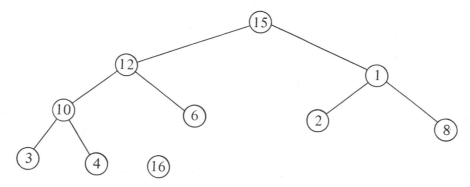

Again, we look at the (1) node and its offspring. By interchanging (1) and (8) the tree becomes partially ordered again:

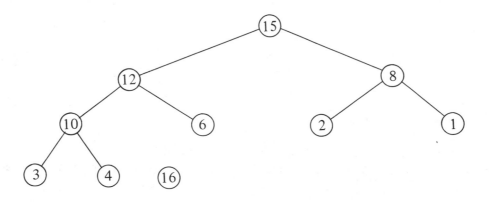

The process is then repeated. The first and last elements are interchanged, and the last element is then ignored:

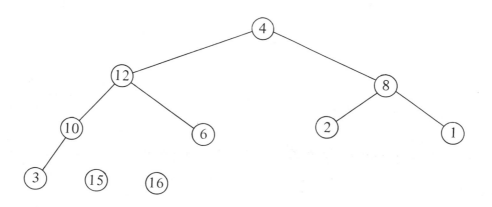

Again we work down the heap, comparing the (4) node with each of its offspring, and then swapping the (4) with the larger of the two offspring when necessary. In this case, the (4) moves along the left-most edge until it reaches the present (10) node. The result is:

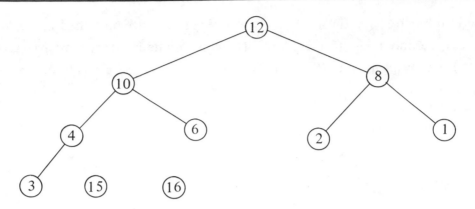

At this point, ④ is larger than its offspring, the tree is partially ordered, and the swapping process stops.

The ⑫ and ③ are then interchanged, the ⑫ ignored, and the ③ is moved down the tree. This process continues until there are no more elements remaining on the tree, e.g., we have:

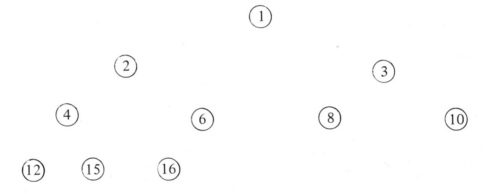

The ordered elements can then be read off one row at a time, from top to bottom.

Next, we return to our initial condition that the tree begins partially ordered. Suppose we are given:

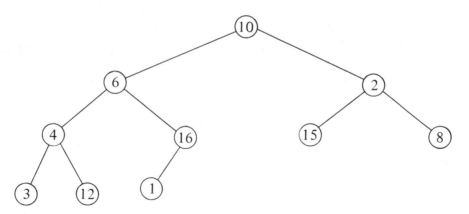

We must create the partially ordered tree we first illustrated. To do this, we work up from the bottom. The last node with offspring is

which is already partially ordered.

Next we consider

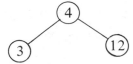

Here, we must interchange ⑫ and ④ to get a partial ordering. The ②

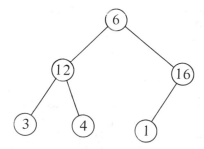

is considered next, with ② and ⑮ swapped. The tree from the next node is:

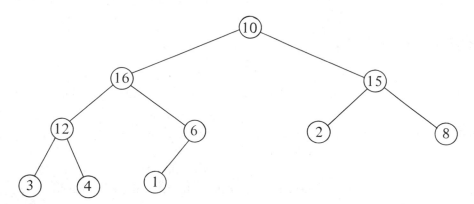

Here ⑥ and ⑯ are swapped and this tree is partially ordered. Finally, we consider the entire tree:

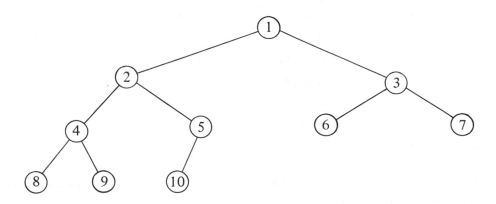

Again we work the ⑩ down, swapping it with the ⑯ and then with the ⑫ to obtain the partially ordered tree we began this section with.

Finally, we must decide how to relate the binary tree above to an array A(1), . . . , A(N). To see the relation, we look at the above tree, numbering the nodes from top to bottom along the rows. We obtain:

For each node $\text{\textcircled{I}}$, we note that its offspring, if any, are 2*I and 2*I+1, and its parent is INT(I/2). Thus, by simple arithmetic, we can convert between the array elements and a corresponding tree.

Programming Notes for a Heap Sort

A Heap Sort is reasonably easy to program using a function DOWN(T, B) which searches down the tree beginning at the node $\text{\textcircled{T}}$, until it gets to the end of the tree (node $\text{\textcircled{B}}$).

The array can then be partially ordered initially by using DOWN(T, B) with T starting at N/2 and moving to 1.

Once the array is partially ordered, the first and last elements are swapped, and DOWN(T, B) is used with T=1 and B equal the last element on the tree that is not being ignored. This is continued until the array is ordered.

Analysis of the Heap Sort

The Heap Sort can be shown to require about K*N*logN comparisons, where K is a known constant, and this number of comparisons can be shown to remain reasonably constant regardless of how the numbers are placed in the array initially. Thus, for arrays of random numbers, this method is much better than the previous methods. (However, if the array already is nearly in order, the Improved Bubble Sort would be better, since this Bubble Sort could stop after a few sets of comparisons.)

Section 3.2:   GENERAL PROBLEMS

Problem 1
    Write a program to compute and print the circumference and area of a circle once the radius of the circle is given.

Problem 2
    Write a program to compute and print a person's weight in grams given the weight in pounds (1 pound avoirdupois = approximately 453.59 grams).

Problem 3
    Write a program to compute and print a person's height in centimeters given the height in feet and inches (1 inch = approximately 2.54 centimeters).

Problem 4
    Use **WRITE** and **FORMAT** statements to write out the message

```
H   H  EEEE  L     L      OOOO
H   H  E     L     L      O  O
HHHH   EEEE  L     L      O  O
H   H  E     L     L      O  O
H   H  EEEE  LLLL  LLLL   OOOO
```

Problem 5
    Write a program to READ three integers and two real numbers from a data card of the form:

columns 1–8:	integer 1
columns 9–20:	integer 2
columns 31–40:	real 1
columns 43–51:	integer 3
columns 61–68:	real 2

and WRITE out the numbers in the order integer 1, real 1, integer 2, real 2, integer 3 in fields 10 columns wide, with the real numbers printed to 2 decimal places.

Problem 6   *Temperature Table*

Write a program that will READ (from DATA cards) a set of temperatures expressed in Fahrenheit and print them and their centigrade equivalents. Then use the program to convert some Fahrenheit temperatures of your own choosing into centigrade. When you have successfully written and tested the program, alter it so that the columns are labeled 'FAHRENHEIT' and 'CENTIGRADE'.

Problem 7

Write a program that will READ a set of real numbers from DATA cards and, using the built-in function SQRT, will compute and print each number and its square root. Then use this program to find the square roots of 2, 3.7, 11.5, 92, and 0.0004.

Problem 8

Prepare a program to compute the fee of a baby-sitter whose rate is 90 cents per hour until 9:00 p.m. and 60 cents per hour thereafter. One READ statement should call for four numbers: the starting time in hours and minutes, and the ending time in hours and minutes. Assume all times are between 6:00 p.m. and 6:00 a.m.

Problem 9   *Tabulate Mortgage Payment*

The monthly payment PAY on a mortgage which will amortize (be paid off) in N years with an interest rate of PERCNT % per year is determined by the formulas:

$$RATE = PERCNT/1200.$$
$$PAY = AMOUNT*RATE/[1. - (1. + RATE)**(-12. *N)]$$

where AMOUNT is the amount borrowed.

(a) Write a program that uses a READ statement to compute PAY for various combinations of PERCNT, N, and AMOUNT. Print the results in the form of a labeled table using at least the values indicated below:

PERCENT	YEARS	AMOUNT	PAYMENT
8.75	25	26000	213.76
9.25	20	30000	
7.00	20	30000	
7.00	25	30000	

(b) [*Optional:* Also print in the table the total amount paid over the life of the loan.]

Problem 10   *Compound Interest Tabulation*

If an amount of money A is deposited in a savings account which earns interest at the rate of R percent per year compounded quarterly (four times a year), then after N interest payments the bank account will contain the amount

$$A*(1. + R/400.)**N$$

Write a program that will READ the initial amount A and the annual interest rate R and then use a DO loop to print a labeled table illustrating the growth of the savings.

Problem 11   *Status of Credit Balance*

If $190.40 for airline tickets is charged on Master Charge, the company requires a minimum monthly payment of $6.00. This problem asks you to investigate the 'cost' of making only the minimum monthly payment. Interest is charged at the rate of 1.5% on the outstanding balance at the end of a month. The balance for the next month is computed by the formula:

$$New\ balance = Old\ balance + Interest - Payment$$

Write a program that will READ the amount borrowed, the monthly interest rate and the constant monthly payment. Have the program print a labeled table showing the month number and the balance at the beginning of that month (the balance at the beginning of month 1 is the amount borrowed). Continue printing until a payment would cause the balance to drop below zero. Also print the final payment necessary to close the loan, the total amount made in payments and the 'cost' of the loan (total payments – loan).

Problem 12   *Making Change*

Write a program that allows the user to READ the cost of an item and the amount paid by the customer, and then prints out the difference (the amount owed to the customer). Also print out how many bills of each denomination should be given to the customer (ones, twos, fives, and ten dollar bills), and the remainder to be paid in coins. Your computation should use the fewest number of bills. [Do not try to compute how many of each type coin should be given to the customer (pennies, nickels, dimes, quarters).]

Problem 13   *Insipid Integers*

Consider the iteration procedure which begins with a positive integer $n(1)$ and generates a sequence by the rule:

$$n(j+1) = \text{sum of the squares of the digits of } n(j)$$

Remarks.

1. If any term in the sequence equals 1, then all successive terms are 1.
2. If any term in the sequence equals 58, then the sequence cycles:

$$\ldots 58, 89, 145, 42, 20, 4, 16, 37, 58, 89, \ldots$$

3. It is known that either (1) or (2) must occur.

Definition. An integer $n(1)$ is called 'insipid' if (1) occurs.

Problem: Find all integers between 1 and 99 which are insipid.

[*Note:* It is interesting to investigate what patterns occur if the integers are represented in a number base other than base 10.]

[This problem was suggested by Professor Arnold Adelberg.]

Problem 14   *6174 Game*

The following iteration procedure begins with any FOUR digit number $n(1)$. The procedure is best explained with an example:

Let $n(1) = 3087$, then $n(2)$ is set equal to the difference of two integers formed from 3087. First the digits are arranged in decreasing order (8730) and then the digits are arranged in increasing order (0378). Then

$$n(2) = 8730 - 0378 = 8352$$

and

$$n(3) = 8532 - 2358 = 6174$$
$$n(4) = 7641 - 1467 = 6174$$
$$n(5) = \qquad\qquad = 6174, \ldots$$

It is known that for any four digit number $n(1)$, whose digits are not all the same, the process generates the number 6174 in less than seven iterations.

Problem: Find all integers $n(1)$ between 2000 and 2500 inclusive which initiate sequences for which $n(5) = 6174$ but $n(4)$ is not 6174.

[This problem was suggested by Professor Arnold Adelberg.]

Problem 15   *Improved Bubble Sort*

Write a program that will perform an Improved Bubble Sort and test it on arrays of various lengths. [The Improved Bubble Sort is described in Section 3.1.]

Problem 16   *Straight Selection Sort*

Write a program that will perform a Straight Selection Sort. Test the program with several sets of data. [The Straight Selection Sort is described in Section 3.1.]

Problem 17   *Heap Sort*

Write a program that will perform a Heap Sort. [The Heap Sort is described in Section 3.1.]

Problem 18   *Comparison of Sorting Algorithms*

In the programs for Bubble Sort, Improved Bubble Sort, Straight Selection Sort, and Heap Sort, add counters to measure the number of comparisons and the number of interchanges required. After testing the program, run it on various data sets ranging in length from 8-element arrays to 200-element arrays. Some arrays should be close to being ordered while others should be scrambled. What conclusions can you draw about the relative efficiency of these methods? [Sorting is described in Section 3.1.]

Problem 19

Write a program that READs an integer N.

If N is between 1 and 26, then the program prints the Nth letter of the alphabet.

If N is not between 1 and 26, then the program prints "ERROR".

Problem 20   *Reverse a String*

Prepare a program which will READ a string and print the string in reverse order.

Problem 21   *Name Manipulation*

Write a program that

(a) READs a person's name in the format

$$\text{(last name), (first name) (middle initial).}$$

[i.e., the last name is followed by a comma which is followed by the first name and middle initial. The string ends with a period.]

(b) prints the person's name with the first name first, with the first name and middle initial seaprated by exactly 1 space, with no spaces between the initial and period, and with exactly 1 space between the period and the last name.

Problem 22   *Count Number of 'E's*

Write a program which will count the number of 'E's in any string which is READ.

Problem 23

Write a program that READs a string of characters and then prints out the string with commas between each character.

Problem 24   *Replace Vowels by '*'*

Write a program which will READ a string and replace all occurrences of vowels by the character '*'.

Problem 25   *Alphabetize Names*

Write a program that READs *n* names and alphabetizes them.

Problem 26   *Count Letter Repetitions*

Prepare a program which will accept a line of text and count the number of repetitions of each letter of the alphabet. Print out the results in a table which gives, for each letter, its number of occurrences and its frequency of occurrence (number of occurrences divided by total of all occurrences of all letters).

Problem 27   *Word Counting*

Write a program that will compute word counts and word percentages for English prose that is entered. More precisely, the program should:

(a) Read successive lines of prose, until a blank line is entered. (The program should allow at least 40 lines to be entered.)

(b) Determine each word that appears in the text. (Words may be separated by blanks or by punctuation marks.) (You should allow numbers to be in the text, but you need not count how many times each number appears.)

(c) Count how many times each word appears.

(d) Print a table giving each word, the number of times it appears in the text, and the frequency (or percentage) of times it appears in the text.

Test the program with a text of at least 30 lines. [You may assume that each word will have no more then 16 characters.]

Problem 28   *Permutation Cipher: Subroutine*

Define a subroutine ENCODE which encodes a TEXT according to a substitution cipher. The first line of the subroutine ENCODE should be:

$$\text{SUBROUTINE ENCODE (TEXT, CODED, REALAL, CIPHER)}$$

where:

TEXT is the message to be encoded;
CODED is the coded message;
REALAL is the 'real' alphabet;

and   CIPHER is the 'cipher' alphabet.

Each of these is an array of appropriate dimension.

The subroutine should encode the message by replacing a character in the message by the corresponding character in the cipher alphabet.

Example: If

$$REALAL = 'ABCDEFGHIJKLMNOPQRSTUVWXYZ\ 0123456789'$$
$$CIPHER = '3456217089ACB\ QRSTUVWXYZDEFGHIJKLMNOP'$$

then the message

$$'IN\ 1492\ COLUMBUS\ SAILED\ THE\ OCEAN\ BLUE'$$

becomes

$$'8\ FHKPIF5QCWB4WUFU38C26FV02FQ523\ F4CW2'$$

Write a program which incorporates this ciphering subroutine and which READs a single line of text (no embedded commas) and prints both the original text and the encoded form of the text. Before reading in the text to be transformed, the program should READ in the cipher alphabet.

Test your program with the example above and then encode the message

$$'TSQ24964XMTUUNSL4IF2X4ZSYNQ4J1FRX'$$

using the cipher alphabet

$$'56789ABCDEFGHIJKLMNOPQRSTUVWXYZ\ 01234'$$

Problem 29   *Credit Bureau File*

A data file, CREDIT.DAT, has been created for the problem, and it contains data from a replica of a credit bureau data file. In the file, each record can be obtained using

```
        INTEGER ADDRES, GROSS, RATING, BALANCE
        DIMENSION NAME(32), ADDRES(64)
        READ (  , 1) NAME, ADDRES, GROSS, RATING, BALANCE
   1    FORMAT (32A1, 64,A1, 3I5)
```

The file has been organized so that it contains information about 200 fictitious individuals. Each record contains data on a separate individual, as follows:

NAME = person's name (last name starting with NAME(1), first name starting with NAME(17). The middle initial, if any, follows the first name by a single blank);
ADDRES = person's address (house number and street starting with ADDRES(1), town with ADDRES(34), state abbreviation in ADDRES(57) and ADDRES(58), and zip code in the remaining 5 array elements;
GROSS = gross income in dollars;
CREDIT = credit rating (between 0 and 100);
BALANC = outstanding credit balance in dollars.

Your program should do the following:

1. Find all people who live in the state of Iowa (IA), whose gross income is above $15,000, whose credit rating is greater than 75, and whose outstanding balance is less than $1000.
2. Find all people who live in the state of California (CA), whose gross income is above $20,000, whose credit rating is greater than 90, and whose outstanding balance is between 15% and 25% (inclusive) of their gross income.
3. Determine and print the total number of people found in (1) and (2).
4. Print out address labels for all people located in (1) and (2). Note that it is not necessary to alphabetize labels according to last names. Format for the label is shown by the example:

<pre>
          JACK S. BACH   GROSS INCOME: $16890
          168 PASSION MATTHEW ST.   BALANCE: $673
          LEIPZIG, IA 51750   % OF INCOME: 3.98
                                          CREDIT RATING: 95
               !__ column 1   !__ column 31   !__ column 46.
</pre>

Problem 30

A file is to be created, containing information on 200 people. The data on each person is to include:

(a) full name (first name, middle initial, last name)

(b) age

(c) occupation

(d) employer

Write a program that will READ the appropriate data from a terminal and place the information in a disk file. Write a second program that will print the name of each person in the file who is a teacher and who is over 40 years old.

CHAPTER 4

Algebra and Trigonometry Problems

Section 4.1: GREATEST COMMON DIVISOR (EUCLIDEAN ALGORITHM)

Let N and M be two positive integers. The greatest common divisor of M and N, denoted gcd(M, N), is defined to be the positive integer D such that

1. D divides M and D divides N, and
2. D is the largest integer dividing both M and N; i.e., every integer E that divides both M and N also divides D.

For example: $2 = \gcd(6, 8)$
$4 = \gcd(4, 12)$
$1 = \gcd(8, 9)$
$6 = \gcd(66, 24)$

In the following algorithm for computing gcd(M, N), we assume that $M \leqslant N$. The approach for $N \leqslant M$ is similar.

We proceed by long division:

Step 1: Write $N = Q_1 {}^* M + R_1$ where $0 \leqslant R_1 \leqslant M{-}1$

Step 2: Write $M = Q_2 {}^* R_1 + R_2$ where $0 \leqslant R_2 \leqslant R_1 - 1$

Step 3: Write $R_1 = Q_3 {}^* R_2 + R_3$ where $0 \leqslant R_3 \leqslant R_2 - 1$

$\cdot$ $\quad\quad\quad\quad$ $\cdot$ $\quad\quad\quad\quad\quad\quad$ $\cdot$
$\cdot$ $\quad\quad\quad\quad$ $\cdot$ $\quad\quad\quad\quad\quad\quad$ $\cdot$
$\cdot$ $\quad\quad\quad\quad$ $\cdot$ $\quad\quad\quad\quad\quad\quad$ $\cdot$

Step i: Write $R_{i-2} = Q_i {}^* R_{i-1} + R_i$ where $0 \leqslant R_i \leqslant R_{i-1} - 1$

Step $i{+}1$: Write $R_{i-1} = Q_{i+1} {}^* R_i + R_{i+1}$ where $0 \leqslant R_{i+1} \leqslant R_i - 1$

To find gcd(66, 24):

Divide 66 by 24: $66 = 2{*}24 + 18$
remainder is 18
Divide 24 by 18: $24 = 1{*}18 + 6$
remainder is 6
Divide 18 by 6: $18 = 3{*}6 + 0$
remainder is 0
so we can stop.

Thus, $6 = \gcd(66, 24)$

This process continues until we find a remainder R_{i+1} which is 0. Then $R_i = \gcd(M, N)$ by the following proof:

First, R_i divides R_{i-1}, since $R_{i-1} = Q_{i+1} * R_i$. Then R_i divides R_{i-2}, since $R_{i-2} = Q_i * R_{i-1} + R_i$ and R_i divides both R_{i-1} and R_i. Continuing up the steps, step 2 shows that R_i divides M and step 1 shows that R_i divides N, so that R_i divides both M and N, satisfying condition 1.

Further, if any integer E divides both M and N, then E divides $N - M*Q_1$ and thus E divides R_1 by step 1. Next, since E divides M and R_1; E divides $M - Q_2 *R_1 = R_2$ by step 2. Continuing down the steps, E divides R_i by step i, satisfying condition 2.

Programming Hint

Given N and M, the long division $N = Q*M + R$ can be performed by computing the integer quotient $Q = (N/M)$ and the integer remainder $R = N - Q*M$. Steps $i+1$ should be performed in a single loop, using the same letters N, M, Q, R every time through the loop, but changing their values each time.

Section 4.2: THE BISECTION METHOD FOR APPROXIMATING ROOTS

Suppose that we are given a function $y = f(x)$ on the interval $[a, b]$, and we want to find a root of f [i.e., we try to find a number x_0 in $[a, b]$ where $f(x_0) = 0$].

Our approach is to find better and better approximations to x_0 in the case that f is a continuous function (i.e., f does not have any jumps). Our work uses the fact that if the root is known to be in a small interval of length L, the midpoint of the interval must be within L/2 of the root.

The following discussion is based on the fact that if f is positive at one endpoint of an interval and negative at the other endpoint, d must cross the axis somewhere within the interval (by the Intermediate Value Theorem). (See Figure 4.2–1.)

To start this method, we suppose that we have already found a and b so that $f(a)$ and $f(b)$ must have opposite signs. Thus, we know that f must have a root in $[a, b]$.

For the first step, we consider the midpoint c of the interval $[a, b]$ [*Note:* $c=(a+b)/2$] and we compute $f(c)$. There are three possibilities (Figure 4.2–2):

1. If $f(c) = 0$, we have found a root.
2. If $f(a)$ and $f(c)$ have opposite signs, a root must be in $[a, c]$.
3. If $f(c)$ and $f(b)$ have opposite signs, a root must be in $[c, b]$.

In case 1, we can stop. Otherwise, we have cut the interval containing a root in half, from $[a, b]$ to either $[a, c]$ or $[c, b]$.

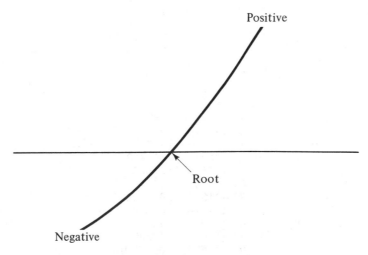

Figure 4.2–1

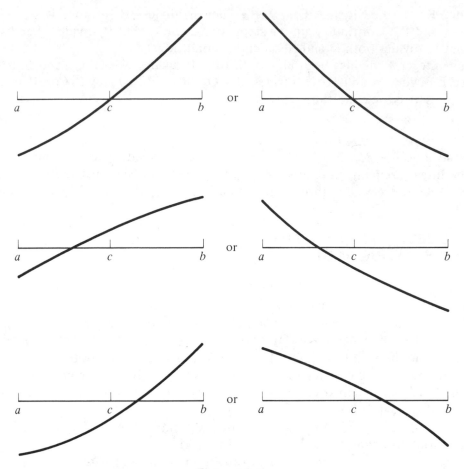

Figure 4.2–2
Cases in The Bisection Method

For the next steps, the above process is repeated, with the interval containing the root being halved each time. Once the root has been trapped in a very small interval, we use the midpoint of the interval to approximate the root.

Example. The following table indicates the steps used to approximate $\sqrt{2}$, a root of $f(x) = x^2 - 2$. The first two steps are illustrated in Figure 4.2–3. Here we find $\sqrt{2}$ to two decimal places (error < 0.005), so the interval we stop with must have length < 0.01.

We know that $1 < \sqrt{2} < 2$, so we begin with $[a, b] = [1, 2]$.

Step	Interval	Midpoint	Function Values	Root Lies in Subinterval
1	[1, 2]	1.5	$f(1)=-1; f(1.5)=0.25; f(2)=2$	[1, 1.5]
2	[1, 1.5]	1.25	$f(1)=-1; f(1.25)=-0.4375; f(1.5)=0.25$	[1.25, 1.5]
3	[1.25, 1.5]	1.375	$f(1.25)=-0.4375; f(1.375)=-0.119375$ $f(1.5)=0.25$	[1.375, 1.5]
4	[1.375, 1.5]	1.4375	$f(1.375)=-0.119375$ $f(1.4375)=0.06640625; f(1.5)=0.25$	[1.375, 1.4375]
5	[1.375, 1.4375]	1.40625	$f(1.375)=-0.119375$ $f(1.40625)=-0.0224609375$ $f(1.4375)=0.06640625$	[1.40625, 1.4375]
6	[1.40625, 1.4375]	1.421875	$f(1.40625)=-0.0224609375$ $f(1.421875)=0.021710415625$ $f(1.4375)=0.06640625$	[1.40625, 1.421875]
7	[1.40625,1.421875]	1.4140625	$f(1.40625)=-0.0224609375$ $f(1.4140625)=-0.00042724609375$ $f(1.421875)=0.021710415625$	[1.4140625, 1.421875]

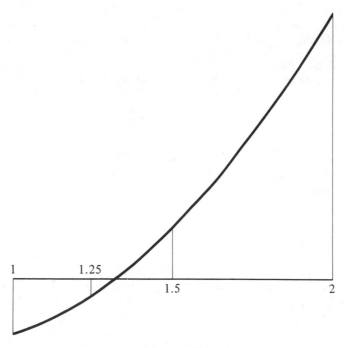

Figure 4.2–3

The last subinterval has length 0.0078125, which is less than the 0.01 required. Thus, the midpoint 1.41796875 of this last subinterval [1.40625, 1.421875] is within 0.005 of the desired root. We use 1.41796875 as our approximation of $\sqrt{2}$. (*Note:* This agrees, to two decimal places, with the true value of $\sqrt{2}$, which is 1.41431.)

Section 4.3: ALGEBRA AND TRIGONOMETRY PROBLEMS

Problem 1

Write a program to compute the volume and surface area of a right circular cylinder, given its radius and height.

Problem 2

Write a program to compute the area of a trapezoid, given the two bases and the height.

Problem 3

Modify the preceding programs so that all required quantities are READ from data cards with numbers in columns 1–10, 11–20, etc.

Problem 4

Use WRITE and FORMAT statements to write out the message:

```
AA   L      GGGG EEEE BBBB RRRR   AA
A  A L      G      E    B  B R  R  A  A
AAAA L      G GG EEEE BBB   RRR   AAAA
A  A L      G  G E    B  B R  R   A  A
A    A LLLL GGGG EEEE BBBB R    R A    A
```

Problem 5   *Sum of Cubes*

For $n = 1, 2, 3, \ldots, 49, 50$, compute both $n**3$ and the sum

$$1**3 + 2**3 + 3**3 + \ldots + (n-1)**3 + n**3$$

Print the results in a table, with headings 'N', 'N CUBED', and 'SUM'.

Problem 6   *Table of Roots and Powers*

Write a program that will print a table, where each row contains a number N together with its square, square root, cube, and cube root. The table should include $1 \leqslant N \leqslant 50$. Label each of the columns in the table appropriately.

Problem 7   *Largest Root of Quadratic Equation*

Write a program that will compute and print the largest root of the quadratic equation

$$a*(x**2) + b*x + c = 0$$

using the formula

$$r = [-b + SQRT(b**2 - 4*a*c)] /(2*a)$$

Use a READ statement with data cards to enter the values of *a*, *b*, and *c*. Compute square roots using the built-in function SQRT. The output should be in the form of a table (with labels):

A	B	C	ROOT
2	5	-3	0.5
1	0	-4	2

Run the program on the following sets of triples *a, b, c*: (2, 5, –3), (1, 0, –4), (1, –2, 1), (3, 17, 2), (4.2, 11.6, 5.07). [*Note:* If *a* is negative the formula for *r* may not give the largest root, so this program is only known to give correct results for positive values of *a*.]

Problem 8   *Quadratic Formula*

Write a program that will input the coefficients of a quadratic polynomial

$$a*(x**2) + b*x + c$$

The program then should check the discriminant, print out how many roots the polynomial has, and then compute any existing real roots. The program should allow for the possibility that $a = 0$.

Problem 9   *Composition of Functions*

Write a program which contains two functions F and G. For various values of X, compute F(X), G(F(X)), G(X), F(G(X)). Run the program several times using different functions for F and G. Compare the values of F(G(X)) and G(F(X)).

Problem 10   *Tabulation of Functions*

Write a program which computes the values F(X) of a function F for X = L, L+H, L+2*H, . . . , U. Use a statement function to define F(X) and use a READ statement to determine L, U, H.

Problem 11

Write a program that READs three numbers and prints out the smallest of these numbers.

Problem 12

Write a program that READs an integer N and then N numbers on separate cards and computes and prints the largest of these numbers. (You should not assume the numbers will be entered in order.)

Problem 13

A positive integer N is divisible by another positive integer I if the remainder after dividing N by I is 0. Write a program that will READ two positive integers and compute if either is a divisor of the other. [*Hint:* The remainder after dividing N by I can be computed with integer arithmetic by N – (N/I)*I. (Why?)]

Problem 14   *Integer Factoring*

Write a program that will compute all factors of a given positive integer. [*Hint:* N is divisible by I if the remainder after dividing N by I is 0.]

Problem 15   *Prime Numbers*

An integer is prime if it is greater than 1 and if it is divisible only by 1 and by itself. Thus 7 and 23 are prime while 22 and 30 are not (both 22 and 30 are divisible by 2). Write a program that will find the first 100 prime numbers. Use DO loops.

Problem 16   *Perfect Numbers*

A perfect number is one such that the sum of its divisors (not including itself) equals the number itself. Thus 6 and 28 are perfect numbers (6 = 1 + 2 + 3 and 28 = 1 + 2 + 4 + 7 + 14). Write a program to compute and print the first 5 perfect numbers.

[This problem was suggested by Mr. Kurt F. Welsch.]

Problem 17 *Euclidean Algorithm*
Write a program that will read two positive numbers and compute their greatest common divisor. [A technique for computing the greatest common divisor is described in Section 4.1.]

Problem 18 *Unusual Cancelling*
The fraction 64/16 has the unusual property that its reduced value of 4 may be obtained by 'cancelling' the 6 in the numerator with that in the denominator. Write a program to find the other fractions, whose numerators and denominators are each two digit numbers and whose values remain unchanged after 'cancelling'.

Problem 19 *Syracuse Numbers*
Consider the following iteration procedure applied to a positive integer $n(1)$ to generate a sequence

$$n(1), n(2), n(3), n(4), \ldots$$

Once the integer $n(j)$ is known, the next integer, $n(j+1)$, is computed by the rules:
  (1) $n(j+1) = n(j)/2$ if $n(j)$ is even;
  (2) $n(j+1) = 3*n(j)+1$ if $n(j)$ is odd.
The original number, $n(1)$, is called 'Syracuse' if the number 1 appears in the sequence $n(1), n(2), n(3), n(4), \ldots$

  Example: The number 5 is 'Syracuse' because if the iteration begins with $n(1) = 5$, the sequence is 5, 16, 8, 4, 2, 1, ...

Problem: Write a program to show that all integers between 1 and 2000 inclusive are 'Syracuse'. [*Note:* You do not have to use dimensioned variables.]

[This problem was suggested by Professor Arnold Adelberg.]

Problem 20 *Polynomial Multiplication*
Compute the degree and coefficients of the product of each of two polynomials given the degree and coefficients of each of the original two polynomials.

Problem 21 *Polynomial Division*
Write a program that will READ the degrees and coefficients of two polynomials and then will divide the first polynomial by the second, giving the quotient and the remainder.

Problem 22
Write a program that will:
  (1) print out the (names of the) numbers from zero to ninety-nine;
  (2) alphabetize these numbers.

Problem 23
Define a function subprogram that calculates the absolute value of its argument wihout using the built-in function ABS. The function you create will have to be a function subprogram. Write a program to check your function against ABS for a variety of arguments both positive and negative.

Problem 24
Write a program that READs an integer and then prints out the integer with commas inserted between every third integer. Thus, 123456789 should be printed 123, 456,789 and –654321 should be printed –654,321. [*Hint:* Consider the integer as a string of characters, not as a number.]

Problem 25
Write a program that will READ an expression for a function F(X) as a string of characters and will replace all occurrences of the variable X by the variable Y. (Thus, the program reads a function F(X) and prints F(Y).)

Problem 26
Write a program that will READ an expression for a function F(X) as a string and an expression E and will replace all occurrences of the variable X by the expression. (Thus, the program will input a function F(X) and will print F(E).) Test the program for F(X) = (X + 1)/(X**2 + X + 1) and E = (Y**2 – Y – 5). [*Note:* This problem is a little tricky.]

Problem 27   *Nth Roots*

Write a program that computes the Nth root of the positive number R to 3 decimal places using the bisection method. Use a READ statement to obtain the values of N and R. Check your program using R**(1./N). [The Bisection Method is described in Section 4.2.]

Problem 28   *Bisection Method on Polynomials*

Write a program that uses the bisection method to compute a root (to three decimal places) of a polynomial given:
   (1) the degree of the polynomial;
   (2) the coefficients of the polynomial;
   (3) an interval [*a, b*] that a root lies in.
Use a function subprogram to evaluate the polynomial. [See Section 4.2 for a description of the Bisection Method.]

Problem 29   *Alphabetize Numbers*

Write a program that will:
   (1) print out the (names of the) numbers from zero to nine hundred ninety-nine;
   (2) alphabetize these numbers.
[*Note:* Due to storage requirements for these words, you may wish to use disk storage in this program.]

CHAPTER 5

Calculus Problems

This chapter was written with Eugene Herman and John Vogel.

Section 5.1: **NEWTON'S METHOD**

The following algorithm, which is credited to Newton, can often be used to approximate the roots of a differentiable function efficiently and accurately. In the algorithm we begin by making a guess x_0 for the root of the function $f(x)$. The algorithm then gives us a "closer" approximation x_1 to the root. We can then use x_1 as our guess, apply the algorithm again, and get a still better guess. This process continues until we are satisfied with our approximation.

The key, therefore, is to decide how to improve a guess a. Here we observe that the tangent line to a curve is usually a good approximation to the curve "near" the point of tangency. Thus, if the point of tangency is near the root, the tangent line will cross the horizontal coordinate axis near the point where the curve crosses the axis. (See Figure 5.1–1.)

We look at the equation of the tangent line to the curve $y = f(x)$ at the point where $x = a$. The point of tangency is $(a, f(a))$ and the slope at this point is $f'(a)$, so by the point-slope form of a line, the equation of the tangent is given by

$$y - y_0 = m(x - x_0)$$

or

$$y - f(a) = f'(a)(x - a)$$

This tangent crosses the x-axis at a point $(b, 0)$, and since this point is on the tangent, we must have

$$0 - f(a) = f'(a)(b - a)$$

or

$$b = a - f(a)/f'(a) \tag{*}$$

We can now describe Newton's Method more precisely.

First, choose an initial approximation, call it x_0, for the root (this may be only a blind guess or it may be based on some knowledge, such as a rough sketch of the graph). Secondly, construct the sequence of numbers

$$x_1 = x_0 - f(x_0)/f'(x_0)$$
$$x_2 = x_1 - f(x_1)/f'(x_1)$$
$$x_3 = x_2 - f(x_2)/f'(x_2)$$
$$.$$
$$.$$
$$.$$

Because the formula (*) gives the x-intercept of the tangent to the curve corresponding to $x = a$, the above iterative process can be graphically described by the dotted path in Figure 5.1–2.

The general form of Newton's Method can be written:

1. x_0 arbitrary
2. $x_{n+1} = x_n - f(x_n)/f'(x_n);$ $(n=0, 1, 2, \ldots)$
3. stop when you are close to the root

We expect that for reasonably shaped curves, such as in Figure 5.1–2, the x_n values approach the actual root as n increases.

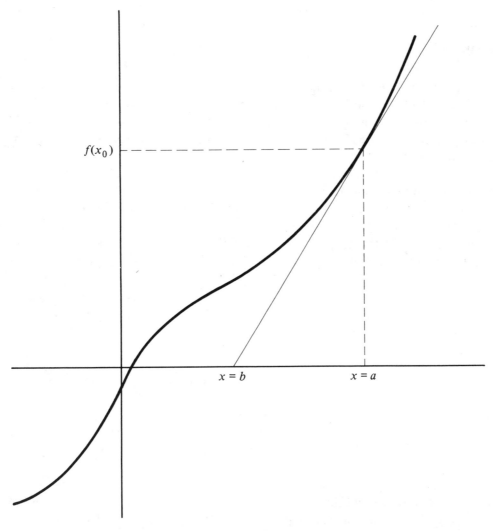

Figure 5.1–1

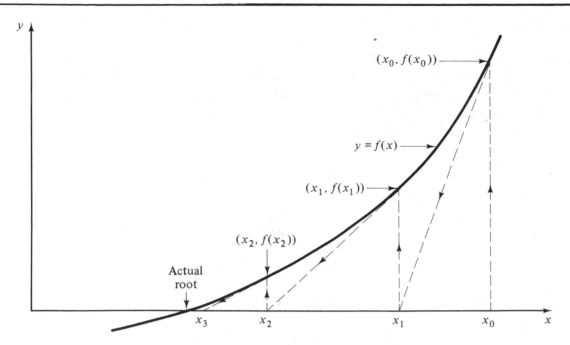

Figure 5.1–2
A Case where Newton's Method Converges

Notes

1. When do you stop the process? There are various ways of deciding when you are close to the root. None of them is completely satisfactory. The procedure that we will use is to choose some measure on the error that we are willing to tolerate, for example,

$$\epsilon = 10^{-6}$$

and continue the iteration process until

$$|f(x_n)| \leqslant \epsilon$$

This procedure cannot give acceptable results for every function because it states that $x = 1$ is an acceptable approximation to the root $x = 0$ of the function $f(x) = \epsilon x$.

2. Figure 5.1–3 indicates a situation where Newton's Method fails completely because of an unfortunate initial guess of either $x = a$ or $x = b$.

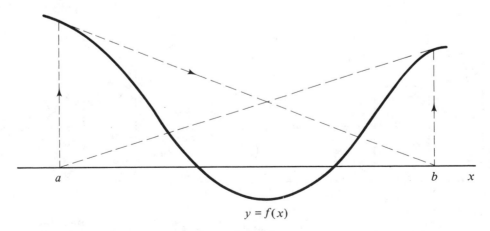

Figure 5.1–3
A Case where Newton's Method Fails

Section 5.2: UPPER AND LOWER SUMS

The following simple method for approximating areas uses only the notion of upper and lower sums, but applies *only* to monotonic (either increasing or decreasing) functions f. Two more sophisticated methods are the Trapezoidal Rule and Simpson's Rule which will be discussed later.

Assume that f is decreasing on an interval $[a, b]$. (The treatment when f is increasing is similar.) Divide the interval $[a, b]$ into n equal parts, each of length h, to obtain the partition

$$\{x_0, x_1, \ldots, x_n\}$$

of $[a, b]$. When this is done, we have

$$h = (b-a)/n$$

and

$$x_j = a + jh \qquad (j = 0, 1, \ldots, n)$$

From Figure 5.2–1 we see that the upper sum (the area of the rectangles above the curve) is

$$U = f(x_0)h + f(x_1)h + \ldots + f(x_{n-1})h$$
$$= \sum_{j=0}^{n-1} f(x_j)h$$

while from Figure 5.2–2 we see that the lower sum (the area of the rectangles below the curve) is

$$L = f(x_1)h + f(x_2)h + \ldots + f(x_n)h$$
$$= \sum_{j=1}^{n} f(x_j)h$$

Let A_a^b be the required area, i.e., the area bounded by the curve, the x-axis, and the lines $x = a$ and $x = b$. Then

$$L \leqslant A_a^b \leqslant U$$

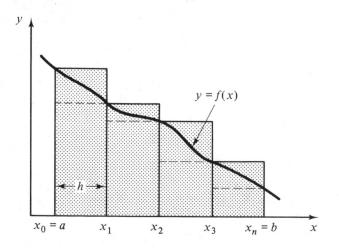

Figure 5.2–1
Upper Sum
(*Note:* $n = 4$ in each figure.)

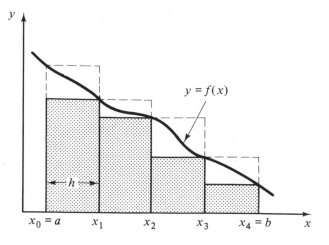

Figure 5.2–2
Lower Sum

We can now determine how good an approximation L or U really is, because it follows from the previous line that

$$0 \leqslant A_a^b - L \leqslant U\!-\!L$$

The expression $U\!-\!L$ has a simple form because U and L are very similar:

$$
\begin{aligned}
U\!-\!L &= f(x_0)h + f(x_1)h + \ldots + f(x_{n-1})h \\
&\qquad\quad - f(x_1)h - \ldots - f(x_{n-1})h - f(x_n)h \\
&= f(x_0)h - f(x_n)h \\
&= h[f(a) - f(b)] \\
&= h|f(b) - f(a)|
\end{aligned}
$$

Thus,
$$|L - A_a^b| \leqslant h|f(b)\!-\!f(a)|$$

Similarly, it follows that

$$|U - A_a^b| \leqslant h|f(b)\!-\!f(a)|$$

So that if S is either the upper sum or the lower sum, we have the estimate of accuracy:

$$|S - A_a^b| \leqslant h|f(b)\!-\!f(a)|$$

This estimate is useful because in a given situation we know the function f and the values b and a, and can make h as small as we please by choosing a large enough number of subintervals in the interval $[a, b]$. To be more specific, suppose we decide beforehand that we want the error of approximating the area by either an upper or a lower sum S to be less than some number ϵ. We must choose h so small that

$$h|f(b)\!-\!f(a)| \leqslant \epsilon$$

But since

$$h = (b\!-\!a)/n$$

this is accomplished if n is chosen so that

$$n > |f(b)\!-\!f(a)|(b\!-\!a)/\epsilon$$

Since FORTRAN does not allow the definition of numbers by inequalities, and since n must be an integer as well as satisfy the above inequality, choose n to be the value obtained when the built-in function INT is applied to the expression

$$1 + |[f(b)\!-\!f(a)]\ (b\!-\!a)|/\epsilon$$

When this value of n is used to compute h, and then to compute either the upper or lower sum as an approximation to the area under the curve, the result will be in error by no more than ϵ.

**THE TRAPEZOIDAL RULE AND
SIMPSON'S RULE**

If we are given a function $f(x)$ (with a continuous second derivative), either the Trapezoidal Rule or Simpson's Rule gives an efficient way of approximating

$$\int_a^b f(x)\, dx$$

These methods do not require that the function f be monotonic as does the method of upper/lower sums. The one practical drawback—that we cannot easily predict the accuracy of the approximation—is studied in some calculus and numerical analysis textbooks.

When using upper or lower sums, we approximated the area under the curve by rectangles. With the Trapezoidal Rule or Simpson's Rule, we use trapezoids or parabolas. As is shown in Figure 5.3–1 below, we can expect these approximations to be much closer than the rectangles used previously.

For either the Trapezoidal Rule or Simpson's Rule, we divide the interval $[a, b]$ into n subintervals of equal length h. (For Simpson's Rule, n must be *even*.) It is easy to see that $h = (b-a)/n$.

These subintervals determine a partition

$$\{x_0, x_1, \ldots, x_n\} \text{ of } [a, b]$$

where $x_j = a + jh$ for $j = 0, 1, 2, \ldots, n$.

Let $y_j = f(x_j)$. We are now ready to approximate area.

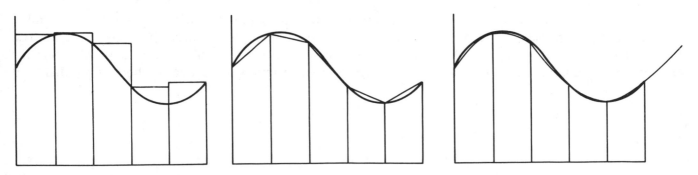

Figure 5.3–1
Approximating Area with Rectangles, Trapezoids, and Parabolas

For the Trapezoidal Rule, we approximate the area under $y = f(x)$ by trapezoids with sides y_i and y_{i+1} as shown in Figure 5.3–2.

From geometry, we know that the area of a trapezoid with parallel sides y_i and y_{i+1} and with width h is $(y_i + y_{i+1})h/2$. Thus, we have

$$\text{area I} = (y_0 + y_1)h/2$$
$$\text{area II} = (y_1 + y_2)h/2$$
$$\text{area III} = (y_2 + y_3)h/2$$
$$\vdots$$
$$\text{area N} = (y_{n-1} + y_n)h/2$$

Adding, we get a total approximation

134

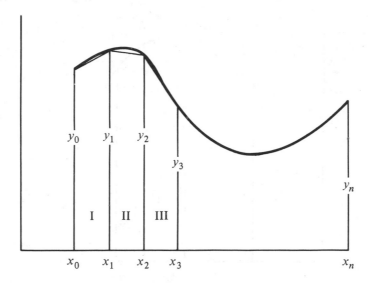

Figure 5.3–2

$$A_t = (y_0 + y_1)\, h/2 + (y_1 + y_2)\, h/2 + (y_2 + y_3)\, h/2 + \ldots + (y_{n-1} + y_n)h/2$$
$$= h/2\, (y_0 + y_1 + y_1 + y_2 + y_2 + y_3 + \ldots + y_{n-1} + y_n) \qquad \text{factoring out } h/2$$
$$= h/2\, (y_0 + 2y_1 + 2y_2 + 2y_3 + \ldots + 2y_{n-1} + y_n) \qquad \text{combining terms}$$

Thus, the Trapezoidal Rule for approximating area under a curve is given by the formula

$$\frac{h}{2}(y_0 + 2y_1 + 2y_2 + 2y_3 + \ldots + 2y_{n-1} + y_n)$$

For a better approximation, we could pass parabolas through points of the curve. This gives rise to Simpson's Rule. The steps are outlined below, but we avoid the messy algebra. The reader should refer to calculus or numerical analysis textbooks if he wishes to see all of the algebra.

We look at the points x_j in groups of three, i.e., we consider (x_0, x_1, x_2), (x_2, x_3, x_4), (x_4, x_5, x_6), $\ldots, (x_{n-2}, x_{n-1}, x_n)$.

In each set (x_i, x_{i+1}, x_{i+2}), we fit a parabola to the points (x_i, y_i), (x_{i+1}, y_{i+1}), and (x_{i+2}, y_{i+2}), as seen in Figure 5.3–3.

If the parabola is $Ax^2 + Bx + C$, then A, B, and C must satisfy the equations

$$y_i = Ax_i{}^2 + Bx_i + C$$
$$y_{i+1} = Ax_{i+1}{}^2 + Bx_{i+1} + C$$
$$y_{i+2} = Ax_{i+2}{}^2 + Bx_{i+2} + C$$

and we can solve for A, B, and C. Then, from calculus, we can compute

$$\int_{x_i}^{x_{i+2}} (Ax^2 + Bx + C)\, dx$$

The result is that the area under the parabola is $(y_i + 4y_{i+1} + y_{i+2})\, h/3$. [*Note:* The 3 comes from the integral of the x^2 term.]

We now proceed as in the Trapezoidal Rule, computing the area for each set:

$$\text{area between } x_0 \text{ and } x_2 = (y_0 + 4y_1 + y_2)\, h/3$$

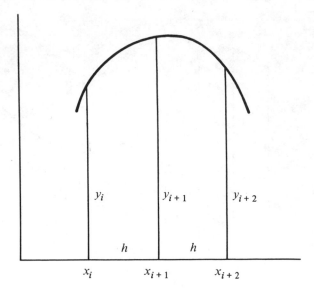

Figure 5.3-3
A Parabola through Points
$(x_i, y_i), (x_{i+1}, y_{i+1})$, and
(x_{i+2}, y_{i+2})

area between x_2 and $x_4 = (y_2 + 4y_3 + y_4) h/3$
area between x_4 and $x_6 = (y_4 + 4y_5 + y_6) h/3$

$$\cdot \qquad \qquad \cdot$$
$$\cdot \qquad \qquad \cdot$$
$$\cdot \qquad \qquad \cdot$$

area between x_{n-2} and $x_n = (y_{n-2} + 4y_{n-1} + y_n) h/3$

As with the Trapezoidal Rule, we add these terms together for a total approximation, and we simplify the resulting expression. When we finish, we find that Simpson's Rule for approximating area under a curve is given by the formula

$$\frac{h}{3}(y_0 + 4y_1 + 2y_2 + 4y_3 + 2y_4 + \ldots + 2y_{n-4} + 4y_{n-3} + 2y_{n-2} + 4y_{n-1} + y_n)$$

This formula is valid for even $n > 2$; for example, when $n = 4$ the approximation is $(h/3)(y_0 + 4y_1 + 2y_2 + 4y_3 + y)$.

It turns out that Simpson's Rule often gives a substantially more accurate approximation than the Trapezoidal Rule, although Simpson's Rule does require a little more programming.

Section 5.4: CALCULUS PROBLEMS

Problem 1
Write a program to compute the slope and y-intercept of a line through two points.

Problem 2
Write a program to compute the slope and y-intercept of a line perpendicular to a given line and through a given point.

Problem 3
Modify each of the preceding programs to READ the required data from cards.

Problem 4

(a) Write a program that will READ an angle in radians and will compute the measure of the angle in degrees.

(b) Write a second program that will READ the angle in degrees and will compute the angle in radians.

Problem 5

Use WRITE and FORMAT statements to write out the message:

```
CCCC   AA    L      CCCC   U  U  L      UUUU   SSSS
C      A  A  L      C      U  U  L      U  U   S
C      AAAA  L      C      U  U  L      U  U   SSSS
C      A  A  L      C      U  U  L      U  U      S
CCCC   A  A  LLLL   CCCC   UUUU  LLLL   UUUU   SSSS
```

Problem 6

Write a program that READs the lengths of the legs of a right triangle from a DATA card and computes the angles (in radians) and the length of the hypotenuse. Use the built-in function ATAN to compute the arctangents.

Problem 7   *Tabulate Function*

Tabulate the function

$$y = [x**3 - 17*(x**2)+42*x - 2]/[5*(x**4)+12]$$

for $x = -20, -19, -18, \ldots, 19, 20$. Output should be in the form of a table with labels. Use this information to sketch (by hand) the graph of this function (on graph paper) and submit the graph with the program. Use a function statement to evaluate the function.

Problem 8   *Tabulation of Functions*

Write a program which computes the values F(X) of a function F for X = L, L+H, L+2*H, . . . , U. Use a statement function to define F(X) and use a READ statement to determine L, U, H.

Problem 9   *Fibonacci Sequence*

Write a program to compute and print the first twenty terms of the Fibonacci sequence. This sequence 1, 1, 2, 3, 5, 8, . . . has the property that each number (beyond the first two) is the sum of the two previous numbers. Also print the ratio R of successive numbers and (2*R-1)**2. [*Note:* It is known that R approaches

$$[1 + SQRT(5)]/2.$$

Thus, (2*R-1)**2 should approach 5.]

Try running this program for the first 40 terms of the sequence.

Problem 10

For each of the following functions and *x*-values, compute:

$$\frac{f(x + h) - f(x)}{h}$$

for $h = 1, 0.5, 0.1, 0.05, 0.01, 0.001, 0.0001$
and for $h = -1, -0.5, -0.1, -0.05, -0.01, -0.001, -0.0001$.

(a) $f(x) = x**2 + 2*x - 5$ and $x = 1$.

(b) $f(x) = x$

Problem 11

Write a program to approximate

$$\lim_{x \to 0} f(x)$$

by choosing values of x that converge to 0. Print your results in a table with appropriate headings. Test your program with the functions $f(x) = (x + 1)**2, f(x) = (\sin x)/x,$ and $f(x) = (1 - \cos x)/x$.

Problem 12   *Tabulate Near a Singular Point*

Write a program to tabulate the function

$$y = [1 - x**(1/2)]/[1 - x**(1/3)]$$

for the values:

$$x = 0.00, 0.50, 0.90, 0.95, 0.99, 0.999, 1.001, 1.01, 1.05, 1.10, 1.50, 2.00.$$

Use a READ statement with data cards to enter the values of x. The output of the program should be in the form of a table with labels:

X	Y
0	1
0.5	...
.	
.	

Use the output to guess the limit of the function as x approaches 1.

Problem 13   *Roundoff Error*
Use a DO loop to tabulate the function

$$y = [1 - x**(1/2)] / [1 - x**(1/3)]$$

when

$$x = 1 + (0.1)**j \quad \text{for } j = 1, 2, 3, \ldots, 17.$$

Tabulate the output with labeled columns for j, x and y. Can you use the output to guess the limit of the function as x approaches 1? Attempt to explain any erratic behavior of the values for y.

Problem 14   *Newton's Method*
Write a program that will use Newton's Method to find approximations to the roots of a differentiable function. [Newton's Method is described in Section 5.1.] Use function statements to give the definitions of the function and its derivative (so the program may be easily altered and applied to other functions). Use the program to find the roots of the function

$$[x**3 - 17*(x**2) + 42*x - 2] / [5*(x**4) + 12]$$

to such a degree of accuracy that the absolute value of the difference of two successive approximations is less than 0.00004. Print the value of each approximation as it is generated; also print the corresponding value of the function. [*Note:* You should also submit the output of two test cases and hand computations which show the values to be expected for each test.]

[*Note:* If you are currently taking Calculus I you may not have covered the material required to write this program by this time.]

Applications of Newton's Method
In the following several problems, use calculus to obtain an equation for the quantities requested. Then use Newton's Method to solve the equation.

Problem 15
Find two positive numbers whose sum is 3 and whose fourth powers add up to 26. Hand in a copy of the algebraic manipulations which lead to the program you submit. As a check on your answer, have the program print the numbers, their sum, and the sum of their fourth powers.

[*Note:* If you are currently taking Calculus I you may not have covered the material needed to write this program by this time.]

Problem 16
We know that $\sin x = \cos x$ when $x = \pi/4$ radians. Use Newton's Method to find a value of x in the interval $(0, \pi/2)$ for which

$$\cos x = \tan x.$$

Problem 17   *Minimize Sum of Fourth Powers*
The sum of a number and twice another number is 5. Use calculus to choose the numbers so that the sum of their fourth powers is a minimum. Hand in a copy of the algebraic manipulations which led to the program you submit, but don't prove that the results you obtain actually minimize the sum.

Problem 18   *Minimize Cost of Cylinder*

A cylindrical can with bottom, but no top, is to be fabricated from sheet metal which costs $0.40 per square foot. The two seams (see the figure) each cost 5 cents per linear foot. Assuming no waste when the bottom disk is cut, find the dimensions which minimize the total cost of the can if the volume of the can is to be 1.5 cubic feet. What are the radius, the height, and the minimum cost?

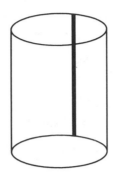

Hand in a copy of the algebraic manipulations which lead to the program you submit.

Problem 19

Locate all local maximums and minimums of the function

$$f(x) = 3/(x+3)**2 + 4/(x-4)**4 + 40/(x**2+4)$$

and decide which are the maximums and which are the minimums.

Problem 20   *Critical Points of a Function*

Locate all local maxima and minima of the function

$$f(x) = (\cos x)**2 + \sin x + \cos x \quad 0 < x < 2\pi$$

and decide which are maxima and which are minima.

Problem 21   *Implicit Function*

When x is greater than or equal to zero, the equation

$$(y-x)**3 \ (y**2+x**2) = 1$$

defines y as a function of x. Tabulate this function for $x = 0.0, 0.1, 0.2, \ldots, 2.0$.

Problem 22   *Norman Window—Fixed Area*

A Norman window, a rectangle surmounted by a semicircular disk, is to be constructed from two different types of glass. The glass for the disk costs $2.50 per square foot while the glass for the rectangle costs $2.00 per square foot. The lead which joins the two pieces of glass and surrounds the whole window costs $0.30 per linear foot.

If the total area of the window is to be 48 square feet, choose the dimensions to minimize the total cost of the materials. What is this minimum cost?

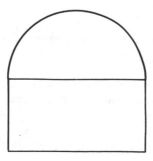

Problem 23   *Norman Window—Fixed Illumination*

A Norman window is to be constructed with no restriction on its size or total area. The amount of light passing through each type of glass in the window is proportional to the area of that glass. The glass for the semicircular disk passes 2 foot-candles per square foot and costs $1.00 per square foot while the glass for the rectangle costs $2.00 per square foot and passes 5 foot-candles per square foot. The cost of the lead that joins the glass and surrounds the whole window is $0.30 per linear foot.

If the window is to pass a total of 297 foot-candles, choose the dimensions of the window to minimize the total cost of the materials. What is this minimum cost?

Problem 24

Determine the constant K so that the line $y = x$ is a tangent for the curve

$$y = K \exp(x/10) - \log x$$

Problem 25 *Minimum of Implicit Function*

When x is nonnegative, the equation

$$y - x = \exp(-4xy)$$

defines y implicitly as a function of x. Find the minimum value of y.

Problem 26 *Bisection Method for Functions*

Write a program that uses the Bisection Method to compute a root (to three decimal places) of a function, given the interval [A, B] that the root lies in. The function should be specified in a FUNCTION statement or subprogram. [The Bisection Method is described in Section 4.2.]

Problem 27 *Comparison of Newton's Method and Bisection Method*

Write a program that will perform both Newton's Method and the Interval Bisection Method for computing the roots of the function F(X). In Newton's Method, use FPRIME(X) for the derivative. When performing each method, count the number of iterations required.

Check the program by computing some square roots, comparing your answers with the function SQRT, and print out the number of iterations required. Run the program for some additional functions of your choice.

[*Note:* If you are currently taking Calculus I you may not have covered the material required to write this program by this time.]

Problem 28 *Upper/Lower Sums*

Prepare a program that will use either an upper sum or a lower sum to approximate the integral of a monotonic function $f(x)$ between limits of integration a and b. The error in the approximation should be less than 0.004 in absolute value. Read the limits of integration and the error bound (0.004) using a READ statement, and have the program compute, and also print, the number of subintervals necessary to achieve the required accuracy. Use a function statement for $f(x)$. This program could be applied to approximate the integral of almost any monotonic function by merely changing the statement and supplying limits of integration and an error bound at the keyboard.

Test the program by applying it to:
(a) $f(x) = 1/x**2$ on the interval (2, 3);
(b) $f(x) = SQRT(x)$ on the interval (1, 4).

Submit the output from these tests along with hand computations to show the values to be expected from each test. Finally, apply the program to

$$f(x) = SQRT(1+x**3)$$

on the interval (-0.5, 1.5). [Upper and lower sums are discussed in Section 5.2.]

Problem 29 *Polynomial Differentiation*

Write a program that will read in: the degree n of a polynomial ($n < 26$); its coefficients $a(1), a(2), \ldots, a(n)$; and a set of values of X. The program should compute, and print out in four parallel columns: the values of X, $p(X)$, $p'(X)$, $p''(X)$, where

$$p(X) = a(1) + a(2)*X + \ldots + a(n)*(X**n)$$

Problem 30 *Symbolic Differentiation*

Write a program that will enter a polynomial as a string of characters and will compute its derivative. Test the program by entering the string 5*X**3 + 3*X – 5. (The answer should be reduced to the form 15*X**2 + 3, rather than being unreduced in the form 5*3*X**2 + 3*X**0 – 0.)

Problem 31   *Symbolic Integration*

Write a program that will enter a polynomial as a string and will compute its antiderivative (with constant term being 0). Test the program by entering the string 5*X**3 + 3*X – 5. (The answer should be in the reduced form 1.25*X**4 + 1.5*X**2 – 5*X, rather than in the unreduced form (5*X**4)/4 + (3*X**2)/2 – (5*X**1)/1.)

Problem 32   *The Trapezoidal Rule*

Write a program which uses the Trapezoidal Rule to approximate the integral of a real-valued function $f(x)$ between limits of integration a and b. Use a function statement or subprogram for the function $f(x)$.

The program should read the limits of integration and number of subintervals using a READ statement. [*Note:* Subscripted variables are not needed in this program.]

Checking of this program is possible because if $f(x)$ is a line, then the Trapezoidal Rule will give an exact value of the integral, regardless of what the limits of integration are or what number of subintervals is used. [The Trapezoidal Rule is discussed in Section 5.3.]

Problem 33   *The Trapezoidal Rule Function Subprogram*

Define a function subprogram TRAPEZ whose value is the Trapezoidal Rule approximation to the integral of a real-valued function $f(x)$ between the limits of integration a and b.

Write a program which incorporates this Trapezoidal Rule function and which READS the limits of integration and number of subintervals.

Problem 34   *Simpson's Rule*

Write a program which uses Simpson's Rule to approximate the integral of a real-valued function $f(x)$ between limits of integration a and b. Use a function subprogram for the function $f(x)$.

The program should read the limits of integration and number of subintervals (an even integer) using a READ statement.

Comprehensive checking of this program is possible because if $f(x)$ is any polynomial of degree three or less, Simpson's Rule will give the exact value of the integral, no matter what the limits of integration or the number of subintervals used (except that the number of subintervals must be an even integer greater than two).

(a) Submit the output of two test cases of your choice along with computations (using antiderivatives) to compute the value expected from each test.

(b) Use the program to approximate the integral of

$$f(x) = 1/(1+x^{**}6)$$

Use –3 and +1 for limits of integration and use 100 subintervals.

[*Note:* Subscripted variables are not needed in this program.]

[Simpson's Rule is described in Section 5.4.]

Problem 35   *Simpson's Rule Function Subprogram*

Create a function subprogram SIMPS whose value is the Simpson Rule approximation to the integral of a real-valued function $f(x)$ between the limits of integration a and b.

Use another function subprogram for the function $f(x)$.

Write a program which incorporates this Simpson-Rule function and which READs the limits of integration and number of subintervals (an even integer).

Comprehensive checking of this program is possible because if $f(x)$ is any polynomial of degree three or less, Simpson's Rule will give the exact value of the integral, no matter what the limits of integration or the number of subintervals used (except that n must be even and greater than two).

(a) Submit the output of two test cases of your choice along with computations (using antiderivatives) to compute the value expected from each test.

(b) Use the program to approximate the integral of

$$f(x) = 1/(x^{**}6+1)$$

Use –1 and +1 for limits of integration and use 100 subintervals.

Do not use subscripted variables here.

Problem 36   *Comparison of Integration Approximation Methods*

Write a program that will perform integration by Upper/Lower Sums, the Trapezoidal Rule, and Simpson's Rule, using the same number of subintervals in each case.

Run the program for the functions $f(x) = x$, $f(x) = x**2$, $f(x) = x**3$, and $f(x) = x**4$ between $a = 1$ and $a = 3$. Compare the results with the integrals you compute yourself.

Problem 37   *Arc Length*
Use Simpson's Rule to compute the length of the arc

$$y = x**3$$

for x between –1 and 2.

Problem 38   *Elliptic Integral*
Compute the function F(k) for $k = 0.0, 0.1, \ldots, 0.9, 1.0$ if F(k) is the integral of

$$\text{SQRT}[1 - (k \sin t)**2]$$

from $t = 0$ to $t = \pi/2$.

Problem 39   *Newton and Area Between Curves*
Find the area of the region bounded by the curves

$$y = \exp(-x) \quad \text{and} \quad y = 2 - x**2$$

Problem 40   *Functions Defined As Integrals*
Write a program to tabulate a function $g(x)$ which is defined to be the integral of a given function $f(t)$ between the limits of integration $t = c$ and $t = x$. (The value for c is a constant but x will vary.) Use Simpson's Rule to produce a table of values with two labeled columns for x and $g(x)$. The program should read the following values using a READ statement:

N = number of subintervals (must be even);
C = lower limit of integration;
F = first value of x in the table;
D = increment for x in the table;
L = last value of x in the table.

Use N = 100 and run the program for each of the following cases to create tables of $g(x)$ for the indicated values of x:

(a) $g(x) = \int_0^x 1 \, dt$ for $x = -3, -2, \ldots, 8$.
        This is a test case since $g(x) = x$.

(b) $g(x) = \int_3^x (3/t**2)dt$ for $x = 2.0. 2.1, 2.2, \ldots, 3.8$.
        This is a test case since $g(x) = (x-3)/x$.

(c) $g(x) = \int_1^x (1/t) \, dt$ for $x = 0.2, 0.3, \ldots, 4.4, 4.5$.
        (*Note:* $1/t$ has no antiderivative that is a rational function.)

Plot the function $g(x)$ for case (c) on graph paper and submit the graph.

CHAPTER 6

Linear Algebra Problems

This chapter was written with Eugene Herman.

Section 6.1: **GAUSSIAN REDUCTION ALGORITHMS**

In computer work, it is increasingly common for the programmer to have to manipulate very large matrices (1,000 by 1,000 or even larger). Thus, algorithms to reduce matrices and solve systems of equations must be designed to minimize the amount of computer storage and computer time needed so that the computations are feasible. A subtle difficulty, and one often compounded by an algorithm with too many computations, is that round-off error can accumulate to such an extent in a large matrix computation that the results are completely wrong. Here we outline a number of techniques for solving equations. Occasionally we will refer the interested reader to *Linear Algebra and Its Applications* by Gilbert Strang (New York: Academic Press, 1976) for more details.

Although many textbooks discuss ways to reduce a matrix, we will concentrate on procedures that differ from some books. In many ways, our techniques will be similar to other methods, so we will not describe the entire algorithm, but only those parts that may be different. We will allow only two row operations in the reduction process: interchanging two rows or replacing a row by that row plus a multiple of another row. Thus the first non-zero entry (the "leading" entry) in each non-zero row need not equal 1. Further, we create zeros below each leading entry but not above. For example, if the original matrix is square, the reduced matrix is *upper triangular.* Our algorithm is sometimes called strict *Gaussian reduction* to distinguish it from *Gauss-Jordan reduction.* The latter algorithm allows rows to be multiplied by non-zero constants and makes each leading entry equal to one. It also creates zeros both below and above each leading entry. The following example, in which we first reduce a matrix by Gaussian elimination and then reduce it further by Gauss-Jordan elimination, shows the many extra steps that the second algorithm requires. (The circled numbers are called the pivots.)

$$
\begin{bmatrix} ⓪ & 0 & -4 & 1 & -3 \\ 2 & 4 & 2 & 0 & 4 \\ 4 & 8 & 0 & 1 & 7 \end{bmatrix}
\begin{array}{c} R_1 \longleftrightarrow R_2 \\ \longrightarrow \\ R_3 \to R_3 - 2R_1 \end{array}
\begin{bmatrix} ② & 4 & -2 & 0 & 4 \\ 0 & 0 & ㊃ & 1 & -3 \\ 0 & 0 & -4 & 1 & -1 \end{bmatrix}
\begin{array}{c} R_3 \to R_3 - R_2 \\ \longrightarrow \\ \text{(the last step of} \\ \text{Gaussian elimination)} \end{array}
$$

$$\begin{bmatrix} ② & 4 & -2 & 0 & 4 \\ 0 & 0 & ④ & 1 & -3 \\ 0 & 0 & 0 & 0 & ② \end{bmatrix} \quad \begin{array}{l} R_1 \to (\tfrac{1}{2})R_1 \\ \xrightarrow{\hspace{2cm}} \\ R_2 \to (-\tfrac{1}{4})R_2 \\ R_3 \to (\tfrac{1}{2})R_3 \end{array} \quad \begin{bmatrix} ① & 2 & -1 & 0 & 2 \\ 0 & 0 & ① & -\tfrac{1}{4} & \tfrac{3}{4} \\ 0 & 0 & 0 & 0 & ① \end{bmatrix} \quad \begin{array}{l} R_1 \to R_1 - 2R_2 \\ \xrightarrow{\hspace{3cm}} \\ R_2 \to R_2 - (\tfrac{3}{4})R_2 \end{array}$$

$$\begin{bmatrix} ① & 2 & -1 & 0 & 0 \\ 0 & 0 & ① & -\tfrac{1}{4} & 0 \\ 0 & 0 & 0 & 0 & ① \end{bmatrix} \quad \begin{array}{l} R_1 \to R_1 + R_2 \\ \xrightarrow{\hspace{2cm}} \end{array} \quad \begin{bmatrix} ① & 2 & 0 & -\tfrac{1}{4} & 0 \\ 0 & 0 & ① & -\tfrac{1}{4} & 0 \\ 0 & 0 & 0 & 0 & ① \end{bmatrix} \quad \begin{array}{l} \text{(end of Gauss-Jordan} \\ \text{elimination)} \end{array}$$

Because of increased efficiency, we use Gaussian, and not Gauss-Jordan, elimination whenever possible, even (as shown below) when solving a system of equations. We do need Gauss-Jordan elimination to compute A^{-1} by reducing the matrix $[A|I]$. However, A^{-1} rarely needs to be computed, and we shall shortly discuss one way to avoid computing A^{-1}. [See pages 5 and 30–31 of Strang's book *Linear Algebra and Its Applications* for details on the number of operations needed for different algorithms.]

Section 6.2: BACK-SUBSTITUTION FOR UPPER TRIANGULAR MATRICES

If we are given an n by n nonsingular matrix A and column n-triple c, we want to compute effectively the unique solution to the system of equations $Ax = c$. In this section, we assume that we have used Gaussian elimination to reduce the augmented matrix $[A|c]$ to the matrix $[B|d]$ where B is an upper triangular matrix. We consider more general matrices in the following sections.

With the upper triangular matrix B, we can avoid Gauss-Jordan elimination by using *back-substitution*. The equations $Bx=d$ have the form

The Upper Triangular Matrix B

$$\begin{bmatrix} b_{11} & b_{12} & b_{13} & \cdot & \cdot & \cdot & b_{1n} \\ 0 & b_{22} & b_{23} & \cdot & \cdot & \cdot & b_{2n} \\ 0 & 0 & b_{33} & \cdot & \cdot & \cdot & b_{3n} \\ \cdot & \cdot & & \cdot & & & \cdot \\ \cdot & \cdot & & & \cdot & & \cdot \\ \cdot & \cdot & & & & \cdot & \cdot \\ 0 & 0 & 0 & & & 0 & b_{nn} \end{bmatrix}$$

$$b_{11}x_1 + b_{12}x_2 + \ldots + b_{1n}x_n = d_1$$
$$b_{22}x_2 + \ldots + b_{2n}x_n = d_2$$
$$\vdots$$
$$b_{nn}x_n = d_n$$

where every b_{ii} is non-zero.

We can solve this system from the bottom up, i.e.,

$$x_n = d_n / b_{nn}$$

$$x_{n-1} = (d_{n-1} - b_{n-1,n}x_n)b_{n-1,n-1}$$

$$x_j = d_j - \sum_{k=j+1}^{n} b_{jk}x_k / b_{jj} \text{ for } j = n, n-1, \ldots, 1$$

[*Note:* A similar approach can be used for *lower triangular* matrices.]

**LOWER-UPPER DECOMPOSITION
FOR GENERAL MATRICES**

Now suppose that we want to solve many equations of the form $Ax = b$ where A is fixed but b changes. We might suspect that it is fastest to compute A^{-1} and then, since $x = A^{-1}b$, simply multiply A^{-1} and b together for each of the different right-hand sides b. This, however, is not the case. It turns out that it is faster to factor A as a product $A = LU$ where U is an upper triangular matrix and L is a lower triangular matrix. We then solve $Ax = b$ or $LUx = b$ by two successive back-substitutions: solve $Ly = b$ for y, and then $Ux = y$ for x. These two systems are solved as explained at the end of the preceding section since both coefficient matrices are triangular. Further, the factors L and U are easy to find, as is shown below. The algorithm for finding L and U is called the *lower-upper decomposition* or *L-U decomposition.*

We will use Gaussian elimination to reduce A and let U be the reduced matrix. Recall, however, that no row interchanges are allowed in the reduction process. If a zero pivot occurs, the decomposition fails and the algorithm must be terminated. [See page 27 of Strang's book *Linear Algebra and Its Applications* for a way to overcome this failure.]

The diagonal entries of L are all equal to 1. We find the entries in the jth column of L below the diagonal as follows. Imagine that we are reducing A to U and are working now on the jth column (with all the preceding columns in their final form). To get zeros below the diagonal, we must perform row operations of the form $R_i \rightarrow R_i - c_i R_j$ for each i for $i = j+1, \ldots, n$. The numbers c_i are the (i, j) entries of the matrix L for $i = j+1, \ldots, n$.

Example. Let

$$A = \begin{bmatrix} 2 & 3 & 4 \\ 4 & 4 & 6 \\ 6 & 10 & 8 \end{bmatrix}$$

let $U_1 = A$, and let $L_1 = I$ (the identity matrix). Then $A = L_1 U_1$ is a (very) modest first step in our factorization algorithm. We now want to use row operations to reduce the first column of U_1. We need

$$U_1 \xrightarrow[\substack{R_2 \longrightarrow R_2 - 2R_1 \\[4pt] R_3 \longrightarrow R_3 - 3R_1}]{} \begin{bmatrix} 2 & 3 & 4 \\ 0 & -2 & -2 \\ 0 & 1 & -4 \end{bmatrix}$$

We name the result U_2. We can go back from U_2 to U_1 if we add $2R_1$ to R_2 and if we add $3R_1$ to R_3. Thus, if

$$T_2 = \begin{bmatrix} 1 & 0 & 0 \\ 2 & 1 & 0 \\ 3 & 0 & 1 \end{bmatrix}$$

we have

$$U_1 = T_2 U_2 \quad \text{and} \quad A = L_1 U_1 = L_1 T_2 U_2 = L_2 U_2$$

where $L_2 = L_1 T_2$.

We now want to reduce the second column of U_2. We need

Step 1

$$
L_1 \qquad\qquad U_1
$$

$$
\begin{bmatrix} 1 & 0 & 0 \\ 0 & 1 & 0 \\ 0 & 0 & 1 \end{bmatrix}
\qquad
\begin{bmatrix} 2 & 3 & 4 \\ 4 & 4 & 6 \\ 6 & 10 & 8 \end{bmatrix}
$$

Step 2

$$
L_2 \qquad\qquad U_2
$$

$$
\begin{bmatrix} 1 & 0 & 0 \\ 2 & 1 & 0 \\ 3 & 0 & 1 \end{bmatrix}
\qquad
\begin{bmatrix} 2 & 3 & 4 \\ 0 & -2 & -2 \\ 0 & 1 & -4 \end{bmatrix}
$$

$$U_2 \xrightarrow{\hspace{4cm}} \begin{bmatrix} 2 & 3 & 4 \\ 0 & -2 & -2 \\ 0 & 0 & -5 \end{bmatrix}$$
$$R_3 \longrightarrow R_3 + (\tfrac{1}{2})R_2$$

We name the result U_3. We can go back from U_2 to U_1 if we subtract $\tfrac{1}{2}R_2$ to R_3.

Thus, if

$$T_3 = \begin{bmatrix} 1 & 0 & 0 \\ 0 & 1 & 0 \\ 0 & -\tfrac{1}{2} & 0 \end{bmatrix}$$

we have $U_2 = T_3 \, U_3$.

Letting $L_3 = L_2 \, T_3$, we have

$$A = L_2 \, U_2 = L_2 \, T_3 \, U_3 = L_3 \, U_3$$

Then $A = L_3 \, U_3$ is the L-U decomposition.

Step 3

$$L_3 \qquad\qquad U_3$$
$$\begin{bmatrix} 1 & 0 & 0 \\ 2 & 1 & 0 \\ 3 & -\tfrac{1}{2} & 1 \end{bmatrix} \qquad \begin{bmatrix} 2 & 3 & 4 \\ 0 & -2 & -2 \\ 0 & 0 & -5 \end{bmatrix}$$

At each step, we see that L_j is obtained from L_{j-1} by modifying the j–1st column to reflect the row operations needed in reducing the j–1st column of U_{j-1}.

The fact that $A = L_i U_i$ for each i in our example gives a hint of the proof of the algorithm in general. The row operation $R_i \rightarrow R_i - cR_j$, which changes a matrix B into a matrix C, also changes the identity matrix into an elementary matrix E with the property that $EB = C$. So $B = E^{-1} C$, where E^{-1} is the elementary matrix obtained from the identity matrix by the row operation $R_i \rightarrow R_i + cR_j$. Thus, DE^{-1}, for any matrix D, is the matrix obtained from D by the column operation $C_i \rightarrow C_i + cC_j$.

We use these observations to construct the following proof of the algorithm. As in the example, let U_j be the result of having reduced the first j–1 columns of A to their final form, and let L_j be the identity matrix but with the first j–1 columns in final form for L.

We must show that $A = L_n U_n$. We know that $A = L_1 U_1$, since $L_1 = I$ and $U_1 = A$.

We now proceed by induction, showing that whenever $A = L_j U_j$, then $A = L_{j+1} U_{j+1}$. The desired result follows easily. We know that $A = L_1 J_1$, since $L_1 = I$ and $U_1 = A$. We must show that $A = L_n U_n$. This will follow easily by induction if we can show that whenever $A = L_j U_j$, then $A = L_{j+1} U_{j+1}$. Since $E_1 \ldots E_k U_j = U_{j+1}$ for some elementary matrices E_i, described in the preceding discussion, we have $L_j U_j = L_j E_k^{-1} \ldots E_1^{-1} U_{j+1}$. In addition, by our remarks above, $L_{j+1} = L_j E_k^{-1} \ldots E_1^{-1}$, since the jth column of L_j is the jth standard basis vector in R^n with a zero in every position except the jth, which has a one. Thus, $L_j U_j$ implies $L_{j+1} U_{j+1}$ and our induction proof is complete.

Section 6.4: SOLVING SYSTEMS BY ITERATION

Even "exact" algorithms, such as solving a system of equations by Gaussian reduction and back-substitution, often yield only approximate solutions when executed by a computer (because of round-off error). Thus, an iterative method (one where we make successively better approximations to the solution) may give solutions that are as accurate and may be much faster.

Given an n by n nonsingular matrix $A = (a_{ij})$ and a column n-tuple b, we want to approximate successively the unique solution to the equations $Ax = b$. We write $A = D + R$, where

$$
D = \begin{bmatrix}
a_{11} & 0 & . & . & . & 0 \\
0 & a_{22} & 0 & . & . & 0 \\
. & & . & & & . \\
. & & & . & & . \\
. & & & & . & 0 \\
0 & . & . & . & 0 & a_{nn}
\end{bmatrix}
$$

is the matrix with the same diagonal entries as A and zeros elsewhere and where $R = A - D$. Our first algorithm, called *Jacobi iteration*, is:

1. let $x^0 = (0, \ldots, 0)$ (a rather arbitrary initial guess at the solution)
2. let $x^{k+1} = D^{-1}(b - Rx^k)$ for $k = 0, 1, 2, \ldots$ (the iterative step)
3. stop and declare x^{k+1} a satisfactory solution if $\|x^{k+1} - x^k\| < \epsilon$, where we have chosen ϵ in advance to be some small positive number.

Notes

(a) We can understand why this method might work by considering what happens in step 2, if for some vector x, $x = D^{-1}(b - Rx)$. Then $Dx = b - Rx$ or $Ax = b$, so x is the desired solution. Thus, we hope to get nearer the exact solution by successively computing $D^{-1}(b - Rx^k)$.

(b) Jacobi iteration is possible only when D^{-1} exists, i.e., when the diagonal entries of A are all non-zero. Even then, the successive approximations x^k may not be getting close to the exact solution x or may be getting close to x too slowly. [See Section 7.4 of Strang's book *Linear Algebra and Its Applications* for theorems in which the vectors x^k do get closer and closer to the exact solution.]

(c) There is clearly no unique way to decide when to stop iterating. Not only is the choice of ϵ rather arbitrary, but criteria other than $\|x^{k+1} - x^k\| < \epsilon$ can be used.

(d) It may help to write out step 2 in coordinates. Let $x^k = y = (y_1, \ldots, y_n)$ and $x^{k+1} = z = (z_1, \ldots, z_n)$ to avoid mixing superscripts and subscripts. If $b = (b_1, \ldots, b_n)$, then step 2 is $Da = b - Ry$ or

$$
a_{11}z_1 = b_1 - (a_{12}y_2 + \ldots + a_{1n}y_n)
$$
$$
.
$$
$$
.
$$
$$
.
$$
$$
a_{nn}z_n = b_n - (a_{n1}y_1 + \ldots + a_{nn-1}y_{n-1})
$$

Divide the *i*th equation above by a_{ii} and we have the *i*th component of z ($= x^{k+1}$) for each $i = 1, \ldots, n$.

(e) A slight variation of Jacobi iteration, called *Gauss-Seidel iteration*, is faster and easier to program, and takes less computer storage. In the system of equations in note d, we see that each equation computes one coordinate of the new iterate x^{k+1}, but uses none of these new coordinates in the right-hand side (in place of the coordinates of y) until all n coordinates of x^{k+1} are computed. Instead, we can call the solution of the first equation y_1, not z_1. We use this new y_1 in the second equation to compute z_2 (but call it y_2); we use the new y_1 and y_2 in the third equation, etc. Step 2 of Gauss-Seidel iteration is:

$$a_{11}y_1 = b_1 - (a_{12}y_2 + \ldots + a_{1n}y_n)$$

.

.

.

$$a_{nn}y_n = b_n - (a_{n1}y_1 + \ldots + a_{nn-1}y_{n-1})$$

Section 6.5: **COMPUTING EIGENVALUES**
BY ITERATION

Machine computation of eigenvalues done by computing the characteristic polynomial and then finding its roots is undesirable, because the procedure is very slow and round-off errors are likely to accumulate rapidly. The iterative *power method,* which we discuss here, often leads rapidly to a good approximation to the eigenvalue with the largest absolute value and a corresponding eigenvector.[†] (This eigenvalue is usually the most significant in applications.)

Given an n by n matrix A, we want to solve the equation $Ax = cx$ or $(1/c)Ax = x$ for the vector x and the scalar c, where $x \neq 0$. (c is called an *eigenvalue* corresponding to the *eigenvector x.*). Our algorithm is:

1. Let $x^0 = (1, 0, \ldots, 0)$ [a rather arbitrary initial guess at the desired eigenvector].
2. Let $a_k =$ the first component of Ax^k and let $x^{k+1} = (1/a_k)Ax^k$ for $k = 0, 1, 2, \ldots$ [the iterative step].
3. Stop when $|a_{k+1} - a_k| < \epsilon$, where we have chosen ϵ in advance to be some small positive number. Declare a_{k+1} and x^{k+1} to be satisfactory approximations to the eigenvalue with the largest absolute value and a corresponding eigenvector, respectively.

We sketch a proof that a_k and x^k do get closer and closer to the exact solutions of the problem under certain circumstances. Suppose A has n linearly independent eigenvectors $u^1, \ldots, u^n$. Let $c_1, \ldots, c_n$ denote the corresponding eigenvalues and suppose further that $|c_1| \leqslant |c_2| \leqslant \ldots \leqslant |c_{n-1}| < |c_n|$. Then

$$(1, 0, \ldots, 0) = x^0 = r_1 u^1 + \ldots + r_n u^n$$

for some scalars $r_1, \ldots, r_n$, since we assumed that the eigenvectors form a basis. So

$$Ax^0 = r_1 Au^1 + \ldots + r_n Au^n = r_1 c_1 u^1 + \ldots + r_n c_n u^n$$

and $$x^1 = (1/a_0)Ax^c = (1/a_0)(r_1 c_1 u^1 + \ldots + r_n c_n u^n)$$

where x^1, like x^0, has 1 as its first component because of the division by a_0. Continuing, we get

$$x^k = (1/a_0 \ldots a_{k-1})(r_1 c_1^k u^1 + \ldots + r_n c_n^k u^n)$$

or $$(1/c_n^k)x^k = (1/a_0 \ldots a_{k-1})(r_1 (c_1/c_n)^k u^1 + \ldots + r_{n-1} (c_{n-1}/c_n)^k u^{n-1} + r_n u^n)$$

Since $|c_i/c_n| < 1$, $(c_i/c_n)^k$ gets very small as k gets large (for all $i < n$). Thus,

$$(1/c_n^k)x^k \approx (1/a_0 \ldots a_{k-1})r_n u^n$$

where $\approx$ means approximately equal to. So x^k is nearly a scalar multiple of the eigenvector u^n. Since,

[†]See Section 7.4 of Strang's book for a more detailed discussion of this and other methods, including some which yield all the eigenvalues.

however, for large k, x^k, and x^{k+1} are both nearly scalar multiples of u^n, and since both have 1 as their first component, they must both be nearly the *same* scalar multiple of u^n. Thus,

$$x^{k+1} \approx x^k \approx ru^n \quad \text{for some scalar } r$$

And since $a_k x^{k+1} = Ax^k$, then

$$a_k ru^n \approx Aru^n = rAu^n = rc_n u^n$$

and so $a_k \approx c_n$.

Section 6.6: LINEAR ALGEBRA PROBLEMS

Problem 1
Write a program that computes the components of the vector that goes from one point in the plane to a second point.

Problem 2
Write a program that computes the components of the vector in space that goes from one point to another point.

Problem 3
Use WRITE and FORMAT statements to write out the message:

```
L        III    N  N    EEEE    AA       RRRR
L        I      NN N    E       A  A     R  R
L        I      N NN    EEEE    AAAA     RRR
L        I      N  N    E       A  A     R  R
LLLL     III    N  N    EEEE    A  A     R  R
```

Problem 4
Write a program that will READ two points in the plane from data cards and will find a vector from the first point to the second one.

Problem 5
Write a program that will READ two points in space and compute a vector from the first point to the second one.

Problem 6
Write a program that will compute the product of any scalar and any ordered triple (a vector in space). Read in the scalar 3.5 and the vector (−2.99, 0, .603) from two data cards.

Problem 7
Write a program that will compute the length of any ordered triple. READ in the vector (−2, 6.1, 0.023) from a data card.

Problem 8
Do the same as in the preceding problem, but compute instead a vector of length 1 in the same direction as the given vector (assuming the given vector is non-zero).

Problem 9
Write a program that will compute the sum of any two ordered triples. READ in the vectors (2.179, −5, 6.33) and (−5.322, 14, 3.67) from data cards.

Problem 10
Do the same as in the preceding problem, but compute instead the dot product (i.e., inner product) of the two vectors.

Problem 11
Do the same as in the preceding problem, but compute instead the projection of the first vector onto the second vector (assuming the second vector is non-zero).

Problem 12
Write a program that will compute the cosine of the angle between any two non-zero ordered triples and also the degree measure of that angle. Read in the two pairs of vectors:

$$(3.2, 4.31, -5.05) \quad \text{and} \quad (6.22, 0.17, -2.39)$$
$$(3.2, 4.31, -5.05) \quad \text{and} \quad (-5.93, 0.08, 1.87)$$

Hint: Once you have the cosine of the angle, the angle (in radians) can be found using the built-in function ATAN, since

$$(\sec x)^{**}2 + (\tan x)^{**}2 = 1, \quad (\tan x)^{**}2 = 1 - 1/(\cos x)^{**}2$$

Problem 13
Write a program that will compute the product of any scalar and any *n*-tuple. Use the program to compute:

$$3.625*(5.01, 5.02, 5.03, \ldots, 5.12)$$

Problem 14
Write a program that will compute the length of any *n*-tuple. Use the program to compute the length of:

$$(5.01, 5.02, 5.03, \ldots, 5.12)$$

Problem 15
Write a program that will compute the vector of length 1 in the same direction as any given vector (i.e., *n*-tuple where *n* < 31). Use the program on the vector:

$$(5.01, 5.02, 5.03, \ldots, 5.12)$$

Problem 16
Write a program that will compute the sum of any two *n*-tuples. Use the program to compute:

$$(5.01, 5.02, 5.03, \ldots, 5.12) + (6.8, -6.7, 6.6, -6.5, \ldots, 5.8, -5.7)$$

Problem 17
Do the same as in the preceding problem, but compute instead the dot product (i.e., inner product) of the two vectors.

Problem 18
Write a program that will compute the projection of one *n*-tuple onto another (assuming the second *n*-tuple is non-zero), where *n* < 31. Use the program to compute the projection of:

$$(1.01, 2.02, 3.03, \ldots, 2.12) \quad \text{on} \quad (0.15, 0.14, 0.13, \ldots, 0.04)$$

Problem 19
Write a program that will compute the cosine of the angle between any two non-zero *n*-tuples and also the degree measure of that angle. Use the program to find the angle between:

$$(1.01, 2.02, 3.03, \ldots, 12.12) \quad \text{and} \quad (0.15, 0.14, 0.13, \ldots, 0.04)$$

Problem 20
Write a program that will compute any linear combination of *m* *n*-tuples, where *m, n* < 21. Use the program to compute:

$$3.1*(1, 2, \ldots, 11) + 6.8*(0.11, 0.10, 0.9, \ldots, 0.1) - 5.3*(-7, -6, -5, \ldots, 2, 3) + 0.32*(0.6, 0.8, 0.10, \ldots, 1.6)$$

Problem 21   *Gram-Schmidt*
Write a program that uses the Gram-Schmidt process to find an orthonormal basis for the subspace spanned by any given set of *m* linearly independent *n*-tuples, where *m, n* < 21. Use the program on the vectors:

$$(1.01, 1.02, 1.03, \ldots, 1.12), \quad (1.1, 1.2, 1.3, 0.04, 0.05, 0.06, \ldots, 0.12),$$
$$(0.9, 0.8, 0.07, 0.06, 0.05, \ldots, 0, -0.01, -0.02), \quad (-5, 0.2, 0.3, 0.4, \ldots, 1.2)$$

Problem 22
Write a program that will compute the product of any scalar and any *m* by *n* matrix, where *m, n* < 21. Use the program to compute:

$$7.65 * \begin{bmatrix} 0.1 & 0.2 & \cdots & 1.0 & 1.1 \\ 0.2 & 0.4 & \cdots & 2.0 & 2.2 \\ 0.3 & 0.6 & \cdots & 3.0 & 3.3 \\ \cdot & \cdot & & \cdot & \cdot \\ \cdot & \cdot & & \cdot & \cdot \\ \cdot & \cdot & & \cdot & \cdot \\ 1.2 & 2.4 & \cdots & 12.0 & 13.2 \end{bmatrix}$$

Problem 23

Write a program that will compute the sum of any two m by n matrices, where $m, n < 16$. Use the program to compute:

$$\begin{bmatrix} 0.1 & 0.2 & \ldots & 1.0 & 1.1 \\ 0.2 & 0.4 & \ldots & 2.0 & 2.2 \\ 0.3 & 0.6 & \ldots & 3.0 & 3.3 \\ \cdot & & & \cdot & \cdot \\ \cdot & & & \cdot & \cdot \\ \cdot & & & \cdot & \cdot \\ 1.2 & 2.4 & \ldots & 12.0 & 13.2 \end{bmatrix} + \begin{bmatrix} 0.0 & \ldots & 0.0 \\ 0.1 & \ldots & 0.1 \\ 0.2 & \ldots & 0.2 \\ \cdot & & \cdot \\ \cdot & & \cdot \\ \cdot & & \cdot \\ 1.1 & \ldots & 1.1 \end{bmatrix}$$

Problem 24

Write a program that will compute the product of any m by n matrix and any n by p matrix, where $m, n, p < 16$. Use the program to compute:

$$\begin{bmatrix} 0.1 & 0.2 & \ldots & 1.0 & 1.1 \\ 0.2 & 0.4 & \ldots & 2.0 & 2.2 \\ 0.3 & 0.6 & \ldots & 3.0 & 3.3 \\ \cdot & \cdot & & \cdot & \cdot \\ \cdot & \cdot & & \cdot & \cdot \\ \cdot & \cdot & & \cdot & \cdot \\ 1.2 & 2.4 & \ldots & 12.0 & 13.2 \end{bmatrix} * \begin{bmatrix} 1 & 0.5 & 0.25 & 0.125 \\ 2 & 1.0 & 0.50 & 0.250 \\ 3 & 1.5 & 0.75 & 0.375 \\ \cdot & \cdot & \cdot & \cdot \\ \cdot & \cdot & \cdot & \cdot \\ \cdot & \cdot & \cdot & \cdot \\ 11 & 5.5 & 2.75 & 1.375 \end{bmatrix}$$

Problem 25 *Projection of Vectors*

Write a program that computes the projection of a given vector in R^n onto the column space of a given $n \times m$ matrix (i.e., the subspace of R^n generated by the columns of the specified $n \times m$ matrix).

Problem 26 *Back-substitution*

Write a program that will solve any system of n equations with n unknowns, where $n < 21$ and where the matrix of coefficients is upper triangular and non-singular, using only back-substitution. (This program will be useful as part of later programs.) Use the program on the system $Ax = b$, where

$$A = \begin{bmatrix} 1 & 2 & 3 & \ldots & 11 \\ 0 & 2 & 3 & \ldots & 11 \\ 0 & 0 & 3 & \ldots & 11 \\ \cdot & \cdot & \cdot & & \cdot \\ \cdot & \cdot & \cdot & & \cdot \\ \cdot & \cdot & \cdot & & \cdot \\ 0 & 0 & 0 & \ldots & 11 \end{bmatrix} \quad \text{and} \quad b = (0.1, 0.2, 0.3, \ldots, 1.1)$$

[See Section 6.2 for a description of back-substitution.]

Problem 27 *Lower-Upper Decomposition*

Write a program that will perform the L-U decomposition on any non-singular n by n matrix with non-zero pivots, where $n < 16$. (This program will be useful as a part of later programs.) Use the program on the 11 by 11 matrix $A = [a(i, j)]$, where

$$a(i, j) = i*(12{-}j) \quad \text{when } i < j \text{ and}$$
$$a(i, j) = j*(12{-}i) \quad \text{otherwise}$$

[Lower-upper decomposition is discussed in Section 6.3.]

Problem 28 *Gaussian Reduction*

Write a program that will reduce any m by n matrix (where $m, n < 21$) using strict Gaussian elimination. (This program will be useful as a part of later programs.) Use the program on the matrix

$$\begin{bmatrix} 1 & 2 & 3 & 4 & 5 & \ldots & 11 \\ 2 & 4 & 3 & 4 & 5 & \ldots & 11 \\ 3 & 6 & 3 & 4 & 5 & \ldots & 11 \\ 1 & 2 & 1 & 2 & 3 & \ldots & 9 \end{bmatrix}$$

[See Section 6.1 for some comments on Gaussian reduction.]

Problem 29   *Gauss-Jordan Reduction*

Do the same as in the Gaussian reduction problem, but use Gauss-Jordan elimination instead of strict Gaussian. [See Section 6.1 for some comments on Gauss-Jordan reduction.]

Problem 30   *Solving a System by Factoring*

Write a program that uses your back-substitution and L-U decomposition programs as subprograms to solve any system of n equations with n unknowns, where $n < 21$ and where the matrix of coefficients is non-singular and has non-zero pivots. Use the program on the system $Ax = b$, where A is the matrix in the L-U decomposition problem and where

$$b = (1, 0.2, 3, 0.4, 5, 0.6, 7, 0.8, 9, 1, 11)$$

[See notes in sections 6.2 and 6.3 for comments on these techniques.]

Problem 31   *Solving a System by Reduction*

Do the same as in the preceding problem, but use back-substitution and Gaussian reduction as subprograms instead. [See notes in Sections 6.1 and 6.2 for a discussion of these techniques.]

Problem 32

Do the same as in problem 30 above, but use your Gauss-Jordan reduction program as a subprogram instead.

Problem 33   *Determinants*

Write a program that uses your Gaussian reduction program as a subprogram to compute the determinant of any n by n matrix, where $n < 21$. Use the program on the matrix A in the L-U decomposition problem. [*Note:* The determinant of a triangular matrix is just the product of the diagonal entries.]

Problem 34   *Linear Independence of n-tuples*

Write a program that uses your Gaussian reduction program as a subprogram to test whether any given set of m n-tuples is linearly independent (where $m, n < 21$). Use the program to test whether the following vectors are linearly independent:

$$(1.01, 1.02, 1.03, \ldots, 1.12), \quad (1.1, 1.2, 1.3, 0.04, 0.05, 0.06, \ldots, 0.12)$$
$$(0.9, 0.8, 0.07, 0.06, 0.05, \ldots, 0, -0.01, -0.02), (-5, 0.2, 0.3, 0.4, \ldots, 1.2)$$

Problem 35

Write a program that uses your Gaussian reduction program as a subprogram to select a set of basis vectors for a vector space V from a given set of m n-tuples with span V (where $m, n < 21$). Use the program on the vectors:

$$(1.01, 1.02, 1.03, \ldots, 1.12), \quad (1.1, 1.2, 1.3, 0.04, 0.05, 0.06, \ldots, 0.12),$$
$$(0.09, 0.18, 0.27, -1, -1, \ldots, -1), \quad (0.09, 0.08, 0.07, 0.06, \ldots, 0, -0.01, -0.02).$$
$$(-5, 0.2, 0.3, 0.4, \ldots, 1.2), \quad (0.815, 0.621, 0.035, 0.084, 0.133, 0.182, 0.231, 0.28, 0.329, 0.378, 0.428, -1.602)$$

Problem 36

Write a program that uses your Gauss-Jordan reduction program as a subprogram to find a basis for the solution space of any homogeneous system of m equations with n unknowns, where $m, n < 21$. Use the program on the system $Ax = 0$, where

$$A = \begin{bmatrix} 1.01 & 1.02 & 1.03 & & & & & \cdots & & & & 1.2 \\ 1.1 & 1.2 & 1.3 & 0.04 & 0.05 & 0.06 & & \cdots & & & & 0.12 \\ 0.09 & 0.18 & 0.27 & -1 & -1 & -1 & & \cdots & & & & -1 \\ 0.09 & 0.08 & 0.07 & 0.06 & 0.05 & 0.04 & & \cdots & 0.0 & -0.01 & -0.02 \\ -5 & 0.2 & 0.3 & 0.4 & & & & \cdots & & & & 1.2 \\ 0.815 & 0.621 & 0.035 & 0.084 & 0.133 & 0.182 & 0.231 & 0.28 & 0.329 & 0.378 & 0.428 & -1.602 \end{bmatrix}$$

Problem 37 *Matrix Inverses*

Write a program that uses your Gauss-Jordan reduction program as a subprogram to compute the inverse of any n by n non-singular matrix, where $n < 12$. Use the program to invert the matrix A in the L-U decomposition problem.

Problem 38 *Solving Systems by Iteration—(i)*

Write a program that uses Jacobi iteration to try and solve any system of n equations with n unknowns, where $n < 21$. The program should read in the error bound. Use the program with the error bound 0.00001 on the system $Ax = b$, where A is the matrix with

$$A(i,j) = \begin{cases} i + j & \text{if } i = j \\ 1/(i+j) & \text{if } i \neq j. \end{cases}$$

and where

$$b = (1, 0.2, 3, 0.4, 5, 0.6, 7, 0.8, 9, 1, 11)$$

[Jacobi iteration is discussed in Section 6.4.]

Problem 39 *Solving Systems by Iteration—(ii)*

Write a program that uses Gauss-Seidel iteration to try and solve any system of n equations with n unknowns, where $n < 21$. The program should read in the error bound. Use the program with the error bound 0.00001 on the system $Ax = b$, where A and b are the matrices used in Problem 38.

[Gauss-Seidel iteration is discussed in Section 6.4.]

Problem 40 *Eigenvalues*

Write a program that uses the power method to try to find the eigenvalue with largest absolute value for any n by n matrix, where $n < 21$. The program should read in the error bound. Use the program with the error bound 0.00001 on the matrix A in the L-U decomposition problem.

[The power method is discussed in Section 6.5.]

Problem 41

Write a program to solve the system $Ax = b$, where $A = [a(i, j)]$ is the 30 × 30 matrix with

$$a(i, j) = i*(31 - j) \quad \text{when } i < j.$$
$$a(i, j) = j*(31 - i) \quad \text{otherwise}$$

and where $b = (1, 0.2, 3, 0.4, 5, 0.6, \ldots, 29, 3.0)$. You are to find and use the L-U decomposition of A to solve the problem. *Warning:* A is so large that you will be forced to create a data file to store the factors L and U.

Problem 42 *Matrix Storage on a File*

(a) Write a program that creates a file **MATRIX.DAT** on the disk, and stores the entries of a specified n × n matrix in the file.

(b) Modify each of the following programs so that they will use the matrix stored in the disk file:
  (1) the program 'Solving a System by Factoring';
  (2) the program 'Solving a System by Reduction';
  (3) the program 'Solving a System by Jacobi Iteration';
  (4) the program 'Solving a System by Gauss-Seidel Iteration';
  (5) the program computing 'Eigenvalues' by the power method.

In Parts 2 through 5, check the modified programs by running them with the matrices used previously.

CHAPTER 7

Statistics Problems
(Precalculus Section)

This chapter was written with Thomas Moberg.

Section 7.1: SOME STATISTICAL DEFINITIONS

In definitions 1–9, we assume that a sample of size N is represented by an array X(1), X(2), . . . , X(N). In definitions 3–5, we assume that these numbers have been sorted so that they are in ascending order. In definitions 7–9, we assume that we have a second sample of size M which is represented by an array Y(1), . . . , Y(M). [For definitions 6–9, however, we do not assume that the X array is in order.]

1. Sample Mean

The sample mean is

$$\bar{X} = \frac{X(1) + X(2) + \ldots + X(N)}{N}$$

2. Sample Variance

The sample variance is

$$S^2 = \frac{(X(1) - \bar{X})^2 + (X(2) - \bar{X})^2 + \ldots + (X(N) - \bar{X})^2}{N - 1}$$

3. Sample Median

Roughly, the median of a list of numbers is the middle value of the list. More precisely, suppose X(1), . . . , X(N) are in ascending order.

If there is an odd number of values in the list, the median is the middle value.
If there is an even number of integers in the list, the median is the average of the two "middle" values.

For example, 8 is the median of the numbers 2, 5, 8, 11, 13, and 6.5 is the median of 2, 5, 9, 11.

[*Note:* If N is odd, then the integer division N/2 does not retain the remainder of 0.5. Thus, if N is odd, (N/2)*2 is not equal to N. Hence, we can determine if an integer N is even or odd in our program by checking if (N/2)*2 $\neq$ N.]

4. Sample Percentile

We let P be a number between 0 and 1, and we want to compute the 100P percentile of the sample. For example, if we want the 50th percentile, then P = .5, and if we want the 75th percentile, then P = .75. We can now give the formula for finding the 100P percentile:

If N*P is an integer, the 100Pth sample percentile is the Kth smallest observation X(K), where

$$K = INT(N * P) + 1$$

If N*P is not an integer, the 100Pth sample percentile is the average of the Kth and K + 1st smallest observation where K = INT(N * P). That is, we must compute:

$$[X(INT(N*P) + X(INT(N*P) + 1)]/2$$

[*Note:* The X array must be in ascending order for this computation.]

5. Sample Trimmed Mean

We compute the mean after deleting some of the elements in the sample. More precisely, a P% trimmed mean is computed by:

(a) Computing P% of N, which we call M.
(b) Deleting M/2 elements from the bottom of our sample and M/2 elements from the top. (If M/2 is not an integer, we take the closest integer.)
(c) Computing the mean on the remaining elements. For example, suppose our sample contains 9 elements 2, 4, 7, 9, 10, 12, 15, 18, 19, and suppose we want to compute a 20% trimmed mean. We take M = 20% of 9 = 1.8. Then M/2 = 0.9. We round M/2 to the nearest integer 1. We then delete 1 element from the bottom of our sample and 1 from the top. We compute the mean of the remaining elements 4, 7, 9, 10, 12, 15, 18 to get a 20% trimmed mean of 10.7.

6. t-Statistic (One Sample)

The *t*-statistic, which under certain conditions behaves like Student's *t*-distribution with $n-1$ degrees of freedom, is defined by

$$t = \frac{\overline{X} - \mu_x}{S/\sqrt{N}}$$

where u_x is the hypothesized mean of the sampled population.

7. t-Statistic (Two Independent Samples)

If the X sample (with sample mean $\overline{X}$ and sample variance S_x^2) is drawn from a population with hypothesized mean μ_x, and if the Y sample (with sample mean $\overline{Y}$ and sample variance S_y^2) is drawn from a population with hypothesized mean μ_y, and if

$$S_p^2 = \frac{(N-1)S_x^2 + (M-1)S_y^2}{N + M - 2}$$

then the t-statistic is defined by

$$t = \frac{(\bar{X} - \bar{Y}) - (\mu_x - \mu_y)}{S_p \sqrt{1/N + 1/M}}$$

with $N + M - 2$ degrees of freedom.

8. t-Statistic (Two Dependent Samples)

Assume that the X sample and Y sample represent paired (dependent) data, with $N = M$. Let $D(I) = X(I) - Y(I)$, $I = 1, 2, \ldots, N$, be the array of differences where the population of differences has a hypothesized mean μ_D. Let $\bar{D}$ be the mean of the sample differences, and let S_D^2 be the variance of the difference values. Then the t-statistic is defined to be

$$t = \frac{\bar{D} - \mu_D}{S_D / \sqrt{N}} \quad \text{with N–1 degrees of freedom}$$

9. Pearson Product-Moment Correlation Coefficient

The Pearson product-moment correlation coefficient is

$$R = \frac{(X(1) - \bar{X})(Y(1) - \bar{Y}) + (X(2) - \bar{X})(Y(2) - \bar{Y}) + \ldots + (X(N) - \bar{X})(Y(N) - \bar{Y})}{(N-1) S_x S_y}$$

where the X sample has mean $\bar{X}$ and standard deviation S_x, and the Y sample has mean $\bar{Y}$ and standard deviation S_Y, and both samples are the same size ($M = N$).

10. Chi-Square Distribution

We measure the frequencies $a_1, \ldots, a_n$ of events that have actually occurred and compare them with the expected frequencies $e_1, \ldots, e_n$ of those events. Then the chi-square statistic is

$$\frac{(a_1 - e_1)^2}{e_1} + \frac{(a_2 - e_2)^2}{e_2} + \ldots + \frac{(a_n - e_n)^2}{e_n}$$

Section 7.2: COMPUTING BINOMIAL DISTRIBUTIONS AND PROBABILITIES

If we have n distinct cards, the number of different hands each containing k cards is expressed by the *binomial coefficient:*

$$c(n, k) = \frac{n!}{k!(n - k)!}$$

Recall: $n!$ is defined to be

$$n(n - 1) : (n - 2) \ldots 3 \cdot 2 \cdot 1$$

and $0!$ is defined to be 1.

When flipping a fair coin n times, the probability of getting exactly k leads is

$$\frac{n!}{k!(n-k)!} \left(\frac{1}{2}\right)^n$$

If the coin is not fair, we let p be the probability that a head will occur. (For a fair coin, $p = 0.5$.) Then the probability of getting exactly k heads is given by the *binomial probability*:

$$B(n, k, p) = \frac{n!}{k! \, (n - k)!} \, p^k \, (1 - p)^{n-k}$$

If n is a rather small number, then these expressions can be computed by machine without difficulty. If n is large, however, $n!$, $k!$ and/or $(n - k)!$ may be too large to store directly in the machine. In this case, we perform some algebraic manipulations so that we can avoid computing these large numbers.

Our approach is based on the observation that for $k \geqslant 1$,

$$c(n, k) = \frac{n!}{(n - k)! \, k!} = \frac{n(n - 1) \ldots (k + 2)(k + 1) \cdot k(k - 1) \ldots 3 \cdot 2 \cdot 1}{(n - k)(n - k + 1) \ldots 2 \cdot 1 \cdot k(k - 1) \ldots 3 \cdot 2 \cdot 1}$$

$$= \frac{n(n - 1) \ldots (k + 2)(k + 1)}{(n - k)(n - k + 1) \ldots 2 \cdot 1}$$

Here we see that there are the same number of factors in the numerator as in the denominator of the fraction. Thus, we could rewrite the expression as:

$$c(n, k) = \frac{n}{n - k} \quad \frac{n - 1}{n - k + 1} \quad \cdots \quad \frac{n - i}{n - k + i} \quad \cdots \quad \frac{k + 2}{2} \quad \frac{k + 1}{1}$$

Hence, we can compute $c(n, k)$ by multiplying the series of fractions $(n - i)/(n - k + i)$ together where i starts at 0 and goes to $n - k - 1$.

Once we have $c(n, k)$, we can obtain $B(n, k, p)$ by noting

$$B(n, k, p) = c(n, k) \, p^k \, (1 - p)^{n-k}$$

Section 7.3: STATISTICS PROBLEMS (WITHOUT CALCULUS)

Problem 1

Use WRITE and FORMAT statements to write out the message:

```
SSSS    TTTTT    AA      TTTTT
S         T     A  A       T
SSSS      T     AAAA       T
   S      T     A  A       T     . .
SSSS      T     A  A       T     . .
```

Problem 2

Write a program that will READ the number of times a coin was tossed and the number of heads that occurred from data cards and then will compute and print the percentage of heads and tails that occurred.

Problem 3

Write a program that will READ (from DATA cards) the number of times a die was rolled and the number of times a 1 resulted. The program then should compute and print the percentage of times the 1 occurred.

Problem 4   *Generating Random Numbers*

On many machines, random numbers can be generated on the computer with the built-in function or subroutine RANDU. The numbers generated are distributed uniformly on the interval from 0 to 1. Write a program which will generate 100 random numbers, and print them out in 5 side by side columns. [*Note:* Before doing this problem, check what random number generating functions are available on your machine.]

Problem 5   *Coin Toss Simulation*

Many random processes can be imitated or "simulated" on a computer by using the built-in random number generator to provide the randomness inherent in the process. For example, coin flipping can be simulated by generating a random number, and calling heads if the random number is smaller than 0.5 and calling tails if the random number is bigger than 0.5. Write a program which will simulate the flipping of a coin, and record the results of "flipping the coin" 100 times. Keep track of how many heads and tails occur. [*Note:* See the note for the above problem.]

Problem 6

Write a program that will generate any number of uniform random numbers.

Problem 7

Write a program which will READ a set of data and will find the smallest value in the data set.

Problem 8   *The Range of a Data Set*

Write a program which will READ a set of data and will compute the range (i.e., the smallest value and the largest value) of the set.

Problem 9

Write a program that will READ (from DATA cards) the number of times a die was rolled and the number of times each outcome (1 through 6) occurred. The program should then compute and print the percentage of the time that each face resulted.

Problem 10   *Dice Toss Simulation*

Dice tossing can be simulated on the computer just as coin tossing can. Write a program which will simulate the tossing of two fair dice 100 times. Record the values appearing on each die and the sum of the two values.

Problem 11   *Dice Tossing Frequency Distribution*

Write a program which tosses a pair of dice N times (with N being specified by the user), and displays the results in a frequency distribution. That is, the program should print a table listing the number of times each sum (from 2 to 12) occurs and the frequency (or percentage) for each sum.

Problem 12   *Relative Frequencies and Probabilities of Events*

Write a program which simulates the tossing of two fair dice 1000 times. Keep track of the number of occurrences of each of the following events:

A: 1 appears on the first die.
B: 2 appears on the first die.
C: 2 appears on the second die.
D: The sum of the values appearing on the dice is 3.
E: 1 appears on the first die and 2 appears on the second (A and C).
F: 1 appears on the first die and the sum totals 3 (A and D).

Calculate and print the observed relative frequency (or percentage) of each event, along with *the true probability* of each event.

Problem 13   *Standard Sample Statistics*

Prepare a program that will READ an integer n followed by n real numbers $x(1), x(2), \ldots, x(n)$ and then compute and print:

1. Sample Mean

$$m = (x(1) + x(2) + x(3) + \ldots + x(n))/n$$

2. Sample Variance

$$v = [(x(1)-m)**2 + (x(2)-m)**2 + \ldots + (x(n)-m)**2]/n$$

3. Standard Deviation

$$s = \text{SQRT}(v)$$

4. Fourth Central Moment

$$f = [(x(1)-m)**4 + (x(2)-m)**4 + \ldots + (x(n)-m)**4]/n$$

Test the program by applying it to:

(a) the six numbers 2, 2, 2, 2, 2, 2

(b) the three numbers 1, 2, 6.

Problem 14

Write a program which will generate any number of uniform random numbers specified by the user, and then calculate the mean and variance of the numbers while they are being generated.

Problem 15

Write a program which computes the values $f(x)$ of a function f for $x = 0, 0.1, 0.2, \ldots, 5$. Use a function statement to define $f(x)$. Test the program on the negative exponential probability function $f(x) = 1 - EXP(-a*x)$.

Problem 16   *Tabulation of a Function*

Write a program which computes the values F(X) of a function F for X = L, L+H, L+2*H, ..., U. Use a function statement to define F(X) and use a READ statement to determine L, U, and H. Test the program on the negative exponential density function $F(X) = A*EXP**(-A*X)$, where $x > 0$.

Problem 17   *Binomial Coefficients*

Write a program to compute and print both $n!/k!$ and the binomial coefficient $C(n, k)$ whose definition is

$$C(n, k) = n!/(k!*(n-k)!)$$

The program should be valid for any pair of positive integers n and k for which k is less than n. Apply the program to the pairs (n, k): (5, 2), (5, 1), (5, 4) and (11, 7).

[*Note:* In this program, compute these numbers by finding $n!$, $k!$ and $(n-k)!$. As long as n and k are relatively small, this approach will cause no difficulties. If either n or k is too large, then $n!$ or $k!$ or both may be too large to be properly stored by the computer. An error message would be printed if this were to happen. We return to an alternative way to compute these values in a later problem.]

Problem 18   *Binomial Distribution*

If one is about to perform N independent experiments, with probability P of success for each experiment, then the probability of a total of exactly K successes in the N attempts is

$$C(N, K)*P**K*(1-P)**(N-K)$$

C(N, K) is the binomial coefficient given by N!/(K!*(N-K)!).

(a) Prepare a program which will compute this probability for given values of N, P, and K.

(b) Modify the program to sum the probabilities for K = 0 to N. Try the program for N = 10. The sum should be 1.

(c) Modify the program to sum the probabilities for K = F to L, where F and L are READ from data cards.

Problem 19   *Generating Normal Random Numbers*

Uniform random numbers can be transformed to other types of random numbers by using the generalized lambda transformation.† That is, if X is a uniform random number, then Y such that

$$Y = A + (X**C - (1-X)**D)/B$$

is a random number from a generalized lambda distribution. By changing A, B, C, D, different distributions can be simulated. For example, by using A = 0, B = 0.1975, C = D = 0.135, standard normal random numbers can be generated.

(a) Write a program which will generate 100 normal numbers and calculate the mean and standard deviation of the sample.

(b) Modify the program in (a) to generate K samples of size N (where K and N are specified by the user) and calculate the mean and standard deviation of each sample. Then calculate the mean of all the means and the standard deviation of all the means.

Problem 20   *Uniform Random Number Frequency Distribution*

Write a program which will generate N uniform random numbers (with N being specified by the user), and record the results in a frequency distribution which has 10 classes, each of width 0.1, with the left endpoint of the smallest class being 0.

---

†John Ramberg et al., "A Probability Distribution and Its Uses in Fitting Data," *Technometrics*, 5, no. 2 (May 1979), 201–204.

Problem 21   *Chi-Square Statistic*

Write a program which will generate a user-specified number of uniform random numbers, construct a frequency distribution with ten equal classes (0.0 to 0.1, 0.1 to 0.2, etc.), and then calculate the chi-square statistic which would be used in a test to determine if a number is equally likely to occur in any of the frequency classes. [See Section 7.1 for the formula for the chi-square statistic.]

Problem 22   *Pearson Product-Moment Correlation Coefficient*

Write a program which will calculate a Pearson product-moment correlation coefficient for two samples. The program must allow the user to input the data from the two samples, calculate the means and variances of the two samples and the correlation coefficient, and print out all the results. [See Section 7.1 for the formula for this correlation coefficient.]

Problem 23   *t-Statistic (1 Sample)*

Write a program which will calculate a one-sample t-statistic, of the type which would be used in testing a null hypothesis stating that a population mean is equal to some fixed constant. The program should:

(a) Allow the user to specify the sample size.
(b) Allow the user to READ the sample values into a data array.
(c) Calculate the sample mean and variance.
(d) Calculate the t-statistic and print out results.

(See Section 7.1 for definitions of various statistics.)

Problem 24   *t-Statistic (2 Independent Samples)*

Write a program which will calculate a t-statistic used in testing the null hypothesis that the means of two independent distributions are equal. The program should:

(a) Allow the user to read the sizes of the two samples.
(b) Allow the user to read the data from the two samples into data arrays.
(c) Calculate means and variances for each sample.
(d) Calculate the t-statistic, and print out all relevant information.

[The t-statistic is defined in Section 7.1.]

Problem 25   *t-Statistic (2 Dependent Samples)*

Do the same as in the preceding problem, but assume the two samples are dependent.

Problem 26   *Ordering Data*

Write a program which will READ a set of sample data and put it into ascending order. [Sorting is discussed in Section 3.1.]

Problem 27   *Sample Percentiles*

Write a program which will find any given percentile of a set of sample data. The program will have to sort the data into ascending order. The program should be tested with both small and large data sets. [Percentile computations are discussed in Section 7.1.]

Problem 28

Write a program which will READ a set of sample data and compute a trimmed mean for the sample. [See Section 7.1 for a discussion of a trimmed mean.]

Problem 29

Write a program which will read a line of text and count the number of repetitions of each letter of the alphabet. Print out the results in a table which gives, for each letter, its number of occurrences and its frequency (or percentage) of occurrence.

Problem 30

Write a program which will read a line of text and record the number of letters in each word. Compute the average number of letters in a word of the text and the standard deviation.

Problem 31

Modify the program for the previous problem so that the sentence can take up more than one line. [You should have to use a blank data card to tell the program you are finished entering lines.]

Problem 32   *Binomial Coefficients, Revisited*
When the binomial coefficient

$$C(N,K) = N! / (K! * (N-K)!)$$

was computed in an earlier problem, the factorials N!, K!, and (N-K)! were computed first. These numbers are too large for the computer to store if N is large. Write a program that computes the binomial coefficients C(N, K) in a single loop. This will allow N to be much bigger. [See Section 7.2 for a discussion of computing C(N,K) without first computing each factorial.]

Problem 33   *Binomial Distribution, Revisited*
Modify the earlier binomial distribution program so that the probability of a success is computed in a single loop, rather than by computing the factorials directly.
    Compare the results of this program with those obtained for the earlier one.
    Then run both programs with relatively large values for *n*.

Problem 34   *Statistics of Numbers on File*
File '#NORMAL.DAT' has been set up containing 500 real numbers, which are the result of a sample from a normally distributed population with unknown mean and deviation. Each record of the file is composed of exactly one of the real numbers.
    Write a program that READs a positive integer *n* with $n < 501$. Then the program
(a) reads the first *n* real numbers from the file;
(b) computes and prints the sample mean, variance, and standard deviation for the sample of size *n* that has been read from the data file;
(c) arranges the *n* numbers of the sample in numerical order and prints them five numbers to a line;
(d) computes and prints the median of the sample;
(e) computes and prints 95% confidence intervals for the population mean and for the population variance.

Run your program with *n* = 5 until you debug it, then use *n* = 30 on the run you submit.

Problem 35   *File Manipulation*
Write a program which READs a positive integer *n* ($n < 501$) followed by *n* positive integers read from an internal disk data file 'INTGER.DAT' that has been set up for this problem. The file has been arranged so that each record of the file contains exactly 1 integer.
    The program you prepare should
(a) compute and print the sum and average of the *n* positive integers;
(b) find and print the following information: the number of integers whose value is in the closed interval [1, 50], in the closed interval [51, 100], or greater than 100;
(c) arrange the numbers that are in the closed interval [51, 100] in decreasing numerical order and print them (but do not order the numbers outside the interval);
(d) compute and print the median of those integers in [51, 100].
Run your program with *n* = 20 until you debug it, then use *n* = 300 on the run you submit.

CHAPTER 8

Statistics Problems (with Calculus Prerequisite)

This chapter was written with John Vogel.

Section 8.1: METHOD OF FALSE POSITION

This method is one of the oldest known for the solution of the equation $f(x) = 0$. Largely because of the efficiency of Newton's Method, the Method of False Position has been surprisingly neglected until recently when its important advantages, particularly for use on computers, have again been realized. In fact, for technical reasons that are beyond the scope of this discussion, False Position is actually more efficient than Newton's Method in many applications.

The method begins with the choosing of two distinct values, say $x\langle 1\rangle$ and $x\langle 2\rangle$. (It is not necessary that $x\langle 1\rangle$ be less than $x\langle 2\rangle$.) If $y\langle 1\rangle = f(x\langle 1\rangle)$ and $y\langle 2\rangle = f(x\langle 2\rangle)$ are not equal, the chord connecting the two points $(x\langle 1\rangle, y\langle 1\rangle)$ and $(x\langle 2\rangle, y\langle 2\rangle)$ intersects the x-axis at a point we shall call $x\langle 3\rangle$. The method continues by throwing away the value $x\langle 1\rangle$ and using the chord connecting the points $(x\langle 2\rangle, y\langle 2\rangle)$ and $(x\langle 3\rangle, y\langle 3\rangle)$, where $y\langle 3\rangle = f(x\langle 3\rangle)$, to generate another value $x\langle 4\rangle$ as the point where the new chord crosses the x-axis. The process continues in this fashion generating a sequence

$$x\langle 3\rangle, \ x\langle 4\rangle, \ x\langle 5\rangle, \ \ldots$$

and terminates if two successive x-values are sufficiently close in absolute value.

Since the point where the chord passing through the points (a, A) and (b, B) crosses the x-axis is determined by the formula

$$x = b - B(b-a)/(B-A) \tag{*}$$

(see proof of this lemma at the end of this section), the Method of False Position takes the form:

(1) choose $x\langle 1\rangle$ and $x\langle 2\rangle$ and let $y\langle 1\rangle = f(x\langle 1\rangle)$ and $y\langle 2\rangle = f(x\langle 2\rangle)$;

(2) let

$$x\langle 3\rangle = x\langle 2\rangle - y\langle 2\rangle(x\langle 2\rangle - x\langle 1\rangle)/(y\langle 2\rangle - y\langle 1\rangle)$$
$$y\langle 3\rangle = f(x\langle 3\rangle);$$

(3) let

$$x\langle 4\rangle = x\langle 3\rangle - y\langle 3\rangle(x\langle 3\rangle - x\langle 2\rangle)/(y\langle 3\rangle - y\langle 2\rangle)$$
$$y\langle 4\rangle = f(x\langle 4\rangle);$$

(4) continue until two successive x-values differ in absolute value by a prechosen small number.

This algorithm may be written more compactly, and in a form more compatible with FORTRAN notation, as:

The Algorithm

1. Choose X1 and X2 and set Y1 = f(X1) and Y2 = f(X2);
2. set X3 = X2 – Y2(X2 – X1)/(Y2 – Y1);
3. if abs(X3 – X2) is small, then stop; otherwise
4. update: replace X1 by X2, X2 by X3, Y1 by Y2, and Y2 by f(X3);
5. go to step 2.

Notice that the method can be programmed without subscripted variables even though the mathematical description of the method uses them.

Lemma

The point where the chord passing through the points (a, A) and (b, B) crosses the x-axis is determined by formula (*).

Proof

The slope of the line connecting (a, A) and (b, B) is

$$m = (B-A)/(b-a)$$

and the equation of the line is

$$y - B = m(x-b)$$

The line crosses the x-axis when $y = 0$, so this condition may be used to solve for the x-coordinate of the crossing:

$$x = b - B/m$$
$$x = b - B(b-a)/(B-A)$$

Section 8.2: ROBUST SAMPLE STATISTICS

Once a sample has been taken and values $x(1)$, $x(2)$, . . . , $x(n)$ are known, an "average" value for the population can be computed to measure "centrality." One obvious candidate for "average" is the sample mean; another is the sample median. These estimators, however, are only two of many possible estimators of centrality. In particular, given $x(1)$, $x(2)$, . . . , $x(n)$, suppose we try to choose a number w to minimize the expression

$$H(w) = \sum_{j=1}^{n} [abs(w - x(j))]^p \qquad (1)$$

where p is a given number. A value w which minimizes H would in some sense be as close as possible to all the values $x(1), x(2), \ldots, x(n)$ and could be used as the "average" we seek.

It is shown below in theorems 1 and 2 that w is the sample mean if $p = 2$ and w is the sample median if $p = 1$. For other values of p, there are no simple formulas for w, and numerical techniques must be used to minimize H, for example, solving the equation $H'(w) = 0$. To put this new problem in a more familiar form, we rename the function $H'(w)$ as $F(w)$. The derivation for $F(w)$ is indicated in the proof of theorem 2 below. Thus,

$$F(w) = H'(w)$$

$$= \sum_{j=1}^{n} p[abs(w - x(j))]^{p-1} \, sgn(w - x(j)) \qquad (2)$$

where sgn is the signum (or "sign") function defined by

$$sgn(u) = \begin{cases} 1 \; ; u > 0 \\ 0 \; ; u = 0 \\ -1 \; ; u < 0 \end{cases}$$

The equation $F(w) = 0$, i.e., $H'(w) = 0$, can be solved by the Method of False Position applied to F. The function F is coded in FORTRAN as a function subprogram, say F(W), and the False-Position portion of the program proceeds as if the function were a simple function:

$$X3 = X2 - F(X2)*(X2 - X1)/[F(X2) - F(X1)]$$

The signum function may be computed with the built-in function SIGN, using 1 as the second argument.

Theorem 1

If $p = 2$, choosing w as the sample mean minimizes the function H defined by equation (1).

Proof

$$H(w) = \sum_{j=1}^{n} (w - x_j)^2$$

$$= \sum_{j=1}^{n} w^2 - 2wx_j + x_j^2$$

$$= nw^2 - 2w \sum_{j=1}^{2} x_j + \sum_{j=1}^{n} x_j^2$$

So $\qquad\qquad\qquad H'(x) = 2nw - 2\Sigma x_j$

and

$$H'(0) = 0 \longleftrightarrow w = \frac{1}{n} \sum_{j=1}^{n} x_j$$

Theorem 2

If $p = 1$, choosing w as the sample median minimizes the function H defined by equation (1).

Proof

$$H(w) = \sum_{j=1}^{n} |w - x_j|$$

and so

$$H'(x) = \sum_{j=1}^{n} \frac{d}{dx} |w - x_j|$$

To continue, we use the chain rule and need to know how to differentiate the absolute-value function.

An Aside

Consider the function

$$g(t) = \text{abs}(t)$$

From the graph of the function g (Figure 8.2–1), we see that $g'(t)$ is defined if t is not 0 and

$$g'(t) = -1 \text{ for } t < 0$$
$$g'(t) = +1 \text{ for } t > 0$$

In order to make g' identical to the signum function which it so closely resembles, we define $g'(0)$ as 0, then $g'(t) = \text{sgn}(t)$ for all t.

The graph of $\text{sgn}(t)$ is shown in Figure 8.2–2. Note that sgn is not continuous at the origin and that sgn is either –1 or +1.

We now return to the proof. We can see by the chain rule that

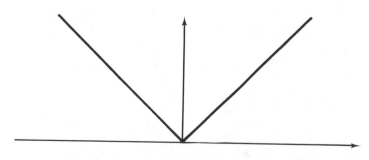

Figure 8.2–1
The Absolute Value Function

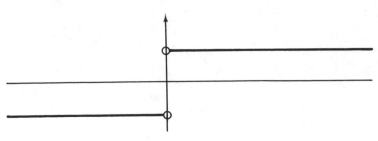

Figure 8.2–2
The Sign Function

$$\frac{d}{dw}\,|w - x_j| = [\text{sgn}(w - x_j)]\,\frac{d}{dw}\,(w - x_j)$$

$$= \text{sgn}(w - x_j)$$

and so

$$H'(w) = \sum_{j=1}^{n} \text{sgn}(w - x_j)$$

We can now choose w to make $H'(w)$ equal to zero. The choice for an even value of n is different from than for an odd value of n, but in each case the key is to recognize that $H'(w)$ is a sum of n values that are each either –1, 0, or +1.

Example 1

Suppose that $n = 3$, $x(1) = 16$, $x(2) = 5$, and $x(3) = 82$. Then

$$H'(w) = \text{sgn}(w-16) + \text{sgn}(w-5) + \text{sgn}(w-82)$$
$$= \text{sgn}(w-82) + \text{sgn}(w-16) + \text{sgn}(w-5)$$

We can make H' zero by choosing w as the middle value, i.e., $w = 16$, because then

$$H'(16) = \text{sgn}(-66) + \text{sgn}(0) + \text{sgn}(+11)$$
$$= -1 + 0 + 1$$
$$= 0$$

No other choice for w will work.

Example 2

Alter the values of example 1 to include $x(4) = 100$. It is not difficult to show that $H'(w) = 0$ for any value of w for which $16 < w < 82$, i.e., for any value of w between the two middle values. The value which is often chosen is $w = (16+82)/2 = 49$.

In each example, the value of w which minimizes H is the median:

1. if n is odd, set w equal to the middle value of the x's;
2. if n is even, set w equal to the average of the two "middle" values of the x's.

A formal proof could be fashioned along the lines indicated by the two examples, and that is why we may conclude our proof outline here.

Section 8.3: METHOD OF LEAST SQUARES (DERIVED FROM CALCULUS)

When we are given a sample containing n points $(x_1, y_1), \ldots, (x_n, y_n)$, we frequently want to find the line which "best fits" or "most nearly passes through" all these points (see Figure 8.3-1). For example, the x- and y-values may be measurements (time, distance, pressure, concentration, population, price, cost, etc.). For n values of x, say, $x_1, \ldots, x_n$, we have n corresponding values of y, say, $y_1, \ldots, y_n$. We have reason to suspect (or we wish to test the hypothesis) that y is a simple linear function of x, i.e., $y = mx + b$ for some constants m and b. We know that our measurements are somewhat inaccurate and that our theory may be imperfect; thus, we do not expect to find m and b so that $y_i = mx_i + b$ for every value of i ($i = 1, \ldots, n$). The problem becomes how to find the best m and b.

The approach that we will take is to consider the distances from the points we have to a line $y = mx + b$. For simplicity, we consider the vertical distances, shown in Figure 8.3-1. Thus, the vertical distance from (x_1, y_1) to the line is $|(mx_1 + b) - y_1|$ and the distance from (x_i, y_i) to the line is $|mx_i + b - y_i|$. We expect that the "best" line should be the one that minimizes these distances.

Our first approach is to let

$$g(m, b) = \sum_{i=1}^{n} |mx_i + b - y_i|$$

The values we want for m and b are those that minimize the distance function. However, we will want to find the minimum by setting partial derivatives equal to 0, and we see that the absolute values here will make this computation quite messy.

Thus, the way in which we normally proceed is to look at the squares $(mx_i + b - y_i)^2$ of the distances instead of the distances themselves. Thus, in our second approach, we try to minimize the function

$$h(m, b) = \sum_{i=1}^{n} (mx_i + b - y_i)^2$$

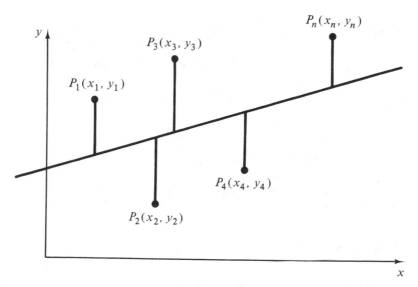

Figure 8.3-1

Here the computations are much easier:

Note: As we are trying to minimize the distances squared, we get the name Method of Least Squares.

$$\frac{\partial h}{\partial m} = \sum_{i=1}^{n} 2x_i(mx_i + b - y_i)$$

and

$$\frac{\partial h}{\partial b} = \sum_{i=1}^{n} 2(mx_i + b - y_i)$$

We can now set those partial derivatives equal to 0 and solve for m and b. Then we can check the second derivative test to be certain that we have, in fact, a minimum.

When we do go through the messy algebra, we find that

$$m = \sum_{i=1}^{n} (x_i - \bar{x})(y_i - \bar{y}) \bigg/ \sum_{i=1}^{n} (x_i - \bar{x})^2$$

and

$$b = \bar{y} - m\bar{x}$$

where $\bar{x}$ and $\bar{y}$ are the averages of the x_i's and y_i's, respectively. (We omit the unenlightening algebra, leaving it to the interested reader. The second equation comes from $\partial h/\partial b = 0$ with little trouble. The first equation is more tedious.)

Thus, *the best line, according to the Method of Least Squares, through the points* (x_1, y_1), . . . , (x_n, y_n) *has the equation* $y = mx + b$, *where m and b are given by the above formulas.*

Section 8.4: TECHNIQUES OF CURVE PLOTTING

In this section, we consider how we might plot each of the following types of graphs on our terminal or printer:

(a)   graphs of functions;
(b)   histograms;
(c)   graphs of data points.

Throughout, we will assume that all functions and data points are given in terms of x- and y- coordinates with functions of the form $y = l(x)$.

We will find it convenient to distinguish two formats for our graphs:

 (i)   the x-axis runs vertically down the page (Figure 8.4-1);
(ii)   the x-axis runs horizontally across the page (Figure 8.4-2).

We may find the second of these cases to be more familiar, due to our experience in algebra. However, the first case is somewhat easier to program.

Plotting with the x-axis Running Vertically

We begin with the simplest plotting. If we want to plot K = L(J) for J = 9, 10, 11, the graph might have the format

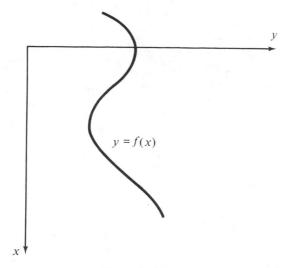

Figure 8.4-1
Case i – x Runs Vertically Down

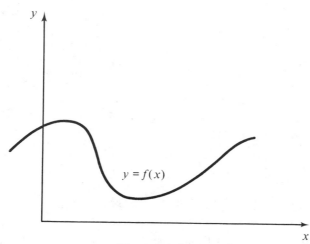

Figure 8.4-2
Case ii – x Runs Horizontally

```
 9  :      *
10  :      *
11  :      *
```

We see that on each line we need to print

1. the J-value
2. a colon :
3. a * at the k-value

This can be accomplished using an array LINE, which contains the characters that we want to print on each line. Our work with LINE consists of two main steps:

(a) setting all entries of LINE to a blank;

(b) changing the entry corresponding to the *k*-value to a *.

These steps are performed in the following lines:

```
        DIMENSION LINE(75)
        DATA IBLANK, ISTAR /' ', '* '/
C START WITH ALL BLANKS
        DO 1 INDEX = 1, 75
   1            LINE(INDEX) = IBLANK

                  .
                  .
                  .

C COMPUTE K VALUE AND SET UP ARRAY, THEN PRINT
        K = L(J)
        LINE(K) = ISTAR
        WRITE (7, 2) J, LINE
   2    FORMAT(1 X, I4, ':', 75A1)
```

Notes:

1. *Non-integer Data*

   If the function is not an integer, as in $y = f(x)$, then we must round off the y value, either with arithmetic or with the INT function. To round down, we may use

   ```
   IY = INT(Y)
   LINE(IY) = ISTAR
   ```

   To round down for 0.0 to 0.5 and up for 0.5 to 1.0, we use

   ```
   IY = INT(Y + .5)
   LINE(IY) = ISTAR
   ```

   You should put values in for Y to convince yourself that these round the way we claim they do.

2. *Scaling*

   If the width of the terminal is only 80 characters, then the above provides room for only $Y = 1$ through $Y = 75$, if we print X in F4.1 format. If y-values are not in this range, we must scale the Y values. For example, for the range $Y = 1$ to $Y = 150$, we should count 1 space horizontally for an increase of 2 in the y-value. Thus, we should plot $Y/2$ instead of Y in this case.

   More generally, if the range is $Y = 1$ to $Y = TOP$, we should plot $Y * 75/TOP$, assuming we have only 75 columns to print in for Y.

   Finally, if y has a range from BOTTOM to TOP, then we should plot

$$\frac{74(Y - BOTTOM)}{TOP - BOTTOM} + 1$$

Note: This is just the formula for the line through (**BOTTOM**, 1) and (**TOP**, 75)

instead of Y. In the formula, we check that when Y = BOTTOM, we plot in column 1 and when Y = TOP we will plot in column 75.

3. *Shading Area*

   If we want the region "under" the graph shaded, we replace

   LINE(K) = ISTAR

by

```
      DO 3 INDEX = 1, K
3           LINE(INDEX) = ISTAR
```

Histograms

When we have a number of readings $r_1, \ldots, r_n$, we sometimes want to see how many times each outcome occurred, as shown in Figure 8.4–3. In constructing a histogram, we proceed down the page. For each *x*-value we can see how many r_i's were obtained with that value. Then, we can print this number of '*'s. Thus, we see that the approach to printing histograms is fundamentally the same as graphing a function; we simply replace the function L(X) with a count of how many r_i's have the value of X on each line.

<u>Notes:</u>

1. The same remarks on non-integer data, scaling, and shading area from graphing functions apply to histograms.

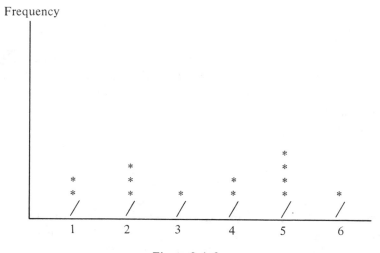

Figure 8.4–3
Histogram Showing Number of
Times Each Outcome Occurred
When a Certain Die was Thrown 13 Times

2. *The Range of the Histogram*

When printing the histogram, we must determine what the smallest and largest x-values are. If we do not know this range ahead of time, the program will have to do this. A simple loop is all that is needed.

3. *Efficiency*

At each line of output, we must have computed the number of R(I) values equal to the x-value for that line. A simple way to do this is:

```
NUMBER = 0
DO 11 INDEX = 1, N
        IF (R(INDEX) .NE. X) GO TO 11
        NUMBER = NUMBER + 1
  11    CONTINUE
```

However, if this is done for each line of printing, our program is performing this computation a great number of times. It is far more efficient to use an array NUMBER(K) to store the number of R(I)'s that have the value of K. If the K values are between 1 and 10, this can be done with

```
DIMENSION NUMBER(10)
DO 12 INDEX = 1, N
        K = INT(R(INDEX))
        NUMBER(K) = NUMBER(K) + 1
  12    CONTINUE
```

For other ranges of X, modifications are needed as described above in the comments on non-integer data and scaling.

To find the largest value, we can use:

```
TOP = R(1)
DO 10 INDEX = 2, N
        IF (TOP .LT. R(INDEX))
   1            TOP = R(INDEX)
  10    CONTINUE
```

Graphs of Data Points

When we want to plot a series of points $(x_1, y_1), \ldots, (x_n, y_n)$, we must remember that the typing on a terminal always goes down the page and from left to right. If the x-axis is going down the paper, this means that we must plot the points with the smallest x-values first. Then, for a given x-value, we need to plot the parts with the smallest y-values first and proceed to larger y-values. This process is rather easy to do if we can put the points in the appropriate order. We need

1. $X_i \leqslant X_{i+1}$ for $i = 1, \ldots, n - 1$
2. if $X_i = X_{i+1}$, then $Y_i \leqslant Y_{i+1}$.

This ordering can be accomplished in two steps. First, we can order the points in terms of the increasing y-value. Then we can order the points again by the increasing x-value. This can be done by a variety of methods: for example, the Bubble Sort or the Improved Bubble Sort described in Section 3.1. We only observe that in this case if we want to interchange y_1 and y_2 when putting the y-values in order, we will also have to interchange x_1 and x_2, so that our data points still correspond with our initial data.

Once this ordering is done, then on a given line corresponding to a given x-value a, we can plot the points (x_i, y_i), (x_{i+1}, y_{i+1}) ... (x_j, y_j) in order, as long as the x-values are equal to a. We just set each entry of the array LINE corresponding to a y-value to the character '*'. When we have covered all of the y-values, we can print our LINE.

Notes

1. The comments on non-integer data and scaling earlier in this section can apply to this case also.
2. If we change the role of the x's and y's, we can use the same techniques as above, but with the x-axis running horizontally across the page.

Plotting with the x-Axis Running Horizontally

When we are plotting either functions or histograms with the x-axis running horizontally, we must realize that before we can print a line, we must know whether to print an '*' or not for each x-value on that line. We cannot print the line on the basis of one x-value and then go on to the next line, because we may have to plot the same y-value for each of several x-values.

For this reason, when plotting functions we usually use an array YVALUE(K) which contains the YVALUE for each x-value on the line. In histograms, we need the array NUMBER(K) that we used earlier. The appropriate array must be set up before any printing occurs.

Once the array is computed, we examine the array on each line for each column of the page. For example, if we are printing a line corresponding to Y = 10, we might use

```
      Y = 10
      DO 1 K = 1, 80                          We assume a page width of 80.
            IF (YVALUE(K) .EQ. Y) GO TO 2
            LINE(K) = IBLANK                   The y-value does not equal Y.
            GO TO 1
2           LINE(K) = ISTAR                    The y-value does equal Y.
1           CONTINUE
      WRITE (7, 3) LINE                        Finally, we print the entire line.
3     FORMAT (1X, 80A1)
```

If we want a graph for a range of y-values, we replace Y = 10 by an appropriate DO loop.

Notes

1. *Shading*
   If we are plotting a histogram or if we want the area under the curve shaded, we only need change the .EQ. to .GE. in the IF statement.
2. The same problems of non-integer data and scaling arise in this setting as they did earlier in this section.

Section 8.5: STATISTICS PROBLEMS (USING CALCULUS)

Problem 1
   Write a program that computes the average of three numbers.

Problem 2
   Modify the previous program so it READs the 3 numbers from data cards.

Problem 3

Use WRITE and FORMAT statements to write out the message:

```
EEEE    X   X   PPPP
E         X X    P  P
EEEE       X     PPPP
E         X X    P     . .
EEEE    X   X    P     . .
```

Problem 4   *Tabulation of the Normal Probability Density Function*

Write a program that tabulates a function for x = –3, –2.9, . . . , 2.8, 2.9, 3. Use a statement function to specify the function and print the results in the form of a table with the columns labeled. Test the program with the function

$$f(x) = [1/\sqrt{2\pi}] *EXP[-(x**2)/2]$$

Use this information to sketch the graph of this normal probability density function.

Problem 5   *Tabulation of a Function*

Write a program which computes the values $f(x)$ of a function f for x = L, L+H, L+2*H, . . . , U. Use a statement function to define $f(x)$ and use a READ statement to determine L, U, and H. Test the program on the following:

(a) Negative exponential density function:

$$f(x) = a*EXP**(-a*x), \quad L = 0, U = 3, \quad H = 0.1$$

(b) Negative exponential probability function:

$$f(x) = 1 - a*EXP**(-a*x), \quad L = 0, \quad U = 3, \quad H = 0.1$$

(c) Normal probability density function:

$$f(x) = [1/\sqrt{2\pi}] *EXP**[-(x**2)/2], \quad L = -3, \quad U = 3, \quad H = 0.2$$

Problem 6   *Standard Sample Statistics*

Prepare a program that will READ an integer n followed by n real numbers $x(1), x(2). . . , x(n)$ and then compute and print:

(1) $m = (1/n) \sum_{j=1}^{n} x(j)$ (sample mean);

(2) $v = (1/n) \sum_{j=1}^{n} (x(j) - m)**2$ (sample variance);

(3) $s = SQRT(v)$ (standard deviation);

(4) $F = (1/n) \sum_{j=1}^{n} (x(j) - m)**4$ (4th central moment).

Test the program by applying it to:
(a) the six numbers 3, 3, 3, 3, 3, 3;
(b) the four numbers 2, 5, 9, 13.

Problem 7   *Least Squares*

Write a program that will read in an integer n followed by n pairs of real numbers

$$x(1), y(1), x(2), y(2), . . . , x(n), y(n)$$

and use the Method of Least Squares to find the slope and y-intercept of the line which best fits the n points

$$x(j), y(j), \quad \text{for } j=1, 2, . . . n$$

Apply this program to the two test cases:

(a) (1, 2), (2, 3), (3, 4), (4, 5), (5, 6)

(b) (-1, 3), (3, 11), (0.5), (-2.5, 0), (-3.5, -2)

Apply the program to the 12 points:

$$(1.0, 3.01), \quad (1.1, 3.23), \quad (1.2, 3.30),$$
$$(1.3, 3.61), \quad (1.4, 3.8), \quad (1.5, 3.77),$$
$$(1.6, 4.22), \quad (1.7, 4.43), \quad (1.8, 4.57),$$
$$(1.9, 4.90), \quad (2.0, 5.01), \quad (2.1, 5.11)$$

[*Note:* See Section 8.3 for further information.]

Problem 8   *Method of False Position*

Write a program that will use the Method of False Position to find approximations to the roots of a function $f(x)$. Use a statement function to give the definition of the function $f(x)$ so that the program may be easily applied to any function by merely changing the one statement. Use the program to find the roots of the function:

$$[x**3 - 17*(x**2) + 42*x - 32]/[5*(x**4) + 12]$$

to such a degree of accuracy that two successive approximations to a root differ by less than 0.00004 in absolute value. You should also submit the output of two test cases and hand computations which show the values to be expected for each test. [See Section 8.1 for further details on the Method of False Position.]

Problem 9

Write a program that uses the Method of False Position to determine when the negative exponential probability function is equal to 0.25, 0.5, and 0.75. Use a statement function to specify the function. Construct the program to READ a value b and then compute an x-value so that $f(x) = b$. [*Note:* $f(x) = b$ when $f(x) - b = 0$.]

[The Method of False Position is described in Section 8.1.]

Problem 10

Modify the preceding program so that it uses Newton's Method instead of the Method of False Position. [*Note:* Newton's Method cannot be used if the function is not differentiable.]

[Newton's Method is discussed in Section 5.1.]

Problem 11

Modify the preceding program so that it uses the Bisection Method instead of the previous methods. [*Note:* The Bisection Method can be used on nondifferentiable functions, while Newton's Method and the Method of False Position do not apply to such functions.]

[The Bisection Method is discussed in Section 4.1.]

Problem 12   *Comparison of Methods to Solve f(x) = b*

Write a program to read a value b and to solve $f(x) = b$ using the Bisection Method, The Method of False Position, and Newton's Method. In each case, count the number of times the program must go through the main iteration process, and print these results. Compare these results for a variety of functions.

Problem 13   *Robust Sample Statistics*

Prepare a program that will READ a positive integer N on one card, and then N real numbers $x(1), x(2), \ldots, x(n)$ on subsequent data cards. Then use the Method of False Position to find a value w which minimizes the function

$$H(w) = \sum_{j=1}^{n} [\text{abs}(w - x(j))] **p$$

when $p = 1.5$ by finding a root of the function $F(w)$ where

$$F(w) = H'(w)$$

(See Section 8.2 for further details.)

(a) Test your program using $n = 3, x(1) = -1.2, x(2) = 3.2, x(3) = 1.5$. The solution is approximately $w = 1.4191$.

(b) Run your program using $n = 12, x(j) = j$ for $j=1$ to 11 and $x(12) = 12.3$.

Problem 14   *The Normal Probability Function, by the Trapezoidal Rule*

We know that the normal probability function $f(x)$ can be computed as the area under the normal probability density function

$$p(x) = [1/\sqrt{2\pi}]*\text{EXP}[-(x**2)/2]$$

Write a program to compute $f(x)$ by approximating the integral

$$0.5 + \int_0^x p(s)\,ds$$

by the Trapezoidal Rule. [The Trapezoidal Rule is discussed in Section 5.3.]

Problem 15   *Normal Probability Function Using Simpson's Rule*

Rewrite the above program using Simpson's Rule. [Simpson's Rule is discussed in Section 5.3.]

Problem 16   *Generating Normal Random Numbers*

Uniform random numbers can be transformed to other types of random numbers by using the generalized lambda transformation.[†] That is, if X is a uniform random number, then Y such that

$$Y = A + (X**C-(1-X)**D)/B$$

is a random number from a generalized lambda distribution. By changing A, B, C, D, different distributions can be simulated. For example, by using A = 0, B = 0.1975, C = D = 0.135, standard normal random numbers can be generated.

(a) Write a program which will generate 100 normal numbers and calculate the mean and standard deviation of the sample.

(b) Modify the program in (a) to generate K samples of size N (where K and N are specified by the user) and calculate the mean and standard deviation of each sample. Then calculate the mean of all the means and the standard deviation of all the means.

Problem 17   *Testing the Central Limit Theorem*

(a) Write a program which generates K samples of uniform random numbers, each sample being of size N.

(b) Calculate the mean of each sample and construct a frequency distribution for the sample means with six frequency classes. The class boundaries are to be MU-3*SIGMA/SQRT(N), MU-2*SIGMA/SQRT(N), MU–SIGMA/SQRT(N), MU, MU+SIGMA/SQRT(N), MU+2*SIGMA/SQRT(N), and MU+3*SIGMA/SQRT(N), where MU and SIGMA are the mean and standard deviation of the population being sampled. (For the uniform distribution, MU = 0.5, SIGMA = 0.2887.) Run the program with K = 100, 500, 1000 and N = 5, 10, 20.

Compare the relative frequency in each class with the theoretical value suggested by the Central Limit Theorem. Set up a chi-square statistic to measure the amount of agreement between the observed relative frequencies and the theoretical.

Problem 18

Repeat the preceding problem, but transform the uniform random numbers to normal random numbers using the generalized lambda transformation.

Problem 19   *Graphing Functions—(i)*

Write a program that prints a graph of the function $f(x) = x**2$ for x = -8, -7, . . . , 7, 8 with the x-axis running vertically down the paper. [*Note:* No scaling is needed for this problem.]

[Graphing is discussed in Section 8.4.]

Problem 20   *Graphing Functions—(ii)*

Write a program that prints a graph of the normal probability density function

$$f(x) = [1/\sqrt{2\pi}]*\text{EXP}[-(x**2)/2]$$

for x = -5, -4.5, . . . , 4.5, 5.

Run the x-axis vertically, and scale the functional values so the graph covers much of the width of the paper. [Graphing is discussed in Section 8.4.]

Problem 21   *Graphing Functions—(iii)*

Modify the preceding program so that the area "under" the curve is shaded. [Shading graphs is discussed in Section 8.4.]

[†]John Ramberg et al., "A Probability Distribution and Its Uses in Fitting Data," *Technometrics,* 5, no. 2 (May 1979), 201–204.

Problem 22   *Die Tossing Simulation*

Many random processes can be imitated or "simulated" on a computer by using the built-in random number generator to provide the randomness inherent in the process. For example, the rolling of a die can be simulated by generating a random number r with $0 < r < 1$. We call the outcome 1 if $0 < r < 1/6$, we call the outcome 2 if $1/6 < r < 2/6$, etc. Alternatively, if we have $0 < r < 1$, then $0 < 6*r < 6$, so $1 < 6*r + 1 < 7$. Thus with integer arithmetic, $(6*r + 1)$ is a random number between 1 and 6 inclusive.

Write a program which will simulate the rolling of a die and record the results of rolling the die 100 times. Keep track of how many times each outcome occurs. [*Note:* Before trying this problem, you should see if a random number generator function is available on the machine you are using. On many machines, this function has the name RANDU.]

Problem 23   *Dice Tossing Simulation*

Modify the preceding program to roll a pair of dice 100 times and record the outcomes.

Problem 24   *Histogram of Dice Tossing*

Write a program that
(a) rolls a pair of dice 100 times and records the sum on the dice;
(b) totals the number of times a 2, 3, . . . , 12 occurred;
(c) prints a histogram of the number of times each outcome occurred, with the outcomes running down the paper.

[Printing histograms is discussed in Section 8.4.]

Problem 25   *Histogram with Random Real Numbers—(i)*

Write a program that
(a) generates 300 real numbers between 0 and 1 (inclusive);
(b) groups the numbers into intervals [0, 0.05), [0.05, 0.1), . . . , [0.95, 1.] ;
(c) prints a histogram of the number of random numbers in each of these intervals. The histogram should run vertically down the page, with one interval displayed for each line of output.

Problem 26   *Graphing Functions—(iv)*

Write a program that prints a graph of $y = f(x) = 20/x$ for $x = 1, . . . , 70$, with the x-axis running horizontally across the paper, and the y-values running from 20 to 0. [Graphing is discussed in Section 8.4.]

Problem 27   *Graphing Functions—(v)*

Write a program that prints a graph of the normal density function

$$f(x) = [1/\sqrt{2\pi}] *EXP[-(x**2)/2]$$

for $x = -3.5, -3.4, . . . , 3.4, 3.5$ with the x-axis running horizontally. Scale the vertical axis so the graph covers at least 20 different lines of output. [See Section 8.4 for a discussion of graphing.]

Problem 28   *Graphing Functions—(vi)*

Modify the preceding program so that the area under the curve is shaded. [Shading is discussed in Section 8.4.]

Problem 29   *Histogram with Random Integers*

Write a program that:
(a) generates integers between 1 and 50 (inclusive);
(b) prints a histogram of the numbers obtained, with the numbers 1 to 50 running horizontally across the paper.

[Graphing is discussed in Section 8.4.]

Problem 30   *Histogram with Random Real Numbers—(ii)*

Write a program that
(a) reads an integer N;
(b) generates N real numbers between 0 and 1 (inclusive);
(c) groups the numbers into intervals of width 0.02, i.e., [0, 0.02), [0.02, 0.04), . . . , [0.98, 1.0] ;
(d) prints a histogram of the number of random numbers obtained in each interval. The histogram should run across the page. Label various points of the horizontal axis, so the output is easy to interpret.

Problem 31   *Count Letter Repetitions*

Prepare a program which will accept a line of text and count the number of repetitions of each letter of the alphabet. Print out the results in a table which gives, for each letter, its number of occurrences and its frequency of occurrence (number of occurrences divided by total of all occurrences of all letters).

Problem 32   *Frequency of Letters in Text with a Histogram—(i)*
    Write a program that will
    (a) read a line of text;
    (b) compute the number of times each letter of the alphabet occurs in the program and the frequency of occurrences;
    (c) prints a histogram of these number of occurrences.

Problem 33   *Frequency of Letters in Text with Histogram—(ii)*
    Modify the preceding program so that it will read several lines of text before finding the frequencies.

CHAPTER 9

Chemistry Problems

This chapter was written with John Vogel.

Section 9.1:   THE METHOD OF LEAST SQUARES (WITHOUT CALCULUS)

In an experiment, we often obtain data containing n points $(x_1, y_1), \ldots, (x_n, y_n)$ and we expect that these points should lie on a line $y = mx+b$. We know that our data contain experimental error, and we therefore do not expect to find values for m and b so that $y_i = mx_i+b$ for each value of i ($i = 1, \ldots, n$). Our problem, then, is to find the line which "best fits" our data. See Figure 9.1–1.

We proceed by considering the vertical distances $|y_i - (mx_i+b)|$ from the point P_i to the line. See Figure 9.1–2. The "best" line should be one where these distances are "small."

Since absolute values are often difficult to work with, we square each term to get $(y_i - mx_i - b)^2$. The sum of these distances now depends only on the values of m and b that we choose [since we know our data $(x_1, y_1), \ldots, (x_n, y_n)$]. This sum is given by the formula

$$\text{Sum} = (y_1 - mx_1 - b)^2 + (y_2 - mx_2 - b)^2 + \ldots + (y_n - mx_n - b)^2$$

A variety of techniques can now be used to find which values of n and b give us the smallest sum. (We

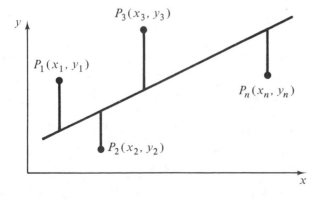

Figure 9.1–1

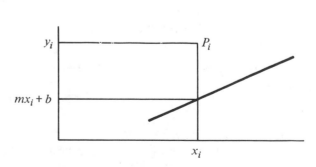

Figure 9.1–2

179

can proceed using only algebra by expanding these terms, making substitutions, completing the square, and examining the result. Alternatively, we can use partial derivatives from calculus. This calculus approach is given in Section 8.3.)

When we apply any of these techniques, we find that the "best" choices for m and b are given by the formulas:

$$m = \frac{(x_1 - \bar{x})(y_1 - \bar{y}) + (x_2 - \bar{x})(y_2 - \bar{y}) + \ldots + (x_n - \bar{x})(y_n - \bar{y})}{(x_1 - \bar{x})^2 + (x_2 - \bar{x})^2 + \ldots + (x_n - \bar{x})^2}$$

and $b = \bar{y} - m\bar{x}$, where $\bar{x}$ and $\bar{y}$ are the averages of the x_i's and y_i's, respectively. That is,

$$\bar{x} = \frac{x_1 + x_2 + \ldots + x_n}{n} \quad \text{and} \quad \bar{y} = \frac{y_1 + y_2 + \ldots + y_n}{n}$$

Thus, after some analysis, we find that *using the Method of Least Squares, the line that best fits the points* $(x_1, y_1), \ldots, (x_n, y_n)$ *has the equation* $y = mx + b$, *where m and b are given by the above formulas*.

Section 9.2: TRANSFORMATION OF DATA

When we have data $(x_1, y_1), \ldots, (x_n, y_n)$, we sometimes want to plot the data on log-log paper or semilog paper (in either variable). If we only have rectangular coordinate paper, however, we can accomplish the same purpose by transforming the data by taking the log of the appropriate variables.

Thus, if we want to plot (x, y) on log-log paper, we can plot $(\log x, \log y)$ on rectangular coordinate paper. If we want to plot on semilog paper, we take the log of only the one appropriate coordinate.

Interpretation of Lines on Log Paper

Normally, if we have a line, its equation is $y = mx + b$ in rectangular coordinates. However, if we see a line in log-log paper or on semilog paper, the equation of the "line" is more complex. We look at the possible cases:

1. *(log x) – (log y) paper*
    Here a "line" will have the equation

    $$\log y = m(\log x) + b \quad \text{or} \quad \log y = \log(x^m) + b$$

    If we take 10 to this power, we get

    $$y = 10^{\log(x^m) + b} = 10^b \cdot x^m$$

    by the properties of logarithms.

2. *(log x) – y semilog paper*
    Here a "line" will have the equation

    $$y = m(\log x) + b \quad \text{or} \quad y = \log(x^m) + b$$

3. *x – (log y) semilog paper*
    Here a "line" will have the equation

    $$\log y = mx + b$$

If we take 10 to this power, we get

$$y = 10^{mx+b} = 10^b \cdot (10^m)^x$$

by the properties of logarithms and exponentials.

Section 9.3: CHEMISTRY PROBLEMS

Problem 1
Write a program which converts a temperature in centigrade into the equivalent temperatures in Fahrenheit and Kelvin.

Problem 2
Write a program that converts the weight of a piece of lead to the corresponding number of moles. [*Note:* The weight of lead is 207.21 grams/mole.]

Problem 3
Use WRITE and FORMAT statements to write out the message:

```
CCCC   H  H   EEEE   M     M
C      H  H   E      MM   MM
C      HHHH   EEEE   M  M  M
C      H  H   E      M     M   . .
CCCC   H  H   EEEE   M     M   . .
```

Problem 4
Write a program that READs a temperature in centigrade from a data card and then computes the equivalent temperature in Fahrenheit and Kelvin.

Problem 5
Write a program that READs the weight of a piece of lead from a data card and prints out the corresponding number of moles. [*Note:* The weight of lead is 207.21 grams/mole.]

Problem 6
Write a program that READs the weight of a molecule obtained in an experiment and the theoretical weight that could be obtained and computes the yield (or percent recovery) obtained in the experiment.

Problem 7
Write a program that READs the number of atoms of carbon, hydrogen, oxygen and nitrogen atoms in a molecule, and computes the molecular weight of the molecule.

Problem 8   *Extended Temperature Table*
Write a program that will produce a table of Fahrenheit temperatures and the corresponding centigrade and absolute (Kelvin) temperatures. The Fahrenheit temperatures in the table should include $0, 1, 2, \ldots, 212$. Label the columns of your table 'FAHRENHEIT', 'CENTIGRADE', and 'KELVIN'.

Problem 9
Write a program that READs a number and computes and prints the common logarithm (log base 10) of the number.

Problem 10   *Ideal Gas Equation*
The ideal gas equation states that

$$PV = 0.082054nT$$

where P is pressure (in atmospheres), V is volume (in liters), and T is temperature (in degrees Kelvin) for n moles of a gas. For $n = 1$, compute P for $V = 0.5, 0.6, \ldots, 2.9, 3$ liters with $T = 300$ degrees Kelvin. Repeat the program for $T = 400$ and $T = 500$ degrees Kelvin. Print the results in a table with appropriate headings.

Problem 11   *Freezing Point Depression and Boiling Point Elevation*
We know that the freezing point of pure water is $0°C$ and the boiling point is $100°C$. Further, we know that each mole of dissolved particles lowers the freezing point of a kilogram of water approximately $1.85°C$ and increases the boiling point by $0.512°C$. (Actually, the freezing point is lowered between $1.85°C$ and $1.87°C$, depending upon the substance.)

Write a program to compute the freezing and boiling points of a kilogram of water when 0, 0.2, 0.4, . . . , 3 moles of particles are added. Print the results in a table with the columns labeled.

Problem 12 *Tabulate the van der Waals Equation*
The van der Waals equation

$$(P + an**2/V**2)\,(V - nb) = nRT$$

relates the pressure, temperature, volume and number of moles of a gas. It includes two numerical constants which are evaluated from experimental data and are different for each gas. The constants for hydrogen are:

$$a = 0.246 \text{ atm–liter}**2/\text{mole}**2$$

$$b = 0.0266 \text{ liter/mole}$$

Solve the equation (by hand) for P and write a program to produce a table of values of T, P, V, and PV for 1 mole of hydrogen occupying 0.5 liters and for T ranging from 100 to 1000 degrees Kelvin in 100-degree intervals. Put labels at the top of each column to identify the output. R is the universal gas constant:

$$0.082 \text{ atm–liter/degree/mole}$$

Problem 13 *Transforming Data*
Write a program that reads a set of data and transforms it for plotting on
(a) log-log paper;
(b) semilog paper.

[See Section 9.2 on transformation of data.]

Problem 14 *Linear Least Squares on Lab Data*
Write a program that will read in an integer N followed by N pairs of real numbers:

$$x(1), y(1), x(2), y(2), . . . , x(N), y(N)$$

and use the method of least squares to find the slope and y-intercept of the line which best fits the N points:

$$x(j), y(j) \quad \text{for } j = 1, 2, . . . , N$$

Apply this program to the two test cases:
(a) (1, 2), (2, 3), (3, 4), (4, 5), (5, 6)
(b) (–1, 3), (3, 11), (0, 5), (–2.5, 0), (–3.5, –2)
From your lab results, select a set of data that you used to determine a straight line. Use this program with this data to determine the slope and y-intercept. Compare the output with your results determined graphically in lab. [*Note:* See Section 9.1 for further information.]

Problem 15 *Least Squares in Log-Log Coordinates*
Write a program that
(a) reads a set of data;
(b) transforms the data for log-log coordinates in rectangular coordinates;
(c) uses the Method of Least Squares to find the "best" line that fits this transformed data;
(d) prints out the best line in the form

$$y = (\text{number 1})*x**(\text{number2})$$

[The transformation of data is discussed in Section 9.2 and the Method of Least Squares is discussed in Section 9.1 and in Section 8.3.]
        Apply the program to the two test cases:
(a) $y = 2x**(-0.5)$; (0.5, 2.82843).(4, 1), (1, 2), (2, 1.41421), (1.5, 1.63299)
(b) $y = 10 \exp(-2x)$: (3, 0.0247), (0, 10), (1, 1.353), (0.5, 3.679), (2.5, 0.067)
From your lab notes, find a set of data that fits each type of "plot" and use the program to predict the best fit for the data. Compare the results of the program with the results obtained graphically in the lab.

Problem 16 *Semilog Least Squares*
Modify the preceding problem to transform the data for semilog coordinates. Write one modification for $(\log x) - y$ semilog paper and write a second modified program for $x - (\log y)$ semilog paper. In each case, print the "best" line in an appropriate format.

Problem 17   *Least Squares in Various Coordinate Systems*
Combine the preceding programs in the following way:
(a) Read the data.
(b) Compute the "best" least squares line in each of the coordinates: rectangular, semilog (in each variable), and log-log.
(c) Print the "best" line for each case in the appropriate format.
[See Section 9.2 for more information on lines in various coordinate systems.]

Problem 18   *Table of Logarithms (base 10)*
Log(x) (base 10) can be shown to be closely approximated by the formula:

$$0.868589*[y + (y**3)/3 + (y**5)/5 + \ldots + y**(2*n-1)/(2*n-1)] \qquad (\dagger)$$

where $y = (x-1)/(x+1)$ for suitably large values of n. Write a program that makes a labeled table of log(x) for $x = 1, 1.1,$ $1.2, \ldots, 4$ using both the formula ($\dagger$) with $n = 8$ and the built-in function ALOG10 in the following format:

X	COMPUTED VALUE OF LOG(X)	MACHINE'S VALUE OF LOG(X)
1.0	0	0
1.1		
1.2		
.		
.		
.		

Use a function subprogram XLOG(X, N) to compute the value of ($\dagger$). [*Note:* You are required in this problem to use multiplication to compute the terms $y**j$ and may not use the power operator (**).]

Problem 19   *Table of Logarithms (base e)*
Log(x) (base e) can be shown to be closely approximated by the formula

$$2.0*[y + y**3/3 + y**5/5 + \ldots + y**(2*n-1)/(2*n-1)] \qquad (\ddagger)$$

where $y = (x-1)/(x+1)$ for suitably large values of n. Write a program that makes a labeled table of log(x) for $x = 1, 1.1,$ $1.2, \ldots, 4$ using both the formula ($\ddagger$) with $n = 8$ and the built-in function ALOG in the following format:

X	COMPUTED VALUE OF LOG(X)	MACHINE'S VALUE OF LOG(X)
1.0	0	0
1.1		
1.2		
.		
.		
.		

Use a function subprogram FNL(X, N) to compute the value of ($\ddagger$). [*Note:* You are required in this problem to use multiplication to compute the terms $y**j$; you may not use the power operator (**).]

Problem 20   *Bisection Method Applied to the van der Waals Equation*
Write a program to apply the bisection method to find the roots of a function defined in a function statement. The program should READ a value for which the function is negative and a value for which the function is positive. Continue iteration until the interval being bisected is smaller than 0.005. At each iteration print the endpoints of the interval and the value of the function at each endpoint.
   Test the program by applying it to two functions whose roots you know and submit the output of the test cases.
   Apply the program to finding the volume of a gas predicted by the van der Waals equation:

$$(P + an**2/V**2)\,(V - nb) = nRT$$

where values of the two physical constants a and b, the pressure P, temperature T, number of moles n and the gas constant R are given. (Take care to use consistent units.)

[*Note:* The Bisection Method is discussed in Section 4.2.]

Problem 21   *Newton's Method Applied to the van der Waals Equation*
Write a program that will use Newton's Method to find approximations to the roots of a differentiable function. Use function statements to give the definitions of the function and its derivative (so the program may be easily altered and applied to other functions). Use the program to find the volume of a gas as predicted by the van der Waals equation:

$$(P + an**2/V**2)\ (V - nb) = nRT$$

to such a degree of accuracy that the absolute value of the difference of two successive approximations is less than 0.00004. Print the value of each approximation as it is generated; also print the corresponding value of the function. Have the program READ values for the two physical constants a and b, as well as values for the pressure P, temperature T and number of moles n. The gas constant R should be defined within the program. Check to make certain you are using consistent units. The ideal gas law, $PV = nRT$, may yield a useful first approximation for V. [*Note:* You should also submit the output of two test cases as well as computations by hand which show the values to be expected for each test.]

[*Note:* Newton's Method is discussed in Section 5.1.]

[*Note:* If you are currently in Calculus I you may not have covered the material required to write this program by the time the program is due. Check with your programming instructor.]

Problem 22   *Plotting the Ideal Gas Equation—(i)*
From the ideal gas equation, plot P versus V for $V = 0.5, 0.6, \ldots , 3$. Use $n = 1$ and try each of the cases $T = 300$ K, $T = 400$ K, and $T = 500$ K. (Have the V-axis run vertically down the paper.) [See Section 8.4 for a discussion of graphing.]

Problem 23   *Plotting Boiling Point Elevation*
The boiling point of a kilogram of water is raised by $0.512°C$ for each mole of dissolved particles. Write a program that plots the amount of particles dissolved down the vertical axis and the boiling point horizontally. Label the axes clearly.

Problem 24   *Plotting the van der Waals Equation*
In an earlier problem, we tabulated van der Waals equation for 1 mole of hydrogen occupying 0.5 liters and for T ranging from 100 to 1000 degrees Kelvin in 100-degree intervals.
    Graph T versus P in this equation, with the T-axis running vertically down the paper, and with T increased in increments of 50 degrees Kelvin.

Problem 25   *Plotting Lab Data*
Write a program that
(a) READs the data points $(x(1), y(1)), \ldots , (x(n), y(n))$ from DATA cards;
(b) plots this data.
[Plotting data is discussed in Section 8.4.]

Problem 26   *Plotting Data on Log-Log Paper*
Write a program that
(a) READs data points from data cards;
(b) transforms the data for log-log coordinates;
(c) plots this data.

Problem 27   *Plotting Data on Semilog Paper*
Write a program that
(a) READs data points from data cards;
(b) transforms the data for $(\log x)$–y coordinates;
(c) plots this data.
Write a second program, replacing the transformation in part (b) to x–$(\log y)$ semilog coordinates.

Problem 28   *Plotting the Ideal Gas Equation—(ii)*
From the ideal gas equation, plot P versus V for $V = 0.5, 0.6, \ldots , 6.9, 7$. Use $n = 1$ and try each of the cases $T = 300$ K, $T = 400$ K, and $T = 500$ K. (Have the V-axis run horizontally across the paper.) [See Section 8.4 for a discussion of graphing.]

Problem 29   *Plotting Boiling Point Elevation*
Write a program that plots the number of moles of particles dissolved in a kilogram of water versus the boiling point of

the water. Graph the number of moles of dissolved particles horizontally. [Recall that one mole of dissolved particles raises the boiling point of water by $0.512°C$.]

Problem 30   *Plotting the van der Waals Equation*

Graph the van der Waals equation for 1 mole of hydrogen occupying 0.5 liters with T ranging from 100 to 1000 degrees Kelvin in 25-degree increments. In the graph, display the T-axis horizontally across the paper.

Problem 31   *Storage of Data on a Disk File*

Write a program that READs an integer n and READs n data points $(x(1), y(1)), \ldots, (x(n), y(n))$.

The program is to store this data in a disk file. On the file, print n on the first line, $(x(1), y(1))$ on the next record, $(x(2), y(1))$ on the record line, etc.

Problem 32   *Least Squares on Stored Data*

Write a program that inputs a set of data points from a disk file (created in an earlier problem), computes the equation of the "best" line that fits this data according to the Method of Least Squares, and prints the equation of the "line" in the appropriate format.

Problem 23   *Plotting of Stored Data*

Write a program to read data from a disk file and plot the data.

Problem 34   *Plotting Stored Data in Various Coordinates*

Modify the preceding program so that the user may specify if the data is to be transformed for semilog coordinates or for log-log coordinates before the data points are plotted.

CHAPTER 10

Physics Problems

This chapter was written with Charles Duke.

Section 10.1: **THE HUNTER AND THE MONKEY PROBLEM**

A hunter, who is standing at the origin, aims his blowgun at a monkey, who is sitting at a point (x_0, y_0) which is on the branch of a tree (see Fig. 10.1–1). The hunter blows the dart at an initial velocity V_0. At the same instant, the monkey drops the banana.

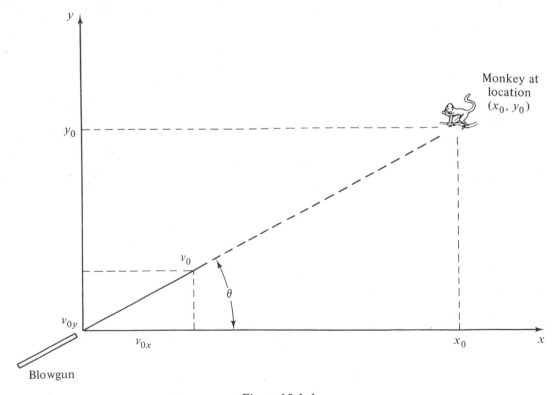

Figure 10.1–1
The Hunter and the Monkey Problem

Since the blowgun must be aimed directly at the monkey, θ, $v_{0\,x}$, and $v_{0\,y}$ can be calculated:

$$\tan \theta = \frac{y_0}{x_0} \quad \text{and} \quad \begin{cases} v_{0\,x} = v_0 \cos \theta \\ v_{0\,y} = v_0 \sin \theta \end{cases}$$

Then for both the dart and the banana, the equations

$$\begin{cases} x = x_0 + v_{0\,x}\,t + \tfrac{1}{2}a_x\,t^2 \\ y = y_0 + v_{0\,y}\,t + \tfrac{1}{2}a_y\,t^2 \end{cases}$$

apply.

Section 10.2: EULER'S METHOD FOR THE SOLUTION OF $F = ma$

We recall that $a = \Delta v/\Delta t$ and $v = \Delta x/\Delta t$, where the only restriction is that Δt must be small enough so that there is no significant difference between average and instantaneous values of the acceleration and velocity within Δt. Thus, we can write:

$$\frac{\Delta v}{\Delta t} = \frac{1}{m}\,F$$

$$\frac{\Delta x}{\Delta t} = v$$

If we rearrange these equations slightly, we can compute the change in velocity and position during any time increment. If these changes are added to the previous values of velocity and position, we can compute new values after which the process is repeated, stepping forward in time:

$$v_{\text{new}} = v_{\text{old}} + \Delta v = v_{\text{old}} + \frac{1}{m}\,F \cdot \Delta t$$

$$x_{\text{new}} = x_{\text{old}} + \Delta x = x_{\text{old}} + v_{\text{old}} \cdot \Delta t$$

where F is evaluated at the beginning of the time interval, Δt. Thus, all that is needed are the initial position and velocity and the force acting during each time increment (see Figure 10.2–1).

$$\Delta v_i = \frac{1}{m}\,F(x_{i-1},\,v_{i-1},\,t_{i-1}) \cdot \Delta t$$

(since in general F can be a function of x, v, and t) and $\Delta x_i = v_{i-1} \cdot \Delta t$.

t	v	v	Δx	x
0		v_0		x_0
$t_1 = \Delta t$	v_1	$v_1 = v_0 + \Delta v_1$	Δx_1	$x_1 = x_0 + \Delta x_1$
$t_2 = 2\,\Delta t$	v_2	$v_2 = v_1 + \Delta v_2$	Δx_2	$x_2 = x_1 + \Delta x_2$
$\vdots$	$\vdots$	$\vdots$	$\vdots$	$\vdots$

Figure 10.2–1
Summary of Euler's Method

This method is easily adaptable to computer methods, since a simple loop can be set up that increments the time and calculates a new Δv and Δx to be added to the previous values of v and x before returning to the beginning of the loop.

Initial Half-step Method

The strategy in this method is to compute a single change in the velocity at the beginning of the program for a half time-step (see Figure 10.2–2). If we then proceed as usual, the velocity and position will be out of step by one-half a time-step. Thus, the change in position will be calculated with a value of velocity that is halfway through the time-step leading to a dramatic increase in accuracy.

For this interval, the proper value for Δx is the slope of the chord times Δt. In our initial discussion, we approximated this slope by the value of v at the beginning of the interval $[v(t)]$. We can now do better because, just by the geometry, the point at which the slope of curve $x(t)$ is equal to the slope of the chord occurs near the center of the interval rather than at the beginning. We should also think about this problem in terms of the Mean-Value Theorem, which states that at some point between t and $t + \Delta t$, the slope of the curve is equal to the slope of the chord. This point is more likely to occur near the center of the interval than at the beginning.

Thus, we should be certain that the velocity is one-half step ahead of the displacement. All we have to do is to replace v_0 by $v_0 + (F_0/m) \cdot (\Delta t/2)$ in our original program before we start the loop to calculate velocities and displacements.

That is,

$$v_0 = v_0 + \frac{F_0}{m} \cdot \frac{\Delta t}{2}$$

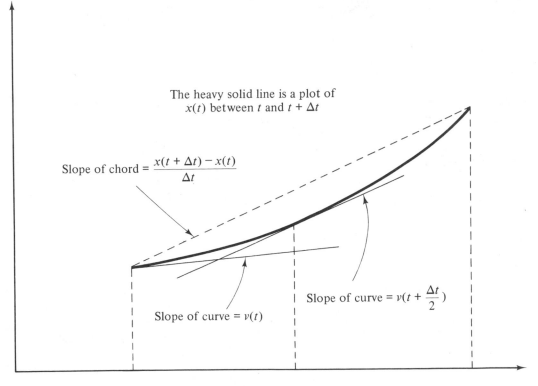

The heavy solid line is a plot of
$x(t)$ between t and $t + \Delta t$

Slope of chord $= \dfrac{x(t + \Delta t) - x(t)}{\Delta t}$

Slope of curve $= v(t + \dfrac{\Delta t}{2})$

Slope of curve $= v(t)$

Figure 10.2–2
The Initial Half-step Method

Section 10.3: **THE PERIMETER OF AN ELLIPTICAL TRACK**

We consider an ellipse centered at the origin (see Figure 10.3-1). The parametric equations for this ellipse are:

$$x = a \cos \phi, \quad a = \text{semimajor axis:} \quad dx = -a \sin \phi \, d\phi$$
$$y = b \sin \phi, \quad b = \text{semiminor axis:} \quad dy = b \cos \phi \, d\phi$$

Hence, we know that the arclength or perimeter of the ellipse is:

$$L = \Sigma \, \Delta \, l_i = \int dl$$

$$dl = \sqrt{dx^2 + dy^2} = \sqrt{(-a \sin \phi \, d\phi)^2 + (b \cos \phi \, d\phi)^2}$$

$$dl = \sqrt{a^2 \sin^2 \phi + b^2 \cos^2 \phi} \; d\phi = \sqrt{a^2 (1 - \cos^2 \phi) + b^2 \cos^2 \phi} \, d\phi$$

$$dl = \sqrt{a^2 - (a^2 - b^2) \cos^2 \phi} \; d\phi = a \sqrt{1 - (a^2 - b^2)/a^2 \; \cos^2 \phi} \, d\phi$$

If

$$\epsilon = \text{Eccentricity of the ellipse} = \sqrt{\frac{a^2 - b^2}{a^2}}$$

then

$$dl = a \sqrt{1 - \epsilon^2 \cos^2 \phi} \, d\phi$$

Thus

$$L = \int_0^{2\pi} dl = 4 \int_0^{\pi/2} dl = 4a \int_0^{\pi/2} \sqrt{1 - \epsilon^2 \cos^2 \phi} \, d\phi$$

an elliptical integral that can be evaluated by Simpson's Rule. (See Section 5.3.)

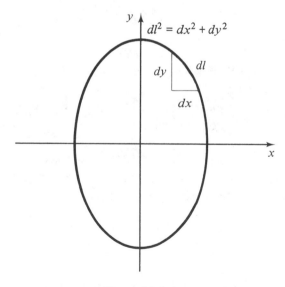

Figure 10.3-1

Section 10.4: **EQUIPOTENTIAL CURVES ASSOCIATED WITH TWO POINT MASSES**

We consider the potential due to gravity associated with two point masses (see Figure 10.4-1). We know that

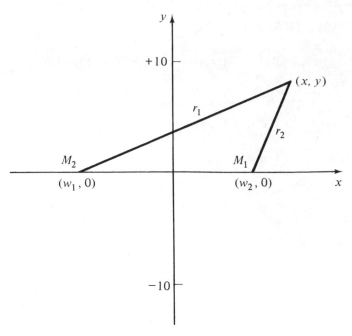

Figure 10.4-1

$$V(x, y) = G \sum \frac{M_i}{r_i} = G \left[\frac{M_1}{r_1} + \frac{M_2}{r_2} \right]$$

We can let the computer calculate the potential at all lattice points within the square defined by:

$$- 10 \leqslant x \leqslant +10$$
$$- 10 \leqslant y \leqslant +10$$

(a) We must give a phony value of V when $r_1 = 0$ or $r_2 = 0$ so that the computer never divides by zero or prints an extremely large number.

(b) After finding the potential at one point, we can move to the next point in the row. When that row is complete, we move to the next row. Thus, in a program, we can use two nested loops.

Remember that the gravitational constant $G = 6.67 \times 10^{-11}$ Newton-Meters^2/Kilogram^2.

Thus, we must be careful to scale the magnitudes so that the computer does not perform the calculations with extremely large or small numbers. We might want to combine the G with M so that

$$V = \frac{GM_1}{r_1} + \frac{GM_2}{r_2} = \frac{M_1'}{r_1} + \frac{M_2'}{r_2}$$

and then use an input statement for the scaled masses. For example, we could enter $M_1' = +1$ and $M_2' = +3$ in our input statement.

Section 10.5: **PHYSICS PROBLEMS**

Problem 1
   Write a program that converts miles to kilometers.

Problem 2

Modify the previous program to READ the number of miles from a data card.

Problem 3

Use WRITE and FORMAT statements to write out the message:

```
PPPP   H   H   Y   Y   SSSS   III   CCCC   SSSS
P  P   H   H    Y Y    S       I    C      S
PPPP   HHHH      Y     SSSS    I    C      SSSS
P      H   H     Y        S    I    C         S
P      H   H     Y     SSSS   III   CCCC   SSSS
```

Problem 4   *Distance Table I*

Write a program that will READ from a data card a distance expressed in feet and print its meter equivalent. Then use the program to convert some feet measurements of your own choosing into meters.

Problem 5   *Distance Table II*

Revise the previous table, so that both feet and inches are entered and centimeters are computed and printed.

Problem 6   *Extended Distance Table*

Write a program that will produce a table of distance equivalents, with feet and inches in the first two columns and with the corresponding distances in centimeters in the third column. Start the table at $0'1''$, and proceed in one inch increments until you reach $3'0''$.

Problem 7

Write a simple program to add a series of 2 dimensional vectors. Use a READ statement for the two components of each vector to be summed. The output should show the components of the sum vector as well as its magnitude and angle with respect to the x-axis.

Problem 8

Write a program to determine the velocity at $t = 0.5$ and at $t = 0.8$ of an object moving according to: $x = 3*\sin(t) + 2*(t**2)$. Your program should calculate the average velocity in a small time interval centered at $t = 0.5$ and at $t = 0.8$. Compare your answer with the result obtained by differentiation.

Problem 9   *Parallel Resistors*

An arbitrary number of resistors (R1, R2, . . . , Rn) are connected in parallel. The first resistor, R1, is 1000 ohms. Each succeeding resistor increases by 50 ohms (R2 = 1050, R3 = 1100, etc.). If n = 10, what is the equivalent resistance? What if n = 100?

As n increases, should the resistance converge to some value? Does the resistance seem to converge? Is there a difference between the expected behavior and the observed behavior? Why or why not?

Problem 10

A radioactive sample decays at the rate of 100,000 events per second (at the present time). It has a half-life of 1 year. Write a program to tabulate its activity for the next 50 years. Plot (by hand) the activity as a function of time; the graph should remind you of the exponential function.

Problem 11   *A Monkey with a Banana*

A monkey is sitting in a tree 10 meters above the ground. He drops a banana with zero initial velocity. Using the standard kinematic expressions, write a program that can calculate the position of the banana as a function of time. Have the program print a table giving the height of the banana every 0.1 seconds. [Section 10.1 discusses some basic kinematic equations.]

Problem 12   *A Hunter with his Blowgun*

A hunter blows a dart from his blowgun. Using the standard kinematic expressions, write a program to calculate the position of the dart as a function of time. Use a READ statement for the initial velocity components. Have the program print a table giving the position coordinates of the dart every 0.1 seconds.

Problem 13   *The Hunter and the Monkey*

Combine the previous two problems by having the hunter aim his blowgun directly at the monkey. The instant the hunter blows the dart, the monkey drops the banana. Have your program follow both the dart and the banana by listing the coordinates every 0.1 seconds. Note from the listing that the dart always hits the banana independent of how hard the hunter blows the dart.

Problem 14   *Model Rocket*
A small model rocket is fired upward from a height of 15 meters. Its height above the ground is given by the expression:

$$y = 15 + 20*T - 4.9*T**2 + 10/(1+T)$$

where T is measured in seconds.
Write a program to follow the trajectory of the rocket every 0.1 seconds. At the same time calculate the average velocity within the 0.1 second interval and print a table showing the location, velocity, and cumulative time. From this table identify: the rocket's initial velocity, the time it strikes the ground, the velocity on impact, the greatest height, and the time to reach maximum height.

Problem 15   *Finding Distance with the Trapezoidal Rule*
A small model rocket with carbon dioxide propellant is fired upward from the ground. Its velocity (measured in feet per second) is given by:

$$V = 55 - 32*T - 30/(1+T)**2$$

Use the Trapezoidal Rule to compute the position of the rocket when $T = 2$. [The Trapezoidal Rule is discussed in Section 5.3.]

Problem 16   *Find Distance with Simpson's Rule*
Repeat the previous problem using Simpson's Rule. [Simpson's Rule is discussed in Section 5.3.]

Problem 17   *Sphere Floating in Water*
A solid sphere of radius ½ is floating in water. How far below the surface is the bottom of the sphere if the density of the sphere is 24% of the density of the surrounding water? [*Note:* Archimedes' principle says that the buoyant force of the water pushing up the sphere equals the weight of the water displaced by the submerged portion of the sphere.]

Problem 18   *Euler's Method in Simple Harmonic Motion*
Write a program using Euler's Method to find the velocity and displacement as a function of time for a simple harmonic oscillator, where $F = -Kx$ or $dV/dT = -Kx/M$. Use a READ statement for M, L, and delta T, and for all initial conditions. The output should be in tabular form giving the time (increasing in equal increments), velocity, and displacement. Do not be surprised if the displacement diverges with time. (Why?)
To eliminate the divergence, use the "initial half-step" method.

[Euler's Method is discussed in Section 10.2.]

Problem 19   *Simple Harmonic Motion with a Simple Damping Force*
Repeat the previous problem with a damping force proportional to the velocity so that $F = -Kx - BV$ and study the output as B is increased from zero.

Problem 20   *Simple Harmonic Motion with Damping and Driving Forces*
Repeat the damped harmonic oscillator (from the previous problem) but add on an oscillating driving force so that

$$F = -Kx - BV + A \text{ SIN}(wT)$$

Use a READ statement for A and w. Study the output for various values of w near the resonance frequency. This problem is particularly appropriate for a graphics terminal.

Problem 21   *Gravitational Motion with Two Force Centers*
Continue the development of gravitational motion by using two force centers fixed in space (see Section 10.4). The orbits obtained in this situation can be very interesting, and you should consider using a graphics terminal, if available.

Problem 22   *Fourier Approximation*
If $y(x)$ is a periodic function with wave length 2π, then it can be represented by a sum of sine and cosine terms where the kth term in the sum is:

$$a(k)*\cos(kx) + b(k)*\sin(kx), \quad k = 1, 2, 3, \ldots$$

This result is known as Fourier's Theorem and is very important in all areas of physics. Normally there are an infinite number of terms in the series. However, in practice, a good approximation is possible using a finite number of the above terms. Write a general program to compute the sum of the first N terms for M evenly spaced values of X in the interval $[-\pi, \pi]$, using any coefficients $a(k)$ and $b(k)$.
Use the program to reproduce a square wave:

$$y(x) = +1 \quad \text{when } 0 < x < \pi$$
$$y(x) = -1 \quad \text{when } -\pi < x < 0$$

for which

$$a(k) = 0$$
$$b(k) = (2/(\pi k))(1-(-1)**k)$$

Run the program for N = 5 and for N = 10, with M at least 20. (You might be interested in plotting the points by hand to see how well the square wave is reproduced. This is an excellent application for a graphics terminal.)

Problem 23

Use Fourier's Theorem to produce a triangular wave:

$$y(x) = 1 - 2*\text{ABS}(x)/\pi \quad \text{where } -\pi < x < \pi$$

for which:

$$b(k) = 0, \quad a(k) = (2/(\pi*k)**2)**(1-(-1)**k)$$

Problem 24

In a Fourier series, the expansion coefficients are given by:

$$a(k) = 1/N, \quad b(k) = 0, \quad k = 1, 2, 3, \ldots$$

Write a program to sum N terms of this Fourier series. Output a table of values for the sum for x in the interval $-\pi <= x <= \pi$. Construct plots of the function for N = 5, N = 10, and N = 20. What kind of function have you reproduced?

Problem 25   *The Perimeter of an Elliptical Track*

Write a function subprogram SIMPS whose value is the Simpson Rule approximation to the integral of a real-valued function $f(x)$ between the limits of integration A and B. [See Section 5.3.] The input to the function should include the limits of integration A and B and the number N of subintervals to be used by Simpson's Rule. Use a function statement for the function $f(x)$.

Write a program which incorporates this Simpson-Rule function and which reads the limits of integration and number of subintervals using a READ statement. Do not use subscripted variables.

Comprehensive checking of this program is possible because if $f(x)$ is any polynomial of degree 3 or less, Simpson's Rule will give the exact value of the integral, no matter what the limits of integration or the number of subintervals used (except that N must be even and greater than 2).

(a) Submit the output of two test cases of your choice along with hand computations (using antiderivatives) to compute the value expected from each test.

(b) Use the program to calculate the length of an elliptical track, given some measurements you have made of the semi-axes (see Section 10.3).

Problem 26   *Moment of Inertia of an Elliptical Plate*

Use Simpson's Rule to calculate the moment of inertia of a thin elliptically shaped steel plate about an axis shown in Figure 10.3-1.

Problem 27   *Electrical Potential Near a Charged Thin Wire*

Use Simpson's Rule to calculate the electrical potential as a function of the distance away from a charged thin wire (see Section 10.4).

Problem 28   *Equipotential Curves Associated with Two Point Masses*

Write a program to find equipotential curves in the x-y plane associated with two point masses placed at two points on the x-axis (see Section 10.4). Have the program calculate $V(x, y)$ for a finite grid of points; use an array $V(i, j)$ where (i, j) labels the point where $V(x, y)$ has been calculated. Once the array is complete, it can be printed out row by row and the equipotential points connected by hand.

Problem 29

Redesign the output for the preceding problem so that the output specifies the grid points where the potential lies between V and $V + \Delta V$. Specify V and ΔV by a READ statement. The grid points can be plotted and connected on graph paper to form the equipotential surface; or better yet, use a graphics terminal, if available.

Problem 30

Extend the preceding problem to include an arbitrary number of point charges located anywhere within your grid.

Index